TEMPERATURE

Temperature Conversion Table

American Oven Temperature Terms	Degrees Fahrenheit	Degrees Centigrade (Celsius)
	160	71
	170	77
	200	93
	212	100
Very Slow	225	107
	230	110
	250	121
Slow	275	135
	300	149
	302	150
	320	160
Moderately Slow.....	325	163
Moderate	350	177
	356	180
	375	190
	390	200
Hot	400	205
	425	218
	428	220
	437	225
	450	232
Very Hot	475	246
	500	260
	525	274
Broil................	550	288

Volume 20

Sou–Syr

WOMAN'S DAY ENCYCLOPEDIA OF COOKERY

**1979 Edition
For WOMAN'S DAY**

JEANNE VOLTZ, *Food Editor*

For FUNK & WAGNALLS, INC.

Supervising Editor—**NORMA H. DICKEY**
Production Editor—**KATHIE L. ATTLEE**
Production Executive—**EDWARD HAAS**
Editorial Staff—**DONNA L. AMOS, JUNE V. ROOK**
Art Director—**MURRAY KESHNER**
Layout Artists—**HERBERT ASCHER, MARTIN GORDON, ERLA SIGURDARDOTTIR**

Special Project Staff:

Contributing Editors—**INEZ M. KRECH, JAMES W. TRAGER**

Original Edition

Prepared and edited by the Editors of WOMAN'S DAY

GLENNA MCGINNIS, *Food Editor*

Special Project Staff:

Editor—**NIKA STANDEN HAZELTON**
Associates—**L. GERALDINE MARSTELLER, HELEN FEINGOLD, SUSAN J. KNOX**

First Revised Edition

Special Project Staff:
Editor—**MARIE ROBERSON HAMM**
Associate Editor—**ISABEL CORNELL**

Copyright © 1966, 1973, 1979 by CBS Publications,
the Consumer Publishing Division of CBS, Inc.,
All Rights Reserved.
Distributed by Funk & Wagnalls, Inc.

HIGHLIGHTS

Volume 20

Southwestern-Syrup

Arranged alphabetically, the articles in this volume fall between the two words listed above. Among the interesting and informative entries found in this volume, several sections are worthy of special attention. We have listed these below for your convenience.

SOUTHWESTERN COOKERY by Sylvia Vaughn Thompson	9
SOYBEAN COOKBOOK	19
SOYBEAN COOKERY by Beverly Bush Smith	21
SPANISH COOKERY by Marcia Colman Morton	28
SPICES—NATURE'S FLAVOR MAGIC by Ethel M. Keating	41
FROM SEED TO SPROUT TO SALAD IN LESS THAN A WEEK by Gay E. Courter	52
STEAKS, CHARCOAL BROILED by Philip S. Brown	61
STRAWBERRY COOKBOOK	74
SUMMER COOKBOOK	89
SWEDISH COOKERY by Nika Hazelton	97
SWEET POTATO COOKBOOK	111
SWISS COOKERY by James A. Beard	115
50 MENUS	124

How to use the Woman's Day Encyclopedia of Cookery

The twenty-two volumes of the Woman's Day Encyclopedia contain a wealth of alphabetically arranged information. If you wish to prepare Apple Pie, look under Apple in volume 1. But to find all of the information in all of the volumes, you should use the twenty-third volume, the Index. Composed of five separate indexes, volume 23 includes: meal and menu planning; information on nutrition and diet; techniques of cookery and equipment use; a listing by author; and an alphabetical listing by ingredients.

This Encyclopedia contains many individual entries that supplement one another. Meal and Menu Planning, for instance, is treated throughout the Encyclopedia in many different entries. The first index in volume 23 collects these entries and lists volume and page numbers for such diverse items as Busy Day Dinners and Low Cost Meals. How to entertain or cook in different national styles will be simplified by consulting such items as Parties or Mexican Cookery. If you want to cook for a crowd or make up a Christmas menu, this index shows you where to find Quantity Cooking and three separate styles of Christmas meals.

If you are learning to cook or beginning to plan diets for a family, two other indexes offer assistance. The Encyclopedia entries that contain information on nutrition and diet are listed in one index, and techniques of cookery and equipment are listed in the other. If you want to know which foods are necessary in your child's diet or how to cut down on cholesterol, see the second index. If you want to find out which pan is appropriate for a layer cake, see Bake in the third index.

The fourth index in volume 23 is a listing by author of all the special articles in the Encyclopedia. Here you will find titles and location of articles by noted cookbook authors and food and health authorities.

A major part of volume 23 is the listing of all the recipes contained in the Encyclopedia, arranged alphabetically by main ingredient and by one or more menu categories. Thus, an Abalone Chowder recipe in volume 1 is listed in this Index under ABALONE and under SOUPS. A Crabmeat Dip recipe appears under CRABS, under DIPS, APPETIZER, and under APPETIZERS.

These volumes offer helpful advice on cooking, meal planning, food budgeting, and entertaining. Brimming with tempting recipes, mouthwatering photos, and interesting tid-bits about the origin and history of some of the ingredients, the Woman's Day Encyclopedia of Cookery is indeed a browsing library for food lovers.

SOUTHWESTERN COOKERY

by Sylvia Vaughn Thompson

SOUTHWESTERN COOKERY

The Spaniards who settled in what is now our Southwest settled a spectacular arid country of dazzling colors, wind-swept arroyos, and sun-drenched wilderness. If the cuisine of today's Southwest owes much to Spain, it is the geography which made it possible.

The Spaniards found in the Southwest Indians who had been living there for thousands of years—cultivated Pueblos, peaceful Hopis and Zuñis, a proud host of agrarian tribes, as well as fearless hostile Comanches and Kiowas, and raiding nomadic Apaches and Navahos—growing corn, beans, and squashes on acres of irrigated land. Maize, which the Spaniards called corn, although once strange, had become familiar to them. In their colonies to the south, the Mayan government had planted corn and beans along the roadways so that a hungry traveler might simply pluck his supper from the stalk and vine. All shapes and sizes and colors of corn that we know today and some which are no more—seven hundred varieties—were grown in New Spain at the time of Columbus. Fossilized grains of corn pollen have been found in Mexico at a geological level 80,000 years old.

The Spanish *conquistadores* had learned about more than all sorts of corn and beans from the Aztecs and Mayans of New Spain. Sweet potatoes, peanuts, cocoa beans, papayas, avocados, tomatoes, and many sweet and hot members of the pepper family were then raised in what today is Mexico. More than four hundred years ago, the Aztecs were serving flat cakes of corn called *tortillas;* chocolate *(xocoatl)* iced with snow brought down from the mountains and spiced with the seeds from the pod of wild orchids which the Spaniards renamed *vainilla;* an appetizer called *guacamole*—puréed avocado seasoned with hot red peppers; *tamallis* of cornmeal covering chopped meat, wrapped in husks of corn; and a sauce for venison made of peppers, herbs, and chocolate like the *mole* sauce today. When Cortés fled Moctezuma's vengeance, he was careful to take back to Spain turkey chicks and brood hens, *cacao* beans, *vainilla* pods, seeds of the *tomatl,* and several sorts of peppers, because neither the turkey nor one plant that the Spaniards found in the New World had ever been known to Europeans.

Within half a century, these fruits and vegetables were among the best gifts the Spaniards had to bestow upon the Indians of their new colony, in what today is our great Southwest. Of their own, the Spanish added some of the foods Columbus had brought from the Old World to the New—oranges, lemons, bananas (from Columbus's stop at the Canary Islands), limes, and melons (most especially well received were the cantaloupes, so called because the Pope had developed the melon at his country place, the castle of Cantalupo). The Spaniards also brought along the first domesticated cattle, sheep, goats, hogs, and chickens the Indians had seen (imagine all those years without the egg of our familiar chicken!).

The Spanish colonists with these presents by no means meant to encourage commerce. And so the Indians of the Southwest passed another two hundred years rather as they had the previous twenty thousand. Then, independence from Spain, annexation of the Southwestern territories, cries of "gold!" in the West, and suddenly there was a rush of people across the land. Some stopped and settled in the golden Southwest instead of fighting their way to doubtful wealth on the coast. These were mostly Anglos, what native Southwesterners affectionately call people of English descent, and they brought with them a whole new color and context of tastes. They wanted to eat oats, wheat, cabbage, and potatoes. They didn't. They wanted to raise cattle and sheep with a vengeance; that they did, with the help of a new breed of man, the cowboy. Cowboys needed to eat on the move, and so the chuck wagon was invented. They liked food that stuck inside them on long cold nights, and found that the beef with chili peppers the Indians ate—add some beans to keep them going—served very well: *chile con carne.* And jerky—pieces of beef hung up to dry much as Indians hung strands of peppers in the sun—kept all winter long in a saddlebag if need be and still gave a man fuel to ride on.

As the railroad was built across the West, it brought more Anglos to build it and more cowboys to drive cattle to it from the territory. When the railroad finally crisscrossed the Southwest itself by 1895, it had the effect on the land of a key in a long-locked door. The mood of expansion and development the railroad excited spread to dam projects and reclamation projects, and suddenly, after thousands of patient years, the door swung open.

But it still is all so new. Arizona and New Mexico didn't become states of the Union, after all, until 1912. And water, if not the source of all good things at least the essential catalyst, is still scarce. Yet from her deficiencies, the Southwest's glories spring. Here, the land, not man, dominates. Its rugged history is so deeply etched in the earth and her people, and so much a part of the everyday, that even though the atomic age was born in the Southwest, descendants of ancient civilizations living within sight of space-age research communities continue very largely in ancient ways. Southwesterners regard the land as their life; they live out of doors a good deal more than in. They eat out of doors—barbecuing, cookouts, picnics, backpacking—as their native predecessors have done. And they dine on a unique combination of culinary traditions—a zesty mixture of Indian, Spanish, Mexican, Southwestern cowboy, Anglo, and of course, 20th-century American.

Southwesterners never seem to feel the press of time or change—a legacy of their imperturbable forebears. What they most enjoy, most often set on their tables, has, somewhere at its heart, a flavor of the East about it.

SOUPS

CHILI PUMPKIN SOUP

Pumpkin was one of the very first crops in our hemisphere. The Indians told of the Great Spirit who came to earth in the shape of a woman. Fatigued by her long journey, she fell asleep. When she arose and walked across the land, pumpkins sprang from the ground by her right hand, beans sprang up by her left, and from her footprints in the earth sprang maize.

Simmer chunks of pared and seeded pumpkin in water until just tender; purée through food mill or in blender. Stir in a mixture of butter and flour to thicken and cook

gently for 10 minutes. Thin with hot milk, season to taste with salt, pepper, ground cloves, and chili powder.
Variation—Summer-squash soup is prepared in the same way.

AVOCADO SOUP

For an elegant patio dinner

Place 1 tablespoon grated Swiss cheese in each soup cup. Pour simmering beef consommé onto it, then slip in slices of ripe avocado. Serve at once.
Variation—Garnish jellied consommé madrilène with avocado and a slice of lemon twisted to make a furl.

RAZOR-CLAM BISQUE

- 24 razor clams
- 1 cup water
- 1 small onion, minced
- 1 tablespoon minced parsley
- 2 whole cloves
- 2 whole allspice
- Dash of ground mace
- 4 cups milk
- ¼ cup all-purpose flour
- ¼ cup heavy cream, whipped

Scrub clams and put in a kettle. Add water, cover, and cook over medium heat until shells open and clams can be easily removed, about 10 minutes. Reserve broth. Chop clams and mix with onion, parsley, cloves, allspice, and mace. Add clam mixture to broth in which clams were cooked. Simmer for 30 minutes. Mix ½ cup milk with flour to make a smooth mixture; add mixture to remaining 3½ cups milk. Cook over low heat, stirring constantly, until smooth and thick. Strain clam broth into milk. Reheat slightly and serve topped with whipped cream. Makes 4 to 6 servings.

SALADS

FRUIT SALADS

The best salads in the Southwest are the simplest

Crescents of fresh grapefruit and casaba melon on romaine lettuce, with a light French dressing.
Alternate sections of white, pink, and red grapefruit on a background of greens, laced with poppy seeds in French dressing. If red grapefruit is unavailable, soak white segments overnight in raspberry juice.
At Christmas, red grapefruit sections alternating with avocado slices are a pretty touch.
Rings of oranges and raw onions seasoned, again, with French dressing accompany rare roast beef.
Try casaba melons sliced and alternated with grapefruit sections.
Ripe tomatoes stuffed with chopped celery, piñons, and the peeled and chopped tomato pulp; a chili-seasoned French dressing ladled on at the last minute.

SOUTHWESTERN COOKERY

Grapefruits one more time: they are by far the favorite salad fruit in the Southwest, being both quenching and abundant; emptied of fruit, filled with brilliant colors of jello, chilled, then sliced into quarters and served on greens with a garnish of grapefruit crescents.

BEAN SALADS

The Southwest's potato salad

To a can of pinto, kidney, or garbanzo beans, well drained, add a spicy oil and vinegar dressing, lots of pressed garlic, fresh or dried oregano, and chili powder, and minced onion and celery to taste. Chill overnight before serving.
Strips of pimiento, canned green chilies, black olives, rings of green peppers, sliced radishes, any of these are handsome additions to a bean salad.

SEAFOOD

TRUCHA FRITA
[Southwestern Fried Trout]

Mountain streams and man-made lakes are stocked with Southwestern finny delicacies, rainbow trout most especially. If you can't catch it yourself and cook it moments later over a campfire, at least try the Southwestern manner of frying trout.

Clean trout at once. Heat bacon drippings over high heat and fry fish and a handful of finely chopped onion for each trout until done, turning once. Remove trout to hot serving dish, swirl in 1 tablespoon cider vinegar, a bit of minced parsley, 1 pressed garlic clove, and 1 tablespoon butter. Heat over high heat, scraping and stirring, then pour over fish and onions. Serve at once with a garnish of lemon twist, capers, and parsley.
Variation—Try boning the fish and skinning it before cooking. Little blue-gills, caught back of Southwestern dams, are heavenly cooked this way, especially when fried until this side of crispness.

SEAFOOD IN CHILI

Since early Colonial days, shrimps have been a favorite food of Southwesterners, even though until recent times the shrimps have been dried, from Mexico. But the habit of taste persists, and many favorite Lenten recipes call for dried or powdered shrimps.

Using canned, reconstituted dried, frozen, or fresh shrimps, fresh-flown-in oysters, or King crab from as far away as Alaska, a refreshing hot-weather supper is a cup of seafood sauced either with a favorite chili sauce, or simply best catsup and a heavy sprinkling of finely chopped canned green chilies. Garnish with lemon and avocado slices. Or serve in an avocado half to begin with. Be sure to use a chili sauce you have made yourself.

SOUTHWESTERN COOKERY

MEAT AND POULTRY

STEAK FRY

Although other cultures may claim the barbecue as their own, it is almost certain the Indians of New Spain initiated the backyard barbecue when they built frames of green wood for smoking their fish. When the Spaniards came with their oversize roasts of meat, they found the barbacoas ideal, making it easy to handle whole animals at once, and giving the meat an incomparable flavor. In most of West Texas and Arizona, barbecue means just one thing: beef. This is the way steaks taste best.

Build a rectangle of rocks about 1 x 2 feet and 6 inches high; make a fire inside of hardwood (mesquite, oak, or hickory preferred) an hour ahead of time, so that it burns down to about 2 inches of glowing embers. Spread the embers evenly. Put a grill on top (an old refrigerator shelf is fine) about 4 inches from the coals. Now put on T-bone steaks 1 inch thick, unseasoned, to "fry." Move steaks as they drip into the fire. When underside is brown and the bone slightly charred, turn. Season well with salt and pepper (never before searing). Turn when the downside is brown, and season that side. Serve the steak while still rare and sizzling.

Variations—Some Southwesterners have to have sop (see Soppin' Sauce) on their beef as it barbecues; if you do, first try just plain melted butter before moving on to something stronger.

Short ribs of beef barbecued either this way or in the patio's barbecue or even on a plugged-in electric roaster are the next most popular cuts in beef country; just be sure the meat is *rare*.

BASQUE BARBECUE

In much of the Southwest, Basque Barbecues are lamb barbecues, often whole 30-pound suckling lambs turning on a spit, so called because many of the sheepmen are of Basque descent. Here is an elegant Southwestern dinner-party meat.

- 1 leg of lamb (7 pounds), boned
  Pork tenderloin, a strip cut to fit the length of the lamb, and thick enough just to be enclosed by it
  Rosemary leaves
  Garlic powder
  Salt and pepper
  Lemon juice
  Worcestershire

Have the butcher bone lamb and cut pork to suitable size; sprinkle inside of lamb with rosemary leaves, garlic powder, and salt and pepper to taste. Lay on pork tenderloin, roll, and tie securely. Rub lamb with lemon juice and Worcestershire all over, then roast over charcoal 4 inches from coals, either on a rack or spit. If on rack, turn occasionally during cooking. It will take about 2 hours, although a meat thermometer is more reliable; thermometer should register 175° to 180°F. Serve with roasted onions. Makes 4 to 6 servings.

CARNE ADOBADA
[New Mexican Cured Pork]

Perhaps feeling most strongly the influences of the early Indian-Mexican cuisine, New Mexicans are less enamored of a big thick steak than they are of a dish of meat skillfully seasoned. Lacking the delicacy of summer's cabrito, kid meat, rural descendants of the conquistadores like to cure winter's pork in this fashion.

Remove fat from any tender cut of pork desired; cut into strips 3 inches long, 2 inches thick. Prepare Green Chili Sauce with fresh peppers, but do not cook, simply combine all ingredients. Marinate meat in sauce for 24 hours, or in refrigerator as long as 1 week. When wanted, cut meat into smaller pieces and sauté in hot lard until done; add some of the Green Chili Sauce, cover, and cook slowly until sauce is thick and meat tender.

CHILE CON CARNE VERDE

After the Spanish conquistadores, came the Spanish padres who established missions for the Indians. Nuns came after the padres, establishing convents and teaching more civilized methods of cooking to the Indian women. It was the nuns who made the first carne con chile, "meat with chili," and whether this recipe is a first or last variation, it's refreshing after so many pots and cans of indifferent red chili with beans.

- 3 pounds beef chuck or lean beef for pot roast
  Water
- ¼ cup drippings or lard
- 2 cups canned green chilies (fresh, of course, may be used)
- 3 garlic cloves, pressed
- 2 cups chopped canned or fresh peeled tomatoes
  Salt

Simmer meat in ample water until tender but not well done; reserve broth and skim off any fat. Cut into small cubes and sauté in fat. Add chopped chilies, garlic, tomatoes, and 2 cups meat broth. Simmer slowly, covered, until meat is done. Season with salt to taste. This, like all stews, is better the second day. Perfect for a casual big dinner. Makes 6 servings.

Variations—In place of beef, use venison to make a fine Deer Chili.

Replace the green chilies with 2 cups or more Red Chili Sauce, or at least ½ cup chili powder (in which case increase the tomatoes by 1 cupful). This is *Chile con Carne Colorado*.

Add either 1½ pounds dried pinto beans which have been properly soaked, cooked, seasoned, and drained, or 6 cans (1 pound 4 ounces each) pinto beans, drained; add to meat with chilies, garlic, tomatoes, and broth, and simmer as above. This is the most famous of Southwestern chilies.

NOTE: *Chile con Carne* must never be made of ground meat, nor be caught with a layer of fat.

Sopaipillas

Tamales

Chile con Carne Verde

Broiled ham slices with sweet potato-stuffed orange shells

SOUTHWESTERN COOKERY

GALLINA RELLENA

[Stuffed Turkey, Southwestern Style]

One of the rare specialities of the Southwest is the turkey population of the Salt River Valley in Arizona. They run free under the olive trees grown there, and gobble up all the olives fallen to the ground. Like the field-salted lambs of Normandy who, nourished on grass growing in salty marshland, come to the table salted to perfection, the olive-fed turkeys are a gourmet-giant's step ahead of their feathered brothers raised on dullard's fare. But whether olive-stuffed or stuffed with this superb Southwestern combination of meat, sweets, chocolate, and spices, there is no roast to rival a perfectly roasted young turkey.

- 1 turkey (12 to 15 pounds)
- Salt and monosodium glutamate (optional)
- ½ cup butter
- 1 pound cooked beef, ground after cooking
- 2 cups golden raisins
- 1 to 2 squares (1 to 2 ounces) unsweetened chocolate, melted
- 1 cup shelled roasted piñons (Italian pignoli may be substituted, but no other nuts)
- 1 cup beef consommé, not too strong
- 1 teaspoon ground cinnamon
- 1 teaspoon ground coriander
- ½ teaspoon ground cloves
- Salt to taste
- ½ cup dry red wine

Clean turkey, rub inside with salt and monosodium glutamate, then rub outside with butter. Wrap in damp cloth and refrigerate on the night before cooking. Remove from refrigerator early next morning, and prepare stuffing. Combine all ingredients except wine; simmer, stirring, until thick. Add wine, bring to boil, then set aside to cool. Stuff turkey as usual and roast as usual, breast side down first half of cooking, basting several times with drippings in pan. Makes 12 to 14 servings.

HOT TAMALE PIE

Here is as good an example as any we have of Indian-Mexican-Anglo-Cowboy cuisines combining to form a Southwestern flavor unique in the world.

Line greased baking dish with cornmeal mush made from *masa harina*, carefully following directions on the package. Fill with *Chile con Carne* with or without beans, as you prefer, fresh chopped tomatoes, chopped raw onions, and chopped canned green chilies; these may be in layers or simply willy-nilly. Top with a pattern of pitted whole ripe olives, add a mountain of grated yellow cheese, then heat in preheated moderate oven (350°F.) for about 15 minutes.

Variation—A good *Last-Minute Tamale Pie* can be put together in no time by breaking frozen or canned tamales into pieces into a greased baking dish, covering with canned *chile con carne*, then with tomatoes, raw onions, green chilies, even a handful of raisins, and the finish of olives and cheese. Or use leftover cooked meat in the pie instead of beef in a tin, and simply season drained canned pinto beans with some good chili sauce in place of a proper *chile con carne*.

HUNTER'S REWARD

The Southwestern mountains, looming large over every desert of the region and resplendent with wild flowers, native shrubs, and songbirds that make Eastern lady sight-seers weak in the knees, hold a wealth of mule deer, white-tailed deer, bear, elk, antelope, bighorn, and peccary to make Eastern hunters dizzy with choice. Here is a campfire stew deliciously typical of the territory.

- 5 pounds stewing game (properly hung if necessary)
- Drippings
- Big handful of raw potatoes, maybe 2 big handfuls, in chunks
- Same of onions, in chunks
- 1 or 2 red chili peppers, seeded
- Salt to taste
- 1 can (1 pound) yellow corn, or more
- 1 can (1 pound) tomatoes, or more
- 1 can (1 pound) hominy, or more
- 1 can (1 pound) okra or fresh summer squash, if available
- ½ pound bacon, cut up

Cut game into 1½-inch chunks. Brown meat in an iron pot over campfire, using just enough drippings to keep meat from sticking. Cover and let mixture simmer in its own juices very slowly until almost tender; if meat is dry by nature, add some water. Add potatoes, onions, chili peppers, and salt. When everything is ready, add the canned vegetables. If using fresh squash, cut into chunks and add to pot 10 minutes before cooked vegetables. Stew gently, covered, while rendering bacon. Add bacon to the pot. When all the hunters are ready, serve. Makes 10 servings.

NOTE: Be sure to let the stew simmer for a nice long time; maybe, if it can be hidden from snoopy night raiders, it should be let mellow overnight.

Variation—Rabbits from the food store rather than from behind a bush are also excellent for this stew, as are tender veal and even kid.

PUEBLO LAMB CHILI

Here is an Indian hominy stew quite similar to the Mexican-Indian pozole, which by now shouldn't surprise anyone at all. Both are made essentially of hominy and meat, with some decorations of green peppers and/or chilies thrown in. As Southwesterners do, mix or match the combinations as the wind and weather move you.

SOUTHWESTERN COOKERY

- 3 pounds lean lamb, cut into 1½-inch cubes
- Bacon drippings
- 8 cups cooked hominy, canned or dried and simmered tender
- 4 cups water
- 10 medium green peppers, seeded and quartered (Indians leave seeds in)
- 3 medium onions, chopped
- 2 garlic cloves, pressed
- Chili powder to taste
- Salt to taste
- Dried oregano to taste

Brown lamb in drippings. Add hominy and water, green peppers, onions, garlic, and seasonings. Simmer, covered, for 1½ to 2 hours, or until tender. Makes 8 to 10 servings.

Variation—Omit green peppers and substitute garbanzos for hominy. Use dry ones, and simmer the meat and other ingredients with the presoaked beans as long as it takes to cook them. Secret of garbanzo cooking: never, never let the water stop simmering, or all is lost.

COWPUNCHER CHILI PIE

Fill greased 8-inch square pan or its equivalent (1½-quart size) with favorite *chile con carne,* with or without beans. Top with Batter and bake in preheated hot oven (400°F.) for 15 minutes. Makes 6 servings.

Batter

- ¾ cup coarse yellow cornmeal
- ½ cup sifted all-purpose flour
- 2 teaspoons baking powder
- 1 tablespoon sugar
- ¾ teaspoon salt
- 1 egg, beaten
- 2 tablespoons melted lard
- ½ cup milk

Mix dry ingredients, then wet ingredients. Combine and pour over chili pie. Smooth even.

VEGETABLES

SWEET POTATOES, NEW INDIAN STYLE

A luxurious dish ancient Indians never knew

Mash cooked sweet potatoes and season; whip with an egg or two, fold in a little whipped cream, then top with chopped garlic that has been browned and some crisp diced salt pork.

QUELITES
[Lamb's Quarters]

Southwesterners so near nature make abundant use of wild greens and herbs in their cooking. Although the tradition of the curandera, *or herb woman, is dying out in villages, fondness for native greens apart from their curative powers endures. Indians prefer* waco, beeweed, *and leaves of wild parsley, but lamb's-quarters is more popular with the Mexicans and Anglos. Beyond the mesas and their wild bounty, substitute spinach, beet, or turnip greens.*

- 2 tablespoons minced onion
- 2 tablespoons drippings
- 2 cups finely chopped steamed greens (about 2 bunches)
- 1 dried red chili, seeds removed
- Salt to taste
- ½ cup or more cooked pinto beans

Brown onion lightly in drippings. Mix in cooked greens, chili, salt, and beans. Makes 4 to 6 servings.

STUFFED TOMATOES, LAS VEGAS

Southern Nevadans have the same feeling for mutton and lamb that Arizonans and West Texans have for beef, even perhaps a little more strongly, since mutton fanciers are generally in the minority. A great pity that most of us never get to savor a flavorsome joint of mutton; few sheepmen can afford to let their lambs go that long. Tomatoes being a Southwestern specialty and combining their sweet-tartness so well with lamb, here is a city-slick version one might find at any barbecue of a warm Las Vegas night.

- 8 large firm tomatoes
- Salt and pepper to taste
- ¼ pound mushrooms, coarsely chopped
- 1 small onion, minced
- 1 cup raw wild rice
- ½ cup minced celery
- 2 tablespoons minced parsley
- Pinch of dried mint
- 3 tablespoons butter
- 1½ cups hot chicken broth
- 4 slices of bacon (optional)

Slice lids off tomatoes, carefully scoop out pulp, and discard seeds. Season insides with salt and pepper and turn tomato cases upside down to drain. Sauté mushrooms, onion, rice, celery, parsley, and mint in butter until all are well coated and begin to take on color; add chopped tomato pulp and boiling broth. Cover and simmer for 20 minutes, or until rice is tender. Season to taste. Fill tomato cases with the mixture. Bake in preheated moderate oven (350°F.) just long enough to heat through. Garnish with a sprinkle of crisp bacon if desired. Makes 8 servings.

SOUTHWESTERN COOKERY

FRIJOLES, FRIJOLITOS, Y FRIJOLES REFRITOS
[Beans, Mashed Beans, and Beans Refried]

Of the Three Sisters of Indian agriculture, corn, beans, and squash, beans are the darling of the family. Everybody in the Southwest eats beans; the Anglos once or twice a week, the cowboys every day, and the Indians and Spanish-Mexicans twice, maybe three times daily. And there is really only one bean that means frijoles to Southwesterners: the pinto, or painted bean. Here is the rule for beans for "a frijole man," as J. Frank Dobie called himself.

- 1 pound dried pinto beans
- Water
- 1½ pounds salt pork, cubed
- 12 chiles pequeños (little wild Mexican red peppers)
- Grated raw onion
- Cider vinegar

Wash beans thoroughly; soak overnight in water to cover. Add salt pork and cook beans until tender, from 3 to 6 hours. (If more salt is needed, add during the last hour of cooking.) Add more water during cooking if needed. Add about 2 *chiles* to each plate of beans; mash up on plate along with onion; add vinegar. Makes 6 servings.

Variations—Mr. Dobie added that a distinct addition to *frijoles* is 2 or 3 tablespoons honey cooked in a pound of beans.

Frijoles Refritos

These are the best of all possible beans. Begin with beans that have simmered until all liquid evaporates. Then mash with a potato masher, moisten with melted bacon drippings (not a lot), a little flour, and some salt if necessary. Panfry for 10 to 15 minutes, stirring to keep from scorching. They're even better the next day, with a bit more drippings stirred in and some grated yellow cheese. Heat just enough for cheese to melt.

TAOS TACOS

Of all the cities of the Southwest, probably Taos, an artists' colony set in the mesaland above Santa Fe, is the purest and most practicing example of Southwestern culture. Nearly all the dwellings are adobe. People cherish the country and its heritage, nearly everything the eye falls on is glorious.

Prepare a buffet of tacos by frying corn tortillas in deep lard or oil (plan 2 or 3 for each guest); fold in half. Arrange tacos in hot pottery platter and place in center of buffet. Have fillings lined up for guests to concoct their own tacos: hot cooked chopped beef, pork, chicken and/or turkey seasoned with salt, pepper, and dried oregano; cold diced ripe tomatoes; chopped raw green onions; chopped green chilies; a thick blend of *chile con carne* perhaps; and always shredded lettuce, shredded yellow cheese, and a choice of Green or Red Chili Sauce.

TOSTADAS INDIO

Southern Californians at the very Eastern tip of the state are, through a link with common Indian ancestors, included in the Southwest. Geographically the land is desert and very hot. This is a favorite quick lunch in the heat; yes, old hands in the territory insist that hot food makes them more comfortable.

Spread tortillas with butter, toast in preheated very hot oven (450°F.), then pile into a basket. Serve with a bowl of *Frijoles Refritos* (at left), a bowl of grated yellow cheese, and another of shredded lettuce. Everyone then swipes their *tostadas* through the beans and heaps the cheese and lettuce on top.

SAUCES

SOUTHWESTERN CHILI SAUCE

When an Arizonan, New Mexican, or West Texan runs out of chili pepper sauce, he either has to make up a new batch pronto, or he might as well close up the kitchen; chili sauce is as crucial as salt to Southwestern cooking.

- ½ cup chili powder
- Cold water
- 1 teaspoon salt
- 4 cups boiling water
- 3 tablespoons lard
- 1 garlic clove, pressed

Make a paste of chili powder and a little cold water; add to salted boiling water with fat; stir to blend, then simmer for 15 to 20 minutes to the consistency of tomato sauce. Add garlic. For thicker hotter sauce, add more chili powder. Makes about 3 cups.

GREEN CHILI SAUCE

Found on Mexican tables in the Southwest three times a day.

- 3 green chilies (fresh or canned), seeds included, chopped
- 4 green tomatoes, chopped
- 2 medium onions, chopped
- 1 cup boiling water
- 1 garlic clove, pressed
- 1 teaspoon dried oregano
- Salt to taste

If using fresh chilies, cook for 10 minutes in boiling water to cover; drain. Add tomatoes, onions, and boiling water; simmer for 20 minutes. Press through sieve or food mill; add garlic, oregano, and enough salt to flavor highly. Should be as thick as tomato paste. Keep tightly covered. Makes about 1¼ cups.

SOPPIN' SAUCE

Sop is what cowboys daub on the meat as it barbecues. They use a paint brush, a rag tied to a stick, or for really big doings, new brooms dunked into great tubs of sop.

- 1 cup tomato catsup
- 2 cups Worcestershire
- 1 cup mighty strong coffee beverage
- ½ cup butter (no substitutes)
- 2 tablespoons freshly ground black pepper
- 1 tablespoon sugar (dudes need it)
- 1 tablespoon salt, or to taste

Simmer all ingredients slowly for 30 minutes, stirring occasionally. Best on beef or chicken. Makes about 3 cups.

BREADS

SOPAIPILLAS

These are Southwestern "sofa pillows," deep-fried, hollow like popovers. Yankees butter them, natives don't. They can serve as bread at dinner as an alternative to tortillas, or rolled in cinnamon sugar, they become ethereal buns with coffee, chocolate, or a cup of mocha.

- 4 cups sifted all-purpose flour
- 2 teaspoons salt
- 4 teaspoons baking powder
- ¼ cup lard
- Water
- Lard for deep frying
- Cinnamon sugar (optional)

Sift first 3 ingredients together. Work in lard with fingertips until mixture is the consistency of cornmeal. Add just enough water to hold together. Rest in refrigerator for 10 minutes. Roll dough ⅛ inch thick and cut into 1½-inch squares. Fry in deep lard 2 or 3 minutes on each side, until crisp and brown. Drain and serve hot. For a sweet bread, roll in cinnamon sugar after frying. Makes about 6 dozen.

ARIZONA'S BISCUITS

As Southwestern as chile con carne are the oversize biscuits on Arizona's cattle ranches. Probably they were first cut that big to fit the huge hands holding them!

Prepare your lightest biscuit dough, roll at least ½ inch thick, and cut into circles at least 3 inches wide. Serve with butter and mesquite honey.

Variation—*Calico Biscuits* have finely chopped green and red peppers blended into the flour and shortening, and minced raw onion added to the milk.

SOUTHWESTERN COOKERY

BURRITOS FROM TAOS

Sopaipillas are an historic bread. Here is a contemporary departure.

Cut *Sopaipillas* twice usual size and fry. Then split open a pocket and stuff with a taco blend of meat or poultry and grated cheese. Slip under broiler until cheese melts. Delicious cut very small and stuffed as an hors d'oeuvre for cocktails.

CHUCK WAGON PECAN BREAD

This is a recipe very nearly a hundred years old, from a cook who served it to cowhands along the Pecos River.

- 3½ cups sifted all-purpose flour
- 1 cup sugar
- 1 teaspoon salt
- 3 teaspoons baking powder
- 1 cup milk
- 2 cups chopped pecans
- ¼ cup melted lard
- 1 egg

Combine all ingredients and stir well. Pour into greased baking pan 9 x 5 x 3 inches. Bake in preheated moderate oven (350°F.) for 1 hour. Turn out and cool on rack. Keeps well, wrapped up tightly.

DESSERTS

ICED PINEAPPLE

With such a beautiful bounty of fresh fruits to choose from—Salt River Valley honeydews, casabas, and cantaloupes; Texas watermelons; Oak Creek Canyon peaches; apples, dates, grapes, and raisins from all over the area—Southwesterners enjoy a light simple refreshing bit of fruit to finish every meal. Time was when all the fruits were dried fruits; because there was little sugar for canning, fresh crops were set out in baskets to let the sun do the preserving.

A new twist to a Mexican custom: cut a pineapple lengthwise into halves. Use a knife to slice out the pulp; cut away core, then chop pineapple fruit coarsely. Return to shells and chill. To serve, cover with alternating slabs of pineapple, lemon, and lime ice. Sprinkle with orange-flavored brandy if desired.

SOUTHWESTERN COOKERY

CARAMELA

The lovely bittersweet flavor of caramelized brown sugar is another hallmark of Southwestern cooking. And ice cream, one of the culinary latecomers to the region, naturally was welcomed with open arms. A simple ice cream on a stick finishes many company barbecues, for example, although as with everything else they like best, highly flavored ice creams are more popular with Southwesterners than bland. In Phoenix, one store sells licorice ice cream, but the recipe is a secret, sad to say. Southwesterners have a fondness for airy light creams—Bavarians, the Spanish natillas (Yankees call it Floating Island)—something cool that will float down after a meal of zesty chilies.

- ½ pound light brown sugar
- 4 cups heavy cream
- 4 egg yolks

Follow directions carefully: Melt sugar slowly in large saucepan and cook until it all turns to syrup. With wooden spoon *slowly* stir in cream, blending each trickle of cream thoroughly before adding more. Remove from heat while you whisk egg yolks lightly in a large bowl. Pour sugar and cream into yolks slowly, whisking madly as you go. Freeze in molds or ice-cube tray. Makes 8 to 10 servings.
NOTE: This is as delicious but as ephemeral a frozen cream as ever was; it melts quickly, so serve without dallying on the way. A triumph of simplicity.
Variation—If you can buy *piloncillos*, little pillars of Mexican brown sugar, by all means make the ice cream with them.

ANISEED COOKIES

Cookies, too, outrank cakes in popularity in this part of the country. And aniseeds, from the Mexican influence, are a favorite cookie flavoring.

- ½ cup butter (or half lard, half butter)
- 1½ cups firmly packed brown sugar (white sugar is good too)
- 3 eggs
  Few drops of oil of anise from the drugstore or 1 teaspoon aniseeds
- 3 cups sifted all-purpose flour
  Lots of freshly roasted aniseeds

With your hand, cream butter with sugar. Add eggs, one at a time. When quite creamy, blend in anise oil, then flour. Drop from teaspoon onto greased cookie sheet and sprinkle with aniseeds. Bake in preheated moderate oven (350°F.) until bottoms are golden, tops pale, about 12 minutes. Cool. Let ripen in airtight can for a week before eating. Makes 4 dozen.

"PIEBOX" SPECIAL VINEGAR PIE

"Piebox" is slang for chuck wagon. The range hands called it that with both affection and optimism, hoping there would be a pie in the wagon for their dessert. All the Southwest is pie-eating country; cakes just don't rate as high. In the days when apples hadn't yet been planted in the land, cattlemen loved the Vinegar Pie, its faint but tantalizing smell of apples from the cider vinegar filling the ranch house while the pie baked. Here is a flossy version that would lift a cowboy's eyebrows.

- Pastry for 1-crust 9-inch pie
- ¼ cup all-purpose flour
- 1 teaspoon ground cinnamon
- ¼ teaspoon ground cloves
- ½ teaspoon ground nutmeg
- ¼ teaspoon ground coriander
  Dash of salt
- 4 egg yolks
- 2 egg whites
- 1 cup sugar
- 1 cup dairy sour cream
- 2 tablespoons cider vinegar
- ½ cup seedless raisins
- 1½ cups coarsely chopped pecans
  Whipped cream to garnish

Line pie pan with pastry and freeze pastry while you prepare filling. Sift dry ingredients together. Whisk egg yolks just to blend; beat egg whites until stiff. Fold sugar into whites thoroughly but not overmuch, and stir with wooden spoon into yolks. Add sifted dry ingredients with a few strokes, then sour cream. Mix all remaining ingredients but whipping cream and fold into filling. Spread in pastry-lined pie pan and smooth top. Bake in preheated very hot oven (450°F.) for 10 minutes. Lower heat to hot (400°F.) and bake for 5 minutes. Then bake at moderate (350°F.) about 15 minutes more, or until set. Cool on rack, then garnish border with a flourish of unsweetened whipped cream.

SOUTHWESTERN MOCHA

If chili, oregano, and garlic light the main course, then cinnamon, chocolate, and mocha spell dessert. Here is a dessert in a cup, all warmth and fragrance, very like the Southwest it represents.

- 4 squares (4 ounces) Mexican chocolate or sweet cooking chocolate
- 4 cups rich milk
- ½ teaspoon ground cinnamon, or more to taste if Mexican chocolate is not used
  Sugar (optional)
- 2 eggs
- ½ teaspoon finely grated orange rind
- ½ teaspoon vanilla extract
- ½ cup black coffee

Melt chocolate over boiling water; whisk in milk and cinnamon. Heat in top part of a double boiler over boiling water for 20 minutes. If not sweet enough, add a bit of sugar. Whisk eggs with rind and vanilla and pour hot chocolate onto them in a stream, whisking constantly. Add coffee, and beat, beat, beat to a froth. Serve at once. Makes 4 servings.

SOYBEAN COOKBOOK

SOYBEAN—This bean, also called soya, soy pea, soja, and soi, is found in the hairy pods of an erect bushy legume, native to Asia. Soybeans contain a large proportion of assimilable protein, have a considerable fat content, and are low in carbohydrates, having no starch at all. They form an important part of the daily diet in China and southeastern Asia where they serve as a meat substitute—a role that they are currently taking on in the United States.

In America, too, soybeans are cultivated as a high-protein, low-cost food. Special varieties are grown with a nutty or bland flavor that may be cooked and eaten like navy beans. Soybeans are also grown commercially for making margarine, cooking oils, soaps, emulsifiers, plastics, and many other compound industrial products. Over one third of the edible fats consumed in the United States are made with soybean oil.

A new development which may have considerable effect on our nutrition and market basket economy is the use of soybeans as an extender of ground meat. The product is known as TVP or textured vegetable protein.

Soybeans are processed to produce a texture closely resembling the ground meat which it supplements. Supermarkets sell it already mixed with meat, or packaged plain or seasoned to add to ground meat.

Aside from the welcome savings, because there is less fat there is less shrinkage in meat loaves, patties and meatballs. Fortunately, the protein content is comparable to the meat it replaces. For further information see under the section in vegetables, recipes and discussion of textured vegetable protein, TVP.

Soybean cake is fed to livestock and soybean oil meal for livestock and poultry is the most important of modern high-protein feeds. Soybeans are an essential and exceedingly important crop in states like Michigan, Illinois, Missouri, Iowa, and Minnesota.

Storage—After opening package of dried soybeans, place unused beans in a clean, covered container and store in kitchen shelf. Soybean flour should be refrigerated. It will keep up to 6 months, covered.
Dried beans, kitchen shelf: 1 year
Dried beans, refrigerator shelf, cooked and covered: 1 to 4 days
Dried beans, refrigerator frozen-food compartment, cooked beans and bean dishes, prepared for freezing: 1 month
Dried beans, freezer, cooked beans and bean dishes, prepared for freezing: 4 to 6 months
Nutritive Food Values—Soybeans are high in protein, contain some calcium, phosphorus, a high amount of potassium, some iron, small amounts of vitamin A, thiamine, riboflavin, and niacin.
Soybean flour, 1 ounce, high-fat = 108 calories
Soybean flour, ½ cup, defatted = 165 calories
Canned soybeans, 4 ounces, solids and liquid = 85 calories
Canned soybeans, 4 ounces, drained solids = 117 calories
Dried soybeans, raw, ½ cup (3.7 ounces) = 423 calories
Dried soybeans, cooked, 4 ounces = 147 calories
Soy sauce, 1 ounce = 19 calories
Soybean oil, 1 ounce = 251 calories

Basic Preparation—Packaged dried soybeans are usually sorted and washed before packaging, so need only be rinsed. Beans bought in bulk should be sorted carefully, discarding broken or defective ones, and washed until water is clear. It is necessary to soak beans to replace the water that was lost in drying. In general, 6 cups of water for each 1 pound of beans is the correct amount. Save the nutritious soaking water to use in cooking the beans. There are two methods of soaking:

1. **Quick method:** Measure the soaking water into a large, heavy pot. Add washed beans and bring to a boil. Cover pot and cook for 2 minutes; remove from heat. Let stand for 1 hour, then cook, covered, according to recipe directions, or until tender.

2. **Overnight method:** Measure soaking water into a large pot; add washed beans, cover pot, and let stand for 6 to 8 hours. To prevent souring and hard skins, the 2-minute boil is also recommended, even when beans are soaked overnight. Beans may also be refrigerated to prevent souring. Cook, covered, according to recipe directions, or until tender.

The soybean plant resembles ordinary field and navy beans. There are over 1,000 varieties cultivated in Southeastern Asia, varying from less than one foot tall to five or six feet. Nearly all varieties, however, are covered with fine tawny or gray hair. The pods range in color from tan to nearly black. The seeds, or beans, may be yellow, green, brown, black, or a combination of these colors. The seeds vary in size, weighing anywhere from 1200 to a pound to 3500 to a pound. Wild beans are even smaller.

Soy sauce is no doubt the culinary soybean product best known to Westerners. Orientals have enjoyed the condiment for thousands of years, and some Japanese soy sauce brands are 350 years old. Few are still made entirely by the traditional process of natural aging, but all begin with a mixture of boiled beans and roasted wheat flour. The percentage of each ingredient largely determines the taste, thickness, and color of the final product. Brine is added to the fermented mash of soybeans and wheat flour and this mixture may be allowed to age for eight to twelve months (the best grades may take as much as seven years to reach their peak of perfection). Much less costly than this enzyme hydrolization is the chemical process of using hydrochloric acid or sulfuric acid to hydrolize the protein. Today, almost all brands of soy sauce, even in Japan, contain at least some chemically hydrolized sauce, and while some brands are saltier, thicker, or darker than others, it takes a connoisseur to distinguish between naturally aged soy sauce and the chemically hydrolized variety.

Although soy sauce is the most widely used soybean product in this country, Far Eastern cooking relies heavily on other soy foods. Bean curd, the fermented milk from the bean, is eaten throughout Southeast Asia as a protein

SOYBEAN

food. It may be eaten as an accompaniment to other foods, or used in various dishes. It is sometimes boiled in syrup and eaten as a candy, or soaked in salted water, roasted, and eaten as a nut. The *dow fu pok* of the Chinese and *aburage* of the Japanese is a deep-fried bean curd. In Chinese groceries Americans will find *fooh jook*, the dried "cream" of boiled soybean milk. It is sold in long narrow beige strips, and often used in soups. *Tiem jook* is the sediment of boiled soybean milk. This is dried into stiff shiny tan sheets, and is used in stewed meatless dishes.

Bean sprouts, widely eaten by the Chinese as a green vegetable, either raw or cooked, are grown from the beans. They are available canned or frozen in this country; occasionally fresh soybean sprouts can be found in health-food stores. With soybeans for sprouting available, anyone can grow sprouts at home.

Availability—Fresh soybeans are not generally available. Occasionally they can be bought in the areas where they are grown during the late summer months.

There are almost endless soybean products sold in health-food stores: canned plain; Boston style, with tomato sauce; dried whole and split; soybean flour: full-fat, high-fat, low-fat, and defatted; seeds for sprouting; soybean oil. soybean milk, fluid and powder; sweetened and flavored milk concentrate: liquid and powder. Chinese stores sell **soybean curd** or *tofu*.

Soy sauce is available in most food stores.

FISH IN SWEET-SOUR SAUCE

The fish, served with the Sweet-Sour Sauce which resembles a bed of brightly colored seaweed, is great fun to eat. With your chopsticks, you pick at the fish and fill your plate.

Choose a sea bass, a mullet, or any other fish weighing 2 or 3 pounds complete with head and tail. Remove the fins, and scale and clean the fish.

Prepare a court bouillon for the fish in a kettle with enough water to cover; add 1 garlic clove, 1 tablespoon salt, 1 tablespoon cider vinegar, 1 piece 1-inch gingerroot, and a little orange peel. Bring court bouillon to a boil and cook for 15 minutes. Place fish in the kettle, cover and simmer for 15 to 18 minutes. Remove to a hot platter and serve with Sweet-Sour Sauce.

Sweet-Sour Sauce

- 1 tablespoon each sugar, soy sauce, and Worcestershire
- ¼ cup cider vinegar
- 3 green onions, finely shredded
- 1 garlic clove, finely chopped
- 1 teaspoon chopped preserved gingerroot
- ½ cup fish stock
- ½ cup Chinese sweet pickles

Heat together all ingredients. Bring to a boil and stir. If it is not thick enough, add a bit of cornstarch mixed with a little water. Serve with the fish.

CHINESE-BEEF CASSEROLE

- 1 beef flank steak (about 1¼ pounds)
- 2 tablespoons all-purpose flour
- ½ teaspoon salt
- Dash of pepper
- 1 garlic clove, minced
- 2 tablespoons cooking oil
- 1 can (10¾ ounces) beef gravy
- 2 teaspoons soy sauce
- 1 teaspoon sugar
- 1 green pepper, sliced
- 1 can (8 ounces) tomatoes, drained

Pound steak with edge of saucer or meat hammer; cut diagonally into thin slices. Dredge meat with flour seasoned with salt and pepper. Brown meat and garlic in oil. Add next 3 ingredients; heat and pour into greased 2-quart casserole. Cover and bake in preheated moderate oven (350°F.) for 1 hour. Add green pepper and tomatoes. Bake, covered, for 1 hour longer. Makes 6 servings.

SOY POT ROAST

- 4 pounds boned chuck or rump pot roast
- ¼ cup vegetable oil
- 1 cup soy sauce
- ½ cup sugar
- 1 piece (1 inch) cinnamon stick, or ½ teaspoon ground cinnamon
- 2½ cups water
- 1 cup sherry
- 3 tablespoons cornstarch

Brown meat on all sides in hot oil in large heavy kettle or Dutch oven. Mix soy sauce, sugar, cinnamon, and 2 cups water; pour over meat. Cover, bring to boil, and simmer for 3 hours, or until tender. Add sherry after first 2 hours of cooking. When meat is tender, remove to a hot platter. Pour off liquid from pan, reserving 2½ cups. Bring to boil. Stir in cornstarch blended with remaining ½ cup water. Simmer, stirring, until smooth and thickened. Serve with the pot roast. Makes 6 to 8 servings.

SOYBEAN STEW

- 4 slices of bacon
- 4 raw potatoes, peeled
- 2 large onions, sliced
- 1 green pepper, sliced
- Salt, pepper, and cayenne to taste
- 2½ cups cooked soybeans
- 1 can (1 pound) tomatoes

Cut bacon into 1-inch pieces and cook in heavy skillet until nearly done. Remove bacon. Add potatoes, onions, and green pepper to fat in skillet. Season with salt, pepper, and cayenne. Add beans and tomatoes. Top with bacon, cover, and simmer for about 1½ hours, adding water if necessary. Makes 4 servings.

COMPANY CASSEROLE

2 cups raw long-grain rice
¼ cup butter or margarine
4½ cups hot poultry broth
4 cups diced cooked poultry
2 cans (4 ounces each) sliced mushrooms
⅓ cup soy sauce
1 package (12 ounces) frozen shelled shrimps, cooked and split
8 green onions, chopped
⅔ cup slivered almonds

Put rice in shallow pan. Brown in preheated hot oven (400°F.) for 10 minutes, shaking pan occasionally to brown evenly. Transfer to 3-quart covered casserole. Add butter and stir to coat each grain. Add broth; cover and bake in preheated moderate oven (375°F.) for 35 to 40 minutes, or until rice is tender. Mix in poultry, mushrooms, and liquid, soy sauce, and shrimps. Cool casserole and freeze or refrigerate at this point and reheat later. If frozen, stand at room temperature for several hours before reheating. If refrigerated, heat directly. In either case, stir in green onions; top with almonds. Cover; bake in preheated hot oven (400°F.) for 30 to 40 minutes. If dry, add a little water. Uncover during last 10 minutes. Makes 8 servings.

BAKED SOY CHICKEN

1 frying chicken (about 2½ pounds), cut up
3 tablespoons soy sauce
2 eggs
1 teaspoon water
¾ cup fine dry bread crumbs

Wash chicken and dry on absorbent paper. Brush chicken with soy sauce to cover completely. Beat eggs with water and stir in crumbs. The mixture should be a little thicker than a sauce of pouring consistency. Pat on chicken on all sides to cover. Bake, uncovered, in preheated very slow oven (250°F.) about 2 hours. Makes 4 servings.

SOY-WHEAT MUFFINS

½ cup soybean flour
1½ cups whole-wheat flour
3 teaspoons baking powder
1 teaspoon salt
2 tablespoons sugar
1 egg, beaten
3 tablespoons butter or margarine, melted
1 cup milk

Mix dry ingredients. Add remaining ingredients all at once, stirring only enough to moisten dry ingredients. Half-fill muffin-pan sections with batter. Bake in preheated hot oven (425°F.) for 12 to 15 minutes. Makes 12.

SOYED ALMONDS

4 cups blanched almonds (1¼ pounds)
¼ cup butter or margarine
¼ cup soy sauce

Put almonds in shallow pan 13 x 9 x 2 inches. Roast in preheated hot oven (400°F.) about 15 minutes, stirring several times. Add butter and soy sauce; stir. Roast for 12 to 15 minutes longer, stirring often, until nuts are coated and fairly dry. Makes 4 cups.

SOYBEAN SHEPHERD'S PIE

12 small white onions, peeled
   Water
4 carrots, halved crosswise
2 cups cooked soybeans
2 tablespoons all-purpose flour
2 tablespoons butter or margarine
1 teaspoon salt
⅛ teaspoon pepper
3 cups seasoned mashed potatoes

Cover onions with water and cook, covered, for 20 minutes. Add carrots, cover, and cook for 10 minutes longer, or until carrots are tender. Drain, reserving liquid. Put onions, carrots, and beans in greased 2-quart casserole. Brown flour lightly in butter. Gradually add 2 cups reserved vegetable liquid and salt. Cook for 2 minutes. Add pepper and pour liquid over vegetables. Spread potatoes on top. Bake in preheated hot oven (425°F.) for 15 to 20 minutes. Makes 4 servings.

SOYBEAN COOKERY

by BEVERLY BUSH SMITH

While soybeans are providing high-quality-protein and low-starch nutrition, along with many vitamins and minerals, they're doing wonders for your budget.

Dried soybeans can be used in casseroles, soups, salads—anywhere you'd use a navy or kidney bean. But that's not the only useful form of the soybean. Soy grits are a flavorful addition to soups and meat and fish dishes, and can even be toasted to use like nuts in desserts. Soy flour is a wonderful nutritional addition to baked goods, from breads, waffles and pancakes to desserts. To use soy flour in a favorite recipe, try about ¼ soy flour to ¾ wheat flour. (You need to keep part of the wheat flour which contains gluten; soy flour does not.)

SOYBEAN

BASIC PREPARATION OF SOYBEANS

Rinse beans, put in bowl and add 3 cups water for each cup beans. Let stand 6 to 8 hours or overnight. Drain, reserving liquid for cooking, and remove any loose, fibrous skins. Put beans and soaking water in kettle. Add more water, if needed, to cover. For each cup beans (measured before soaking) add 1 tablespoon vegetable oil, 1 small onion, chopped, ¼ cup diced celery (leaves and all), 1 bay leaf, 2 peppercorns and 1 teaspoon salt. Bring to boil, lower heat and simmer 3 hours, or until very tender.

Soybean Paste

Soak beans and cook as directed above. Drain well. Force through sieve or colander. 1 cup cooked soybeans yields about ⅔ cup paste.

SAVORY SANDWICH SPREAD

- 3 tablespoons braunschweiger
- ¼ cup Soybean Paste
- 1 tablespoon mayonnaise

Mix all ingredients together. Makes about ½ cup spread.

BOSTON BAKED SOYS

- 1½ cups soybeans
- Water
- ¼ pound bacon
- 1 small onion, chopped
- 2 tablespoons molasses
- ½ cup catsup
- ½ teaspoon each dry mustard and Worcestershire
- ½ teaspoon salt
- ¼ teaspoon pepper

Soak and cook soybeans according to directions. Dice all but 2 strips bacon and mix with beans, remaining ingredients and ¼ cup of bean cooking water. Turn into greased 1½-quart casserole. Crisscross the 2 bacon strips on top. Cover and bake in preheated slow oven (300°F.) 30 minutes. Stir, then bake, uncovered, 30 minutes longer, or until thick. Makes 4 servings.

CHILI CON SOYS

- ½ pound ground beef
- 2 teaspoons salt
- 2 tablespoons chopped onion
- Pepper to taste
- 2 to 3 teaspoons chili powder (or to taste)
- 1 can (28 ounces) tomatoes
- 1 can (6 ounces) tomato paste
- 1 teaspoon sugar
- 2 cups cooked soybeans

Brown beef with salt in large saucepan. Add next 6 ingredients. Cook over low heat, stirring occasionally, 1 hour. Add soybeans and cook 15 minutes longer. Serve with whole-wheat crackers. Makes 6 servings.

NOTE: If desired, omit the meat and add a bouillon cube for flavor. Makes 4 or 5 servings.

COLORFUL CALIFORNIA DIP

- ¼ cup Soybean Paste
- ¼ cup mashed avocado
- ¼ cup mayonnaise
- ½ to 1 teaspoon lemon juice
- ½ teaspoon seasoned salt
- Dash of cayenne

Blend all ingredients together. Serve with whole-wheat or corn chips or with rye crackers. Makes about ⅔ cup.

SOUTH-OF-THE-BORDER SOYS

- ¼ cup soy or safflower oil
- 2 cups cooked soybeans, mashed
- 1 teaspoon instant minced onion
- ½ teaspoon chili powder
- Salt to taste
- ¾ cup shredded Cheddar or Jack cheese

Heat oil in skillet. Mix next 4 ingredients together. Cook in oil and, when oil is absorbed, sprinkle cheese on top. Let stand over low heat until cheese is melted. Makes 4 servings.

BONUS BREAD

- ⅓ cup unsulfured molasses
- 2 cups lukewarm water (105°F. to 115°F.)
- 2 packages active dry yeast
- 4 cups whole-wheat flour
- 1 cup unbleached white flour
- 1 cup soy flour
- 1 cup nonfat dry-milk powder
- 3 teaspoons salt
- 3 tablespoons vegetable oil
- 1 egg, slightly beaten
- Sesame seed

Mix molasses and water and dissolve yeast in the mixture. Stir in half the flours and dry milk and beat until smooth. Add salt, oil and remaining flour, or enough to make dough easy to handle. Turn out on floured board and knead 8 to 10 minutes, or until smooth and no longer sticky. Put dough in greased bowl, cover and let rise in warm place 1¾ to 2 hours, or until doubled in bulk. Divide in 2 equal portions and shape in balls. Let rest 10 minutes, then shape in loaves and put in greased 9 x 5 x 3-inch loaf pans. Brush loaves with egg, then sprinkle with sesame seed. Let rise 1 hour, or until doubled in bulk. Bake in preheated moderate oven (375°F.) about 50 minutes. Makes 2 loaves.

DELICATE COFFEE CAKE

- 1 cup margarine
- 1 cup honey
- 2 eggs
- 1 teaspoon vanilla extract
- 1½ cups whole-wheat pastry flour
- ½ cup soy flour
- 2½ teaspoons baking powder
- ½ teaspoon salt
- 6 tablespoons sour milk, buttermilk, yogurt or milk
- ½ cup firmly packed brown sugar
- 1 teaspoon ground cinnamon
- ½ to 1 cup chopped nuts
- ¼ cup wheat germ

Cream margarine and honey, then beat in eggs. Add vanilla. Mix dry ingredients and add alternately with milk, beating after each addition until smooth. Turn half the batter into greased 13 x 9 x 2-inch pan. Mix remaining ingredients and sprinkle half on batter. Carefully spoon on remaining topping. Bake in preheated moderate oven (350°F.) about 30 minutes. Makes 1 large loaf.

NOT-QUITE PUMPKIN PIE

- 2 eggs
- ¾ cup firmly packed brown sugar
- 1½ cups Soybean Paste (cook beans in water only)
- ½ teaspoon ground nutmeg
- ¾ teaspoon ground cinnamon
- ¼ teaspoon each ground allspice and ginger
- ½ teaspoon salt
- ⅓ cup nonfat dry-milk powder
- 1⅓ cups undiluted evaporated milk
- ½ teaspoon vanilla extract
- Whole-Wheat Pie Shell

Beat eggs, then stir in next 8 ingredients. Add evaporated milk gradually, beating until smooth. Stir in vanilla. Pour into pie shell and bake in preheated hot oven (425°F.) 10 minutes. Reduce heat to moderate (325°F.) and bake 30 minutes, or until set. Makes 6 to 8 servings.

Whole-Wheat Pie Shell

Mix 1 cup whole-wheat pastry flour and ¼ teaspoon salt in bowl. Cut in ⅓ cup solid white vegetable shortening until mixture resembles coarse meal. Mixing with fork, add enough cold water to hold ingredients together. Gather into ball and roll on floured board to fit 9-inch piepan. Trim edges and flute.

SPAGHETTI

SPAGHETTI—One of the most popular members of the pasta family, spaghetti is made from a mixture of semolina, the flour that is milled from durum wheat, and water. The dough is passed through metal discs full of holes to emerge as slender solid rods.

The name spaghetti is Italian, from the plural form of *spaghetto*, "string."

Availability and Purchasing Guide—Spaghetti is widely available in different degrees of thickness. In addition to the standard thickness, there are fusilli, short curly spaghetti, the thickest; spaghettini, thin spaghetti; and vermicelli, angel-hair-thin spaghettini, long and straight, or twisted into a birds' nest, used in soups.

One pound uncooked spaghetti equals 4 to 5 cups. One pound spaghetti weighs 4 pounds after cooking and equals 2½ quarts, or 15 servings of ⅔ cup each.

Storage—Spaghetti in its original or other covered container can be stored at room temperature. Prepared dishes should be refrigerated.
Kitchen shelf: 3 to 6 months
Cooked and in prepared dishes, refrigerator shelf: 4 to 5 days
Cooked and in prepared dishes, refrigerator frozen-food compartment: 3 to 4 weeks
Cooked and in prepared dishes, freezer: 1 year

Nutritive Food Values—Enriched spaghetti is a good source of iron and the B vitamins.
1 cup, cooked *al dente* = 216 calories
1 cup, cooked tender = 155 calories

Basic Preparation—Spaghetti should always be freshly cooked in plenty of boiling water salted to taste. To cook 1 pound, it is essential to have a kettle that will hold 6 quarts of water. Add 2 tablespoons salt to 6 quarts water. Bring water to a full rolling boil. Gradually add 1 pound spaghetti, stirring with a long-handled, two-pronged kitchen fork. The water should keep on boiling hard. As the spaghetti begins to soften, fold it over and over in the water so that it won't stick together. Keep on stirring frequently during the cooking process. Occasionally lift out a strand and taste for doneness. Tasting is essential to get the spaghetti right for one's own taste.

When spaghetti is done,* drain it immediately in a large strainer or colander. Return to pot and add seasonings. Stir to coat all strands. Serve immediately on heated platter and heated plates.
*Spaghetti that is to be cooked further in a casserole should not be more than three-quarters done, or the final product will be mushy.

CLAM SPAGHETTI

- ½ cup olive oil
- 1 small garlic clove, minced
- ¼ cup minced onion
- ½ cup minced green pepper or pimiento
- 2 cans (7 ounces each) minced clams
- ¼ cup minced parsley
- ¼ teaspoon dried thyme
- ½ teaspoon salt
- ¼ teaspoon pepper
- ½ cup tomato juice or white wine
- 1 pound spaghetti

Heat olive oil. Cook garlic and onion in it until soft and golden. Add green pepper and cook for 5 minutes. Add clams and juice, parsley, thyme, salt and pepper, and tomato juice. Simmer for 15 minutes, stirring occasionally. Cook and drain spaghetti. Add sauce and toss well. Makes 6 servings.

SPAGHETTI

SPAGHETTI WITH MEATBALLS

- 2 onions, chopped
- 2 garlic cloves, minced
- 2 tablespoons cooking oil
- 1 can (1 pound 12 ounces) tomatoes
- 1 cup water
- 2 leaves fresh or dried basil
- ¼ cup chopped parsley
- ½ teaspoon dried thyme
- 2 teaspoons salt
- ¼ teaspoon pepper
- ¼ teaspoon crushed dried red pepper
- 1 can (6 ounces) tomato paste
- Meatballs
- 12 ounces spaghetti, cooked and hot

Sauté onion and garlic until golden in hot oil in large saucepan. Add tomatoes and bring to boil. Simmer, uncovered, for 20 minutes, stirring occasionally. Add remaining sauce ingredients and browned Meatballs; simmer, uncovered, for 2 hours longer, stirring occasionally. Add more seasoning, if desired. Serve on hot cooked spaghetti. Makes 6 servings.

Meatballs

- ½ pound ground beef
- ½ pound ground pork
- 2 onions, minced
- 1 garlic clove, minced
- ¼ cup chopped parsley
- ½ cup grated Parmesan cheese
- ½ cup fine dry bread crumbs
- 1 egg
- 2 teaspoons salt
- ½ teaspoon pepper
- 2 tablespoons cooking oil

Mix all ingredients except oil thoroughly. Add a little water if mixture seems dry. Shape into 24 balls and brown slowly in hot oil.

TURKEY TETRAZZINI

- ⅔ butter or margarine (about)
- ½ cup all-purpose flour
- 1 cup hot milk
- 1 cup hot chicken bouillon
- ½ teaspoon salt
- ½ teaspoon pepper
- ⅛ teaspoon ground nutmeg
- ¼ cup dry sherry
- ¾ cup heavy cream
- 1 pound thin spaghetti
- ½ pound mushrooms, sliced, or 2 cans (4 ounces each) mushrooms, drained
- 2 to 3 cups diced cooked turkey
- ½ cup grated Parmesan or Romano cheese

Heat ½ cup butter and stir in flour. Combine milk and bouillon; stir into flour mixture. Cook, stirring, until sauce is smooth and thickened. Blend in salt, pepper, nutmeg, and sherry. Stir in cream and remove mixture from heat. Cook and drain spaghetti. Sauté mushrooms in 2 tablespoons butter for 5 minutes. Mix half of sauce with spaghetti and mushrooms. Place in buttered shallow baking dish. Make well in center of spaghetti mixture. Mix remaining sauce with turkey and place in well. Sprinkle with Parmesan cheese. Bake in preheated hot oven (400°F.) for 20 minutes. Makes 6 to 8 servings.

Ham Tetrazzini

Proceed as in Turkey Tetrazzini, but for turkey substitute 2 cups small, thin cooked ham slices. Sauté 1 small green pepper, seeded and cut into rings, with mushrooms. Mix ham with all of sauce, spaghetti, and mushroom mixture. After putting in baking dish, slice 1 large tomato, and arrange slices on top. Sprinkle with grated Parmesan cheese, and put buttered croutons around edge of baking dish. Bake as directed. Makes 6 to 8 servings.

SICILIAN SPAGHETTI

- 3 tablespoons olive oil
- 1 garlic clove, minced
- 2 tablespoons minced parsley
- 1 tablespoon minced fresh basil or 1 teaspoon dried basil
- 1 tablespoon minced celery
- 1 tablespoon capers
- 12 pitted black olives, minced
- 4 anchovy fillets, minced
- Dash of hot pepper sauce
- 3 cans (8 ounces each) plain tomato sauce
- 1 pound spaghetti

Heat olive oil. Over low heat, stirring constantly, cook all ingredients except tomato sauce and spaghetti in oil for 5 minutes. Add tomato sauce and simmer, covered, over low heat for about 30 minutes. Cook and drain spaghetti. Add sauce and toss well. Makes 6 servings.

CARUSO SPAGHETTI

- 2 tablespoons butter or margarine
- 2 medium onions, minced
- 6 fresh tomatoes, peeled, seeded, and chopped
- 1 cup fat-free beef or veal gravy
- ¼ cup olive oil
- 1 can (4 ounces) sliced mushrooms, drained
- 4 canned artichoke bottoms, diced
- 1 cup chopped chicken livers
- 1 teaspoon salt
- ½ teaspoon pepper
- 1 teaspoon grated lemon rind
- 2 tablespoons chopped parsley
- 1 pound spaghetti

Melt butter and cook onions until soft and golden. Add tomatoes and gravy. Simmer for 10 minutes. Heat olive oil and sauté mushrooms, artichoke bottoms, and chicken livers about 5 minutes. Add to tomato sauce together with salt, pepper, lemon rind, and parsley. Cover and simmer for 10 to 15 minutes, stirring frequently. Serve on hot cooked spaghetti. Makes 6 servings.

Ham Tetrazzini

TWO-CHEESE FUSILLI

- 8 ounces fusilli
- 3 tablespoons butter or margarine
- 3 tablespoons all-purpose flour
- 1 cup each hot milk and light cream
- 1 teaspoon salt
- ½ teaspoon pepper
- 2 cups grated Cheddar cheese
- ½ pound Swiss cheese, diced
- Paprika

Cook and drain fusilli. Melt butter and stir in flour. Stir in combined hot milk and cream. Cook until sauce is smooth and thickened. Stir in salt, pepper, and grated Cheddar. Cook until cheese is melted. In buttered dish arrange a layer of fusilli, diced Swiss cheese, and one third of the cheese sauce. Repeat twice. Sprinkle with paprika. Bake in preheated moderate oven (350°F.) for about 20 minutes. Makes 4 to 6 servings.

Olive Two-Cheese Fusilli

Add ¾ cup chopped pitted black or sliced pimiento-stuffed olives to sauce in above recipe. Proceed as directed.

Pimiento Two-Cheese Fusilli

Add ¾ cup chopped pimientos to sauce in above recipe. Proceed as directed.

Poppy-Seed Two-Cheese Fusilli

Add 1 tablespoon poppy seeds to sauce in above recipe. Proceed as directed.

SPAGHETTI

SPAGHETTI SAUCES

Few if any dishes are so satisfying as a dish of steaming spaghetti or other pasta dressed with a lovely sauce. Serve your spaghetti with plenty of grated Parmesan or Romano cheese, preferably freshly grated. And here's an Italian spaghetti trick to make the dish even more succulent. When you've poured the sauce over your spaghetti, add a piece of butter (2 to 4 tablespoons for each pound of pasta) and toss it right in.

MARINARA SAUCE

- ¼ cup olive oil
- 2 tablespoons chopped parsley
- 1 onion, minced
- 1 garlic clove, minced
- 6 anchovy fillets
- 1 can (1 pound 13 ounces) Italian tomatoes
- Salt, pepper, and dried oregano
- 12 ounces spaghetti, cooked
- Grated cheese

Heat olive oil. Add parsley, onion, garlic, and anchovy fillets. Brown lightly. Add Italian tomatoes and salt, pepper, and oregano to taste. Simmer, uncovered, about 20 minutes, stirring occasionally. Serve on spaghetti, sprinkled with grated cheese. Makes 6 servings.

TOMATO SPAGHETTI SAUCE

- 1 garlic clove, minced
- 1 green pepper, minced
- ⅓ cup chopped celery
- 1 large onion, chopped
- 3 parsley sprigs
- 2 medium carrots, diced
- 2 tablespoons olive oil
- 1 can (19 ounces) tomatoes
- 2 bay leaves
- 6 peppercorns
- ¼ teaspoon dried thyme
- 2 teaspoons salt
- Dash of cayenne
- 6 whole cloves
- 1 tablespoon sugar
- 1 can (6 ounces) tomato paste
- ½ pound mushrooms, sliced
- 1 tablespoon butter or margarine

Put first 7 ingredients in kettle. Cover and cook gently for 15 minutes; do not brown. Stir frequently. Add remaining ingredients except tomato paste, mushrooms and butter, and simmer, covered, about 45 minutes. Force through a coarse sieve or food mill. Add tomato paste. Sauté mushrooms in butter about 5 minutes. Add to sauce, and heat. Makes enough sauce for 12 ounces spaghetti, or 4 generous servings.

GARBANZO SAUCE

- 1 onion, chopped
- 1 garlic clove, minced
- ½ cup diced celery and tops
- 3 tablespoons olive oil
- 1 can (1 pound 3 ounces) garbanzos (chick-peas) with liquid
- Water
- 1 can (1 pound 3 ounces) tomatoes
- 1 can (6 ounces) tomato paste
- 1 bay leaf
- 1 teaspoon salt
- Dash of cayenne
- ½ teaspoon dried oregano
- 1 pound spaghetti, cooked
- Grated Parmesan cheese

Sauté onion, garlic, and celery in olive oil until golden. Drain garbanzos, reserving liquid. Measure liquid; add water to make 2½ cups. Mash garbanzos. Add garbanzos, liquid, tomatoes, tomato paste, bay leaf, salt, cayenne, and oregano to onion mixture. Simmer, uncovered, for 2 hours, stirring occasionally. Serve on spaghetti, with a sprinkling of grated cheese. Makes 8 servings.

MUSHROOM-OLIVE SAUCE

- ¼ pound mushrooms, sliced
- 2 tablespoons butter or margarine
- 2 garlic cloves, crushed
- 1 tablespoon dry mustard
- 1 tablespoon water
- 3 tablespoons olive oil
- ½ teaspoon sugar
- 2 tablespoons heavy cream
- 10 diced pitted ripe olives
- 2 to 3 teaspoons capers
- 8 ounces spaghetti, cooked
- Salt to taste

Sauté mushrooms in butter with garlic about 5 minutes; cool. Blend mustard with water. Gradually blend in olive oil. Add sugar, cream, olives, and capers. Add mushrooms, and pour over spaghetti. Toss lightly, and season. Makes 4 servings.

ANCHOVY SAUCE

- 1 tablespoon all-purpose flour
- ¼ cup olive oil
- 2 tablespoons dry wine
- ¾ cup water
- 1 can (6 ounces) tomato paste
- 1 bay leaf
- 1 can (2 ounces) flat anchovy fillets, mashed to a paste
- Salt and pepper
- 8 ounces spaghetti, cooked

Brown flour lightly in oil. Add wine, water, tomato paste, and bay leaf. Simmer, uncovered, for 15 minutes. Add anchovies, anchovy oil, and salt and pepper to taste. Simmer for 5 minutes. Serve on spaghetti, with grated cheese. Makes 4 servings.

SPAGHETTI

WHITE TUNA SAUCE

- 1 onion, chopped
- 1 garlic clove, chopped
- ¼ cup olive oil
- 2 cans (7 ounces each) tuna fish
- ½ teaspoon pepper
- 8 ounces spaghetti, cooked
- Salt to taste

Sauté onion and garlic in oil until golden-brown. Add tuna, and simmer for 5 minutes. Add pepper. Pour over spaghetti. Toss, and add salt. Makes 4 servings.

QUICK WHITE CLAM SAUCE

- 2 tablespoons chopped parsley
- 1 garlic clove, minced
- 1 medium onion, chopped
- 2 tablespoons olive oil
- ½ teaspoon salt
- Dash of pepper
- 1 can (10½ ounces) minced clams
- 8 ounces spaghetti, cooked

Sauté parsley, garlic, and onion in hot oil for 5 minutes. Add salt, pepper, and minced clams with liquid. Simmer for 5 minutes longer. Serve on spaghetti. Makes 4 servings.

STRACOTTO SAUCE

This is one of the best of all Italian pasta sauces. It is really an essence of meat flavored with mushrooms and Marsala. The mushrooms should be the imported dried ones, found in practically all food stores, since they are more flavorful than our fresh ones. Stracotto in Italian literally means cooked for a very long time, and the secret of this sauce is just that—long slow cooking.

- 1 pound beef chuck or round
- ½ cup butter or margarine
- 1 medium onion, minced
- 1 medium carrot, minced
- 1 celery stalk, minced
- ½ cup minced parsley
- ½ cup dry Marsala or Madeira wine
- 1 cup beef bouillon
- 1 ounce dried mushrooms
- Water
- 1 medium tomato, peeled and chopped
- Salt and pepper to taste
- 1 teaspoon grated lemon rind

Cut meat into tiny dice or run through coarse blade of food chopper. It must not be ground as finely as hamburger. Heat butter in heavy saucepan. Add onion, carrot, celery, and parsley and cook over medium heat for 5 minutes, stirring frequently. Add meat, wine, and bouillon. Soften dried mushrooms in water to cover for 5 minutes; chop. Add mushrooms and water to sauce. Add tomato. Season with salt, pepper, and lemon rind. Simmer over lowest possible heat, it should be barely a flicker, for 3 hours, or until meat is almost dissolved. Stir occasionally. Check for moisture; the sauce should be thick. Enough for 1 pound of pasta.

TOMATO PURÉE SAUCE

- 2 tablespoons chopped parsley
- ¼ cup butter
- 1 can (10½ ounces) tomato purée
- 1 tablespoon water
- 8 ounces spaghetti, cooked

Sauté parsley in butter for 2 minutes. Add tomato purée and water; heat. Serve on spaghetti. Makes 4 servings.

PARMESAN PARSLEY SAUCE

- ⅓ cup butter or margarine
- 1 garlic clove, minced
- 8 ounces spaghetti, cooked
- ¾ cup finely chopped parsley
- ½ cup grated Parmesan cheese

Melt butter in small saucepan; add garlic and simmer until butter is lightly browned. Pour over spaghetti. Add parsley and cheese. Toss well; serve with additional cheese if desired. Makes 4 servings.

BOLOGNESE MEAT SAUCE

- ¼ pound bacon or Italian prosciutto, minced
- 1 tablespoon butter
- 1 medium onion, minced
- 1 carrot, minced
- 1 small piece of celery, minced
- ½ pound ground lean beef
- ¼ pound chicken livers, minced
- 1 tablespoon tomato paste
- ½ cup dry white wine
- 1 cup beef bouillon
- Salt and pepper
- ⅛ teaspoon ground nutmeg
- 1 teaspoon grated lemon rind
- 2 whole cloves (optional)
- 1 cup heavy cream

In heavy saucepan cook bacon in butter until soft and golden. Add onion, carrot, and celery. Cook over low heat until browned. Add beef and brown evenly. Add chicken livers and cook for 2 or 3 minutes. Stir in tomato paste and wine and cook for another 2 minutes. Add bouillon, salt and pepper to taste, nutmeg, lemon rind, and cloves, if desired. Simmer, covered, over low heat for 40 minutes. Before serving, heat cream but do not boil. Stir into sauce. Makes enough sauce for 12 ounces spaghetti, cooked, or 4 generous servings.

SPANISH COOKERY

by Marcia Colman Morton

Flamenco, bullfights, dusty olive trees baking in an adobe square, wild-maned girls dressed in polka-dot flounces and with roses in their teeth, spicy food that sets your blood on fire—ah, Spain, that most oversimplified of all European countries.

Spain is no never-never little storybook land, easily grasped in a few phrases. How could it be? For one thing, it's so big—in all Europe, only Russia and France are bigger—and so varied. Its nearly thirty million people live in separate provinces as different as separate countries in their customs, their speech, and their cooking. I, for instance, who am used to the Barcelona dialect, can hardly understand the people of Málaga in the south; while the Catalans in the countryside around Barcelona, and the northern Basques, go far beyond mere dialect shadings—each people has its own ancient distinctive language.

The cooking varies so much that there is even a popular Spanish saying about it: "In the south they fry, in the central regions they roast, and in the north they stew." But whatever they do, the food is seldom really spicy; savory is a more fitting word for what is, after all, European cooking, not Mexican. Just as flamenco is not quite the whole story of Spanish dance. True, the passionate chants and heel stampings of flamenco haunt the gypsy- and Moorish-tinged nights of Andalusia. But other provinces twirl and skip like German or French peasants; while the stately Catalonian *sardana* is measured out to a unique reedy music, more reminiscent of Greek music and dance than of flamenco.

Partly all this variety is a matter of geography, in a country stretching over so many different terrains: the indeed sunny languor of Andalusia, with its white-stucco walls and red-tile roofs; the just-as-authentically Spanish salt-aired Atlantic coast around San Sebastián, with its half-timbered houses so reminiscent of French Normandy; the snowy peaks of the Pyrenees, where Alpine chalets nestle and skiers' cries echo down the slopes; the green fields of Catalonia, where vegetables grow verdant under pleasant rains; the hard-headed businessmen and energetic bustle that make Barcelona "the New York of Spain"; the icy winds of a Madrid winter, and the cosmopolitan chic of that city, with its white skyscrapers and a night life and boulevards and elegant shops to rival Paris itself.

Geography determines the food, too. Spaniards of the central region (fanning out from the center of the center, Madrid) eat roast meats because they have such tender suckling pigs, such delicate young lambs grazing on wild herbs, to work with. And they roast these good things simply, as people do everywhere when the basic ingredients are too delicious to tamper with.

But everywhere in Spain the beef is a tough customer. So the national beef dish is not a roast but a *cocido,* meaning stew. Roughly this is a simmering casserole in which the meats vary according to what is on hand, as do the vegetables. Ingredients and methods change a little from region to region, but always chick-peas are *the* essential ingredient, and always a *cocido* is cooked long and lovingly to make sure the beef is chewable in the end. (The *cocido* recipe given here is as close as you can come to one that most Spaniards would agree to call classic.)

Until quite recently chicken, too, was a matter for casserole cooking and slow coaxing into tenderness. I remember driving for miles to find the occasional farm that raised specially fed pullets and capons for roasting. Then, in the early 1960's, Spain began to import huge quantities of frozen American fowl, and a grateful nation learned the delights of juicy barbecued chicken. Little shops that serve nothing else now dot the Spanish cities the way pizza parlors dot ours.

Just because meats and domestic fowl have been, historically, in short supply, the Spanish cuisine has developed rich substitutes. Toothsome little roasted wild partridge, for instance, appears on the menu of even a rather humble restaurant. And soup—the Spanish are masters at getting a delicious tureen from surprisingly little—a dash of olive oil and a few garlic cloves, or a hambone and some odds and ends of vegetables. Or beans—every tiny village seems to have its own special way of turning this humble staple into a nutritious, rib-sticking meal that costs pennies.

Sweets are the least of Spanish accomplishments; not so surprising in a country where fresh sweet melons, passion fruit, oranges, and bananas make such a stunning final touch to a meal. The cakes are usually of a Byzantine sweetness, running to marzipan and candied fruits, and not very appealing to non-Spanish palates. They are a vestige of the medieval Moorish invasions of Spain, culinary counterparts to the Moorish towers now crumbling along Spain's Mediterranean coasts, or the tiled mosques and palaces of Granada and Córdoba and Seville. The best pastry is borrowed from other European countries, the French or Viennese classic recipes. If there is a national dessert, it is *flan,* which is nothing but a boiled custard, no different from the recipe available in your most basic cook book. And the *churros* sold at street stands—to be eaten at breakfast, teatime, or any other time you want a snack—are merely fried crullers.

I have saved for last the best part of Spanish cooking, the part that has the most to teach Americans. And that, in a word, is fish. The seafood of Spain is a wonder. It is good everywhere, and everywhere it is cooked with love and care and tender appreciation. "In the south they fry . . ." They fry everything from the tiny fresh whitebait to the succulent red mullet; or they grill quickly, with a few drops of olive oil, the sardines fresh from the sea, and wash them down with red wine and hunks of fragrant bread smeared with the pulp of ripe tomatoes.

It's different in the north, where the epicurean Basques have a reputation for being the best cooks in Spain. Appetites whetted by the brisk salt breezes, "in the north they stew" heartily, aromatically.

But however the Spanish cook the sea's bounty, in whatever part of the country—a savoring respect for fish is the Spanish cuisine's most valuable lesson for Americans. We, who have as beautiful a supply of seafood as do the Spanish, but who usually toss it in a skillet and hope for the best, can learn how to prepare fish so that it comes to the table greeted by the smile and the sigh of pleasure it deserves.

APPETIZERS

ALCACHOFAS RELLENOS CON SARDINAS
[Sardine-Stuffed Artichokes]

- 6 whole raw artichokes
- Juice of 1 lemon
- ½ cup olive oil (about)
- Salt
- 1 raw egg yolk
- 1 teaspoon prepared mustard
- 1 teaspoon vinegar
- 3 large canned sardines, boned
- Pepper
- Chopped parsley
- 6 large pitted green olives

Discard tough outer leaves of artichokes. Cut off spiny tips of remaining inner portion of each artichoke and core out center thistles. Sprinkle artichokes with half of lemon juice. Cook with ¼ cup olive oil and remaining lemon juice in salted boiling water to cover until tender, about 20 minutes. Drain thoroughly. Meanwhile, beat together egg yolk, mustard, vinegar, and enough remaining olive oil to make a mayonnaise. Mash sardines with 1 tablespoon of this mayonnaise, or enough to make a velvety mixture. Season with salt and pepper to taste. Heap sardine mixture into artichoke centers and top with remaining mayonnaise. Garnish each with chopped parsley and an olive. Makes 6 servings.

PESCADO A LA VINAGRETA
[Fish Vinaigrette]

- ½ pound fish (scrod, haddock, flounder, etc.), cooked
- 2 tablespoons chopped onion
- 1 garlic clove, minced
- 1 tablespoon chopped capers
- 2 tablespoons chopped parsley
- 1 cucumber, peeled, seeded, and diced
- 1 hard-cooked egg, chopped
- 3 tablespoons olive oil
- 3 tablespoons cider vinegar
- Salt and pepper
- 1 or 2 firm tomatoes, peeled, seeded, and diced

Use leftover cooked fish; or, if you start with raw fish, simmer it gently until it's thoroughly cooked; when cold, cut into cubes. Arrange cubed fish in shallow bowl. Add onion, garlic, capers, parsley, cucumber, and egg. Sprinkle with oil and vinegar. Season with salt and pepper to taste. Toss gently so as not to break up fish. Cover bowl, and marinate salad in refrigerator for about 2 hours. Gently toss in diced tomato. Makes 4 servings.

Anchoas a la Vinagreta
[Anchovies Vinaigrette]

Substitute anchovies for fish in preceding recipe (two or three 2-ounce cans of flat fillets), and omit salt since the anchovies provide their own saltiness.

SALMONETES LEVANTINOS
[Red Mullet Levantine]

For this recipe the Spanish use the smallest red mullet, available all along the Mediterranean coastline of Spain; if unavailable here, substitute small butterfish, porgies, or any small but meaty fish; or use larger fish cut into quarters.

- 12 to 24 small fish or equivalent (about 4 pounds)
- 2 tablespoons olive oil
- Salt
- 2 garlic cloves, minced
- ½ bay leaf, broken up
- 1 teaspoon ground saffron
- Fennel seed, ground cuminseed, and dried thyme to taste
- 2 tablespoons chopped parsley
- 4 tomatoes, peeled, seeded, diced
- ½ bottle dry white wine
- Quartered lemons

Prepare fish for cooking, but do not remove skin or bones. Wash; dry thoroughly. Oil generously a large baking pan. Arrange fish on it so that pieces don't touch. Sprinkle with salt, spices, herbs, and tomatoes. Pour wine over top. Bake in preheated moderate oven (350°F.) for 30 minutes, or until sauce begins to bubble. Continue baking for 10 to 15 minutes longer, or until fish is just done; time depends on size of fish. Let fish cool in sauce. Remove to platter, carefully so as not to break fish. Strain sauce over top. Serve cold, garnished with lemon quarters. Makes 12 servings.

SARDINAS CON SALSA DE TOMATES
[Sardines in Tomato Sauce]

Dry canned whole sardines on paper towels to drain off all the oil. Arrange them on a platter in any attractive pattern desired (a star shape is popular in Spain). Pour tomato sauce, canned or home made, over fish; if sauce is mild, add a little freshly ground black pepper. Split green peppers into flat pieces, halves or thirds; remove seeds and white portion of pulp. Broil under medium heat until the skin browns and puckers. Skin will peel off easily with a thin-bladed knife. Slice peppers and egg white into thin julienne strips, and sprinkle generously over the tomato sauce. Serve cold, accompanied by crackers or thin toast triangles.

SPANISH COOKERY

SALADS

ENSALADA A LA ANDALUZA
[Andalusian Vinaigrette Salad]

- ¼ cup olive oil
- ¼ cup cider vinegar
- ¼ teaspoon pepper
- 2 cucumbers, peeled, seeded, and diced
- Salt to taste
- 6 green peppers
- 3 tomatoes
- ½ garlic clove (optional)
- 2 tablespoons chopped onion

Mix oil, vinegar, and pepper for a dressing; reserve. Heap diced cucumber in a bowl; sprinkle with salt and let stand for 20 minutes, or until water has run out. Drain on paper towels. Remove to small bowl and toss with half reserved dressing. Split green peppers into flat pieces, halves or thirds; remove seeds and white portion of pulp; broil under medium heat until the skin browns and puckers; peel off skin with thin-bladed knife; dice peppers. Heap diced peppers in a bowl; sprinkle with salt and let stand for 15 minutes to drain. Remove to small bowl and toss with remaining dressing. Plunge tomatoes into boiling water for a few seconds to loosen skins; dry with paper towels. Peel and quarter the tomatoes and remove seeds; dice; add salt to taste and let stand for 15 minutes. If you like a touch of garlic (I don't, in this salad), rub a salad bowl with a cut garlic clove. Add diced cucumbers and green peppers (which have been marinating for about 30 minutes by now) and their dressing. Add tomato and onion; toss lightly. Chill before serving. Makes 6 to 8 servings.

ENSALADA DE ARROZ A LA VALENCIANA
[Rice Salad Valenciana]

- 2 quarts water
- 2 tablespoons salt
- ⅔ cup raw rice
- 1 tablespoon dry sherry
- 2 green peppers
- 2 tomatoes
- 1 tablespoon dry mustard
- Water
- ¼ teaspoon pepper
- ¼ cup olive oil
- ¼ cup cider vinegar

Bring water and salt to a boil. Add rice and cook, uncovered, about 20 minutes, or until rice is cooked but still firm. Drain rice and remove to heatproof casserole. Stir in sherry and let rice cool completely. Prepare green peppers and tomatoes as directed in recipe for Ensalada a la Andaluza, above, but do not add any dressing to them; instead, in large bowl, moisten mustard with a little cold water to make a paste; add pepper, oil, and vinegar; mix for a dressing. Stir in diced green peppers, tomatoes, and finally, the cooled rice. Marinate salad in refrigerator for at least 30 minutes. Makes 6 servings.

SOUPS

GAZPACHO
[Cold Salad-Soup]

- ½ cup soft bread crumbs
- Water
- ½ garlic clove, minced
- 1 teaspoon salt
- 3 tablespoons olive oil
- 3 tablespoons cider vinegar
- 1 or 2 tablespoons chopped onion (optional)
- 4 tomatoes, sliced
- 1 canned pimiento, diced
- Green peppers, tomatoes, and cucumbers
- 3 slices of toast, diced
- 3 hard-cooked eggs, chopped

Moisten bread crumbs with ½ cup cold water. Add garlic, salt, oil, vinegar, onion, if desired, tomatoes, and pimiento. Marinate in refrigerator about 30 minutes; then put through fine sieve, food mill, or blender. Blend in up to 2 cups cold water, just enough to make a fairly thick soup. Chill; or use less water, and add a few ice cubes. Serve in large tureen, surrounded by individual small serving bowls containing green peppers, tomatoes, and cucumbers, each prepared separately as in Ensalada a la Andaluza, and each tossed with one-third the dressing specified in that recipe; toast cubes, and chopped hard-cooked egg. Each person is served a plateful of soup and he adds the accompaniments in any proportion he likes. Makes 6 servings.

SOPA DE ALMENDRAS
[Almond Soup]

- 2½ cups blanched almonds, ground
- 1½ quarts cold water
- 1 bay leaf
- Peel cut from ½ lemon
- 1 cinnamon stick
- 5 tablespoons butter
- Salt
- 8 slices of white bread, crusts removed, diced

In large bowl, soak almonds in water for 1 hour. Strain through cheesecloth into soup kettle, squeezing hard to extract all the essence. Add bay leaf, lemon peel, cinnamon stick, and butter. Simmer for 10 minutes. Add salt to taste. Toast diced bread in oven until golden; heap into soup tureen. Strain soup over bread carefully, so as not to break up the toast cubes. Serve immediately. Makes 6 servings.

MEAT

The most classically Spanish meat dish is not a roast or grill but a sort of stew, called cocido *or* puchero, *which provides soup and main course both. The same is true of their fish recipes. So although some of them might technically fit into the Soups category, I am dividing them into Meat and Fish.*

COCIDO
[Spanish Boiled Beef]

- *1 pound beef (chuck, round, rump, etc.)
- *¼ chicken
- 2 beef marrowbones and 1 hambone (optional)
- 1 tablespoon salt
- 2 quarts cold water
- ½ pound dried chick-peas, soaked overnight in water to cover
- 1 onion
- 3 leeks, sliced
- 2 carrots, sliced
- 1 white turnip, sliced
- 1 parsley sprig
- 1 pound raw potatoes, peeled and quartered

In soup kettle, combine beef, chicken, and bones; the hambone, if you have one, adds a nice smokiness. Add salt, and enough *cold* water to cover. Bring to a boil over high heat, and carefully skim off the scum that rises. Reduce heat and simmer, covered, for 1 hour. (This method, starting the meat in *cold* water and bringing it to a boil, is used for beef soups in much of Europe because it lets the beef richness flow into the soup. Starting the meat in *boiling* water seals in the juices and gives you more succulent beef at the end, but the soup suffers. So take your choice.) While the soup is simmering, drain the presoaked chick-peas. Pour boiling water over them so they'll be hot when you add them to the soup, and drain again; wrap loosely but securely in cheesecloth so they won't fall apart in the soup, and plunge into soup kettle. Taste the soup, and correct for salt sparingly (the vegetable side dish for a *cocido,* see Verduras, adds its own considerable saltiness). Skim soup carefully again. Continue simmering, covered, about 1 hour longer. Add onion (pretoasted in oven if you want its brownness to enrich the color of the soup, then sliced), leeks, carrots, turnip, and parsley. Simmer about 1 hour longer. (In Spain the soup is cooked, start to finish, about 5 hours, because it takes that long for the tough Spanish meat to become tender. But most of our superior American beef will be done with about 3 hours of cooking.) Strain off the soup; save to use for stock or to serve as clear consommé or garnished with rice, noodles, toasted bread cubes, etc. Leave everything else in the kettle and add potatoes. Simmer for another 30 minutes, or until potatoes are tender; there will be enough liquid left in the kettle, even after straining the soup, to steam the potatoes.

To serve: Remove cheesecloth package of chick-peas; drain. Heap chick-peas in center of large platter. Slice beef and chicken, and arrange over chick-peas together with slices of Relleno. Garnish with vegetables from soup kettle. In separate bowl, serve Verduras. The Spanish also often accompany a *cocido* with a dish of tomato or other piquant sauce, a serving bowl of one of the bean recipes, and a plate of fried green peppers. Makes 4 to 6 servings.

*This relatively small amount of beef and chicken makes a *cocido* for 6 in Spain, along with all the side dishes. For meat-loving Americans, you may want to increase the quantity.

VERDURAS
[Vegetable Side Dish for Cocido]

- ¼ pound chorizo (Spanish sausage), cubed
- ¼ pound lean ham, diced
- 2 ounces salt pork or bacon, diced
- ¼ pound blood sausage, cubed
- 2 pounds sliced cabbage, green beans, Brussels sprouts, etc. (alone or in combination)
- Cold water

In large saucepan, combine meats and any green vegetable you like. (Personally, I panfry the meats first to get rid of excess fat, but the Spanish use them raw. They like the resulting "richness" in the vegetables.) Cover with just enough cold water to keep from sticking. Simmer until done, about 15 to 20 minutes. Makes 6 servings.

RELLENO
[Pork Roll for Cocido]

- ¼ pound lean pork, chopped fine
- 1 garlic clove, minced
- 2 tablespoons chopped parsley
- 1 egg, beaten
- Soft bread crumbs
- Salt and pepper
- All-purpose flour
- Olive oil

Mix together chopped pork, garlic, parsley, egg, enough bread crumbs to bind, and salt and pepper to taste. Form mixture into thick roll. Dredge lightly with flour. Sauté in hot oil until golden brown. Drain, slice, and serve as described for Cocido. Makes 6 servings.

SPANISH COOKERY

CHULETAS DE CERDO CON ESPINACAS
[Pork Chops with Spinach]

- 4 large thick pork chops
- ¾ teaspoon salt
- 2 tablespoons all-purpose flour
- 3 tablespoons olive oil (divided)
- 1 garlic clove, minced
- Few sprigs parsley, minced
- 1 small onion, chopped
- ¼ cup dry white wine
- ½ teaspoon prepared mustard
- 1 package (10 ounces) frozen chopped spinach, partially thawed
- ½ cup croutons

Trim excess fat from chops. Mix ½ teaspoon salt and flour; rub on chops. Brown on both sides in 2 tablespoons oil in large skillet. Transfer to 2-quart casserole. Add garlic, parsley and onion to drippings in skillet and sauté until soft but not browned. Add remaining ¼ teaspoon salt, wine, mustard and spinach. Cover and cook about 5 minutes. Drain off excess liquid and purée in blender or force through sieve. Pile on chops. Sauté croutons in remaining 1 tablespoon oil and sprinkle on spinach. Cover and bake in preheated moderate oven (375°F.) about 25 minutes. Makes 4 servings.

MARINATED STEAK MADRILENO

- 5 to 10 garlic cloves, minced
- ¼ cup dry sherry
- ¼ cup cider vinegar
- ½ cup olive oil
- ½ cup chopped green olives
- 3 pounds steak with bone
- Salt

Combine all ingredients except steak and salt; marinate steak in the mixture overnight in refrigerator, turning once or twice. Remove from marinade, broil and salt to taste. Simmer marinade 5 minutes or so and serve as sauce. Makes 6 servings.

POLLO A LA PRAVIANA
[Chicken, Asturian Style]

- 1 broiler-fryer, cut up
- 3 tablespoons all-purpose flour
- 1 teaspoon salt
- ¼ cup olive oil
- 1 medium onion, sliced
- ½ cup diced cooked ham
- 1 or 2 garlic cloves, minced
- 1 cup beer or cider
- 1 tablespoon minced parsley
- ½ pound cleaned shelled large shrimps
- ¼ teaspoon paprika

Dust chicken with mixture of flour and salt and brown in oil in large skillet. Remove chicken pieces and add onion, ham and garlic to drippings in skillet. Sauté over low heat until onion is soft. Add remaining ingredients and top with chicken. Bring to boil, cover and simmer 30 minutes, or until chicken is tender. Makes 4 servings.

PAELLA VALENCIANA
[Chicken, Seafood and Rice, Valenciana Style]

- 2 tablespoons olive oil or drippings
- ½ frying chicken
- ½ pound lean pork
- ¼ pound squid or cuttlefish, cut in ¼-inch slices
- 4 medium tomatoes, chopped
- French-style green beans, green peas or quartered artichoke hearts
- Mushrooms
- 1 teaspoon paprika
- 1 small sweet red pepper, chopped
- 1 cup raw rice
- 3 cups boiling water
- 1½ teaspoons salt
- ¾ teaspoon saffron
- 8 to 10 mussels (in shells)
- 6 to 8 large fresh shrimps, cleaned

Heat oil in paella dish. Chop or cut chicken in 1- to 2-inch pieces; cut pork the same size and sauté both until browned and tender. Remove. Add squid and sauté 4 to 5 minutes; remove. Add tomatoes, vegetables (ideally you should have at least 2 different green vegetables, plus the mushrooms, the total to be around 1½ cups), paprika and red pepper and sauté 3 minutes. Return chicken, pork and squid and add rice. Turn heat to high and add water little by little—about a cupful at a time so that it never stops boiling. At first it evaporates rapidly, of course, but by the time the second cup is added you've sufficient liquid to add the salt and saffron. Stir ingredients only enough to distribute and add remaining water. Cook uncovered and as the mixture starts drying (8 to 10 minutes) sample rice. If not almost tender, add another ½ cup or so of water. **Add shellfish.** Cook about 6 minutes. When rice is practically dry and done, remove paella from heat 3 minutes or so before serving. Makes 6 servings.

32

POLLO VALENCIANA
[Chicken Valencia Style]

- ¼ cup olive oil
- 2 tablespoons lard or margarine
- 2 fryers (about 3½ pounds each), cut up
- 2 large onions, sliced
- 2 tablespoons all-purpose flour
- 1 cup dry white wine
- Stock (use giblets to make)
- 8 sprigs parsley
- ¼ teaspoon dried thyme
- 1 bay leaf
- ¼ teaspoon poultry seasoning or pinch of sage
- 1 teaspoon salt
- ¼ teaspoon pepper
- 1 piece of lemon rind
- 1 sweet red pepper
- 2 large oranges, peeled and sliced
- 1 dozen large pimiento-stuffed olives

Heat oil and lard in heavy skillet with cover and brown chicken well. Remove chicken, add onions and sauté until golden. Stir in flour. Stir in wine, then add 1 cup stock, next 7 ingredients and chicken. Clean and cut red pepper in strips and arrange on chicken. Cover, reduce heat and simmer 30 to 35 minutes, or until tender, adding more stock if necessary. Remove chicken to heated serving platter. Remove and discard parsley, lemon rind and bay leaf. Add orange slices and olives to sauce. Boil rapidly 3 minutes, then pour over chicken, arranging orange slices, and olives as garnish. Makes 6 to 8 servings.

FISH

SOPA DE PESCADO A LA VASCA
[Basque Fish Soup]

- 2 medium onions, diced
- 2 leeks (white part), diced
- 3 garlic cloves, minced
- 2 carrots, diced
- ¼ cup chopped parsley
- ¼ cup olive oil
- 2 pounds mixed fish in large hunks or slices (scrod, haddock, bass, etc.)
- 3 large tomatoes, quartered
- 2 quarts boiling water (about)
- Salt and pepper
- 6 slices of French or white bread, crusts on, cubed

Sauté onions, leeks, garlic, carrots, and parsley in hot oil until cooked but not browned. Add fish, tomatoes, and just enough boiling water to cover. Season with salt and pepper to taste. Simmer, covered, for 30 minutes, or until fish is cooked but still firm. Carefully remove fish; discard skin and bones; cut flesh into bite-size pieces; reserve. Meanwhile, let soup continue simmering for 30 minutes or more, to bring out flavor. Arrange cubed bread in flameproof casserole or Dutch oven. Strain soup over bread; bring to a simmer. Add reserved fish; simmer for about 5 minutes. Serve immediately. Makes 6 servings.

MARMITAKO
[Basque Fresh-Tuna Stew]

- 1 medium onion, chopped
- ¼ cup olive oil
- 1 pound fresh tuna, in large pieces (if unavailable, use swordfish)
- 2 garlic cloves, minced
- ¼ cup chopped parsley
- 2 tomatoes, peeled, seeded, and diced
- 2 raw large potatoes, peeled and cubed
- ¼ pound peas, shelled
- ½ cup beef bouillon
- 1 red pepper or canned pimiento, diced
- 1 bay leaf
- Dash of cayenne
- Salt and pepper
- Toast triangles

Sauté onion in hot oil until golden. Add fish and sauté for a few minutes. Add garlic, parsley, and tomatoes; sauté. Add potatoes, peas, bouillon, diced pepper, bay leaf, and cayenne. Simmer, covered, about 1 hour. Season with salt and pepper to taste. Serve, garnished with toast triangles. Makes 6 servings.

ZARZUELA DE MARISCOS
[Literally, Musical Comedy of Shellfish]

- 1 onion, chopped
- ¼ cup olive oil
- 1 or 2 garlic cloves, minced
- ¼ cup chopped parsley
- 2 tablespoons tomato paste
- 1½ pounds small shrimps, shelled
- 1½ pounds lobster or lobster tail, cut into bite-size pieces
- ½ cup dry white wine
- Salt and pepper
- 20 raw clams
- 1 teaspoon ground saffron

Sauté onion in hot oil until golden. Stir in garlic, parsley, and tomato paste. Add shrimps and lobster. Pour wine over top. Season with salt and pepper to taste. Cover, and simmer for 10 minutes, or until shrimps and lobster are half-cooked. Meanwhile, simmer clams in water until they are cooked and open. Remove half shells; add clams, on the half shell, to simmering shrimps and lobster. Sprinkle everything with saffron, and continue cooking until shrimps and lobster are done. Serve hot in soup plates. Makes 6 servings.

SPANISH COOKERY

HALIBUT BAKED IN SALSA GADITANA

- 2 pounds halibut, preferably in one piece
- Salt
- ¼ cup olive oil
- 1 large garlic clove
- ¼ cup pine nuts or blanched almonds
- 2 large onions, chopped
- ¼ cup minced parsley
- 1 can (1 pound) tomatoes with purée
- Pepper
- ½ teaspoon sugar (optional)

Sprinkle both sides of fish with salt and put in shallow baking dish. Heat oil in heavy skillet, add garlic and nuts and sauté over low heat until golden. Remove to mortar or wooden bowl. Add onions to oil remaining in skillet and sauté until golden. Meanwhile, with pestle or back of wooden spoon, crush garlic and nuts to a paste. Gradually work parsley into mixture, along with a little oil from skillet. Add tomatoes to onion and simmer 5 minutes. Then stir in nut paste. Season to taste with salt and pepper. Add sugar, if desired, and pour over fish to cover completely. Bake in preheated moderate oven (350°F.) about 30 minutes. Makes 6 servings.

NOTE: If frozen fish is used, thaw before cooking. For a short cut, mince nuts with knife and crush garlic between two thicknesses of waxed paper. Or force with parsley through fine blade of food chopper.

BACALAO A LA VIZCAÍNA
[Basque Salt-Cod Casserole]

This dish is even better reheated the next day. It may work with fresh cod, although I've never tried it.

- 2 pounds dried salt cod, best quality (use only the lean side portions, not the fatty center)
- ½ cup olive oil
- Lard
- ¼ pound bacon, diced
- ¼ pound smoked ham, diced
- 4 large mild red onions, chopped
- 2 garlic cloves
- 3 parsley sprigs
- 2 cups boiling water
- 8 to 10 canned pimientos (enough to give the finished dish a rich red color), diced
- 3 tomatoes, peeled, seeded, and cubed
- 2 hard-cooked egg yolks
- Water
- ½ cup soft bread crumbs
- Salt and pepper
- Dash of cayenne
- Sugar (optional)

Cut cod into 6 equal servings. To remove salt, soak about 20 hours in fresh cold water, changing water 4 or 5 times. Several hours before you plan to cook the cod, start the sauce (for which they take over 5 hours in Spain, but you may need less). In large skillet with cover, or Dutch oven, heat oil, ¼ cup lard, bacon, and ham. When mixture bubbles, add onion, whole garlic cloves, and parsley. Cover, turn down heat as low as possible, and cook for 3 hours, or until onion is very soft but not at all burned. Add boiling water and continue simmering for 2 hours longer, or until onions are completely fallen apart. Add more boiling water as necessary to keep from sticking. Add pimientos, tomatoes, and egg yolks mashed with bread crumbs and mixed to a fine paste with a little cold water. Simmer for a few minutes longer. Put everything through a sieve, food mill, or blender so you have a smooth sauce. Add salt and pepper to taste, and if you want to be authentic, a dash of cayenne. Meanwhile, when cod has soaked for 20 hours, dry it thoroughly with paper towels. Remove any scales, being careful not to damage the skin (which adds a smooth, gelatinous quality to the finished dish's sauce). In large saucepan, combine cod and unsalted cold water to cover; bring to a boil. As soon as water starts to boil, take out the pieces of cod; carefully remove bones. Grease a heatproof casserole with lard or bacon fat. In it, arrange a layer of cod; pour sauce over; repeat until all the cod and sauce are used up. Sauce should cover the fish, not drown it. Cook slowly until fish is done, about 20 minutes. During cooking, shake the casserole often so the sauce runs to the bottom. Also, with a wide pancake turner or spatula, loosen the bottom layer of fish often to keep it from sticking, being careful not to break the pieces. Taste from time to time, and add salt and pepper if necessary; or a pinch of sugar if the cod is making the sauce too salty. Finished dish should be savory, neither too salty, too peppery, nor too sweet, and of a good red color. Makes 6 servings.

MERLUZA ASADA AL HORNO
[Baked Fish]

The Spanish usually bake a whole fish this way, but I don't see why this recipe couldn't also be used for sliced fish steaks.

- 1 large striped bass
- ½ cup olive oil
- 2 onions, chopped fine
- 2 garlic cloves, minced
- Salt and pepper to taste
- 2 tablespoons bread crumbs
- ¼ to ½ cup dry white wine
- 2 tablespoons chopped parsley
- Juice of 1 lemon

Clean fish and remove scales, but leave it whole. With small sharp knife, make a few slits crosswise along the top. Pour 6 tablespoons oil into a baking dish. Spread an even layer of half the onion and garlic in dish and lay the fish on top. Sprinkle with salt and pepper, the remaining onion, garlic, and 2 tablespoons oil, bread crumbs, and wine. Bake in preheated hot oven (400°F.), allowing 12 minutes per pound. Before serving, sprinkle fish with parsley and lemon juice. Makes 6 to 8 servings.

SPANISH COOKERY

COD BAKED WITH ASPARAGUS

- ¼ cup olive oil
- 1 onion, sliced
- 2 pounds cod fillets
- 2 tablespoons all-purpose flour
- Salt
- 1 can (14½ ounces) sliced tomatoes, drained
- 1 package (10 ounces) frozen asparagus spears
- 2 tablespoon butter or margarine
- 1 to 2 tablespoons grated Parmesan cheese

Put 2 tablespoons of oil in shallow baking dish and cover with onion. Cut fish in 6 serving pieces and dust with flour and 1 teaspoon salt. Arrange on onion. Put tomato slices over and around fish and arrange asparagus spears in empty spaces. Brush vegetables and fish with remaining 2 tablespoons oil. Sprinkle asparagus with salt, dot all ingredients with butter and sprinkle with cheese. Bake in preheated moderate oven (375°F.) about 35 minutes. Makes 6 servings.
NOTE: If fish is frozen, thaw before cooking.

EGGS

HUEVOS A LA FLAMENCA
[Eggs Flamenco]

Omelets of all kinds are very popular in Spain. This egg dish is served throughout the country, and is as authentically Spanish as its name.

- 1 small onion, chopped fine
- 1 garlic clove, minced
- 3 tablespoons olive oil
- ¼ cup chopped ham
- Dash of cayenne
- 1 tomato, peeled, seeded, and diced
- Salt and pepper
- 1 teaspoon sugar
- 1 cup beef bouillon
- ¼ pound green beans, Frenched
- ½ pound green peas, shelled
- ¼ pound asparagus tips
- 6 eggs
- ¼ pound chorizo or smoked pork sausage links, browned whole
- 1 pimiento, cut into julienne strips
- ½ pound ham, cut into julienne strips
- 1 or 2 tablespoons chopped parsley
- 6 to 12 toast triangles

Sauté onion and garlic in hot oil for 2 or 3 minutes. Add ham and continue to cook until onion is translucent but not golden. Stir in cayenne and turn down heat. Stir in tomato, salt and pepper to taste, and sugar. Add bouillon and vegetables. Cook over low heat until vegetables are just tender; do not overcook. (If asparagus tips are canned, add them only after other vegetables are done.) Transfer everything to greased shallow baking dish, arranging vegetables evenly, being careful not to break the asparagus tips. Break eggs onto the bed of vegetables and sauce, spacing eggs out a little. Slice the drained, prebrowned *chorizo*. (In Spain the sausage is cooked along with the vegetables, then removed and sliced, but this procedure makes the sauce too fatty for American taste, so I panfry the sausage separately to remove excess fat.) Garnish each egg with some sliced *chorizo* and a few strips of pimiento and ham. Set baking dish on lower rack of oven; bake until whites of eggs are just set. Sprinkle with chopped parsley, set toast triangles around edge of dish, and serve immediately. (In Spanish restaurants, Eggs Flamenco are usually served in individual little clay baking dishes, 1 or 2 eggs in each. But for most American households, and Spanish, it's easier to serve one large dishful, and it's very attractive, too.) Makes 6 servings.

BEANS

Throughout Spain, bean casseroles are a staple, either as a hearty main dish or an accompaniment to simple meat courses. Here are a few recipes using both fresh and dried beans.

JUDÍAS BLANCAS A LA LERIDANA
[Lima Beans Lérida]

- 1¼ pounds fresh baby Lima beans, or 2 packages (10 ounces each) frozen
- Salt
- Water
- 2 onions, chopped
- 2 tablespoons olive oil
- 1½ pounds raw potatoes, peeled and cubed
- ½ pound German-style salami
- 1 to 2 cups sliced cabbage
- 2 garlic cloves, minced
- 1 teaspoon ground saffron
- Pepper

Combine beans, enough salted water to cover generously, onions, and oil. (In these bean recipes, instead of adding oil and raw onions as the Spanish do, I prefer first to sauté onions in oil until transluscent but not golden and then to add *that* to the beans and fresh cold water; seems to taste better and be less oily.) Simmer, covered, for 15 minutes, or until beans are half cooked. Add potatoes, salami, and cabbage. (Again, the Spanish add raw cabbage; I prefer to precook it for a few minutes first to remove some of the strong odor and make it more digestible, then add the drained cabbage.) Mash together garlic and saffron; mix to a paste with a little cold water; stir into simmering beans. Continue simmering, covered, for 15 to 20 minutes, or until potatoes are completely tender; add boiling water as necessary to keep from sticking. Season with salt and pepper to taste. Makes 8 servings.

SPANISH COOKERY

JUDÍAS VERDES A LA VASCA
[Basque Green Beans]

- 1 pound green beans
- Water
- Salt
- ¼ cup olive oil
- 1 onion, chopped
- 2 garlic cloves, minced
- ¼ pound smoked ham, diced
- 2 or 3 canned pimientos, diced
- Pepper
- 2 tablespoons chopped parsley

Cook green beans in lightly salted water until just tender; do not overcook. Drain; reserve cooking water. In hot oil, sauté onion until golden. Add garlic, ham, and pimiento; sauté until cooked. Add drained green beans, salt and pepper to taste, and parsley. Continue cooking, stirring, until beans are hot. If necessary, add a little reserved cooking water to keep beans from sticking, but this dish should not be very liquid. Makes 4 to 6 servings.

FABADA A LA ASTURIANA
[Asturian Bean Casserole]

- 1 pound white navy beans, soaked overnight in water to cover
- Water
- Salt
- 1 onion, quartered
- ¼ cup olive oil
- ½ pound chorizo
- ½ pound blood sausage
- ½ pound ham
- ¼ pound bacon
- 1 teaspoon ground saffron

Drain beans, cover with cold water and bring to a rolling boil. Drain, and again bring beans to a boil in fresh *salted* cold water. Add onion and oil. When water is at a rolling boil, add meats, cut into large dice, and saffron. Lower heat and simmer, covered, for 2 to 3 hours, or until beans are tender. Add salt to taste. Makes 8 servings.
NOTE: Sometimes a few chopped chili peppers or pimientos are added to the beans during the last few minutes of cooking.

LENTILS MONASTICAS
[Lentils, Monastery Style]

- 1 cup dried lentils
- 5 cups water
- 1 tablespoon salt
- ⅛ teaspoon each dried thyme and marjoram
- 3 large onions, chopped
- 1 carrot, chopped fine
- ¼ cup olive oil
- ¼ cup minced parsley
- 2 canned tomatoes, chopped
- ¼ cup dry sherry
- Grated Swiss or Gruyère cheese

Wash lentils and put in kettle with water, salt and herbs. Bring to boil, cover and simmer 15 minutes. Cook onion and carrot slowly in olive oil until soft. Add to lentils with parsley, tomato and sherry. Cover and simmer 1 hour longer, or until lentils are tender. When ready to serve, put some cheese in each soup bowl and top with lentils. Makes 4 servings.

GARBANZOS CON ESPINACAS
[Chick-Peas with Spinach]

- 2 boxes (10 ounces each) frozen chopped spinach
- 2 hard-cooked eggs, chopped
- 1 onion, minced
- 2 tablespoons olive oil
- 1 tablespoon all-purpose flour
- ½ cup broth or bouillon
- 1 small bunch parsley, chopped
- 2 cans (20 ounces each) chick-peas, drained
- Salt and pepper

Heat spinach until thawed, then cook 2 minutes in its own liquid. Add eggs. Cook onion in oil until soft and yellow. Blend in flour. Gradually add broth and cook, stirring, until thickened. Add parsley and chick-peas and heat. Add spinach and heat if necessary. Season with salt and pepper to taste. Makes 6 servings.

COSTA BRAVA SPECIALTIES

The *Costa Brava*, "Rugged Coast," is a 110-mile strip in the *region* Catalonia, stretching along Spain's southeast corner from, roughly, Barcelona to the Pyrenees, shoreline all the way. Mountains parade spectacularly here beside the Mediterranean under a Riviera sun. Sea meets rock in a twisting, jagged riot of color, pink boulders thrusting out into turquoise grottoes and emerald bays. In the tile-roofed towns, burro-drawn carts still crawl along unpaved roads and automobiles get a second look. The children have yet to catch up with lollipops; they nibble on roses instead.

The women defy their century. They fill their water jugs at the village well, crush garlic with marble mortar and pestle, blend pastry dough with their hands on their marble work tables. Their spice shelves hold only what they've held for centuries: bay leaves, cinnamon, saffron, paprika. But with these and with nuts, olives, and crackers, they simmer marvels on their wood-burning stoves.

When my husband and I rented a house on the Costa Brava one spring, our $18-a-month cook taught me *paella*, of course, but also a gamut of dishes from soup (based on cheese) to nuts (as a steak sauce). Before I went to live in the little Costa town of Bagur, I'd heard the usual horror story about Spain: "They cook everything in rancid olive oil!" Yes, they do, in the very cheap places that use the same oil over and over, from potatoes to fish to veal and back again. But this has nothing to do with the practice in decent restaurants, nor with the fine,

SPANISH COOKERY

fresh golden oil our cook Mela used. As anyone knows who has cooked with olive oil, a good pure grade heats with a beautiful evenness; and it does not intrude its own taste in the robust sort of dishes the Costa loves: fish, for instance.

The sea, as the defining element, gives the Costa Brava its contour and much of its cuisine; the waters teem with luscious food. By day, the village boys go down roads lined with fig trees and the silvery olive to skim mussels from the shore rocks, or *bogavante* (the local lobster variant), or sea urchins, the little orange shellfish that are eaten fresh with a sprinkle of lemon juice, a morsel of the sea itself. Under starlight the fishing boats sail out for sardines, sole, bass; for *rapé* (a kind of codfish) and for the pink-scaled firm-fleshed red mullet, called "redhead" *(cap rox)* in the Catalan language, as opulent a plateful as you'll get from any ocean.

A Catalan housewife prepares her matchless seafood with the simplicity that is a cook's highest praise for her materials. On a bed of red-hot coals she grills fresh sardines or mullet, dry or with a splash of olive oil, to a crackling smokiness. Sometimes she pops slices of *rapé* or sole into an eggy baking-powder batter. Fried quickly in deep olive oil, the dough puffs out, leaving the fish inside white and meltingly tender. Or she tosses a whole basketful of fruits of the sea into the glory that is a *paella*.

Only she calls it by the more usual Spanish name, *arroz*, rice. The word *paella* is derived from the two-eared skillet in which the dish is cooked and served. The name *arroz* explains the philosophy of the *paella* on its native ground: it is, before everything, rice cooked as deliciously as possible. A Spanish cook will use the cheapest chicken and pork cuts for a *paella* because the meats are not primarily meant to be eaten, but rather to flavor the rice. Mela's *paella* is savory and succulent, and not nearly so difficult to prepare as its splendor leads guests to believe. One thing will help a lot: for this recipe you'll need at least a 12-inch skillet, a couple of inches deep. And you cook a *paella* uncovered, from beginning to end.

PAELLA DE LA COSTA BRAVA

Boil cut-up, small chicken 30 minutes, or until thoroughly cooked. In large skillet lightly greased with olive oil, fry for 15 minutes: boiled chicken, ½ pound sausage links, and ½ pound pork (2 center cut chops) cut into small pieces. Add sliced green pepper; ½ pound fish (haddock is wonderful); ½ pound shrimps and/or crayfish, rinsed and dried (add shells and all for flavor); ¼ to ½ pound sliced squid, if you like it and it's available. Fry together (with meats in skillet) for 5 minutes, adding more olive oil if it's needed to keep ingredients from sticking. Add 1 cup raw rice; mix thoroughly with meats. Add 2 dozen mussels or small clams, scrubbed and dried, but with shells. Keep on low heat.

In separate saucepan: Heat ½ cup olive oil; chop in 2 large, ripe tomatoes and 1 onion. Add ¼ teaspoon ground cinnamon, 1 teaspoon paprika, 1 bay leaf, 1 teaspoon salt, ¼ teaspoon dark-red ground saffron, and 2 cups boiling water. Mix thoroughly. Add 1 pound fresh, or 1 package (10 ounces) frozen, peas; cook for 10 minutes. Add mixture slowly to skillet, reserving 1 teaspoon liquid; add 2 sliced, canned pimientos; cook for 10 minutes more, or until rice is soft. (You needn't stir.)

Meanwhile: Mix 2 crushed garlic cloves with 1 tablespoon chopped parsley; add reserved teaspoon of the liquid to make a paste. Stir in to skillet; cook for 5 minutes more, or until all liquid is absorbed by rice, which turns saffron yellow. (By this time, the haddock has probably flaked into the rice, too.) Let stand for 5 minutes. Mussels, peppers, and pimientos act as *Paella's* decorative garnish. Makes 6 servings.

Mela has several chopped-meat extravaganzas up her sleeve. There was, for instance, the dish she called *Guisado de Cosas Rellenas* or "Stew of Stuffed Things," that went the ubiquitous stuffed cabbage one—no, five—better. This was a steaming platter of artichokes, zucchini chunks, onions, potatoes, and green peppers, all scooped out and filled to bursting with diced beef, then steamed together in a big shallow pot. In her *Guisado*, Mela forswore the unfair advantage of *foie gras*. The meat was spiced only with egg, salt, paprika, and a pinch or two of cinnamon. The vegetable jackets were the only flourish needed.

It was not, however, only a hamburger heaven at our house. Mela could do interesting things even to steak intact. Now beefsteak as we know it in the States is unheard of on the Costa Brava as in most of Europe. They have a so-called *entrecot*, but it's closer to veal than to beef. You have to go to Barcelona and order *carne de toro* (bull meat, and usually a late hero of the arena), and that's more like it! Still, our modest little *entrecot* was dressed with walnut-anchovy sauce that almost made my husband forget the royal American sirloin. And a sirloin given this treatment became a downright imperial.

STEAK WITH WALNUT-ANCHOVY SAUCE

- 1 garlic clove, crushed
- 3 anchovy fillets
- 5 walnuts, shelled
- ½ teaspoon vinegar
- ⅓ cup olive oil
- 1 pound steak, broiled to desired doneness

With mortar and pestle blend together garlic, anchovies, walnuts, and vinegar. Drop by drop, add olive oil, mixing constantly. Pour lightly over just grilled steak; oven-heat steak for 1 minute. Serve at once. Makes 4 servings.

For all these strapping meat and vegetable dishes you would, perhaps, expect to use olive oil, buttressed as it is by zesty onion, tomato, and, above all, garlic. Yet our favorite tureen, *Sopa de Queso* (cheese soup) used olive oil even though it wafted, not a garlic tang, but an almost floral perfume; the secret lay in ¼ teaspoon ground cinnamon. Made with the Edam-like Cadi cheese. *Sopa de Queso* was so rich, bland, and soothing to the palate that I have adopted it as the perfect luncheon soup for "the girls."

Paella de La Costa Brava

SOPA DE QUESO
[Cheese Soup]

- 2 tablespoons olive oil
- ½ onion, sliced
- ½ tomato, sliced
- ½ bay leaf
- ¼ teaspoon each paprika and ground cinnamon
- 3 cups boiling water
- ⅓ cup green spinach noodles
- 1 egg
- 1 tablespoon butter, softened
- ¼ cup grated Edam cheese

In olive oil in heavy pot sauté first onion, then tomato with bay leaf. Mix in paprika and cinnamon. Add boiling water; cover and simmer for 1½ hours. Strain, reserve 1 cup clear soup and cool for 15 minutes. Meantime, return remaining clear soup to low heat; add green spinach noodles and cook for 15 minutes, or until done. Beat egg with butter, then with grated Edam until custardy. Add 1 cup reserved soup; blend well. Pour mixture into tureen, then add hot soup with noodles. Blend, season with salt to taste, and serve immediately. Makes 4 servings.

The Spanish stick with olive oil even for pastry. And here I tamper. The crumbly, yolky, miniature doughnuts called *Rosquillas,* delicate even when Mela did them in olive oil, are better with butter.

ROSQUILLAS
[Fried Cakes]

- 1 cup all-purpose flour
- ⅓ cup granulated sugar
- 1 egg
- 1 teaspoon baking powder
- ¼ teaspoon vanilla extract
- 2 tablespoons soft butter
- Hot butter or margarine
- Confectioners' sugar

Sift flour into a bowl; add sugar, egg, baking powder, vanilla, and butter. Mix with wooden spoon until you have a firm dough. Leave in warm room to let dough rise slightly. Shape into circlets or half moons about the diameter of a silver dollar, and as little thicker as you can manage so that they'll cook through. Fry in a small amount of hot butter about 4 minutes on each side, or long enough so they'll brown but not burn. Sift confectioners' sugar over and serve warm. Makes about 18 cakes.

The fragrant little *Rosquillas* (above) take only minutes of actual working time, yet they give you an impressive homemade, warm pastry dessert. Even quicker is the nameless dainty Mela conjured from an unpromising box of ladyfingers.

MELA'S LADYFINGER DESSERT

- 1 cup milk
- 2 eggs, well beaten
- 3 tablespoons granulated sugar
- 1 tablespoon cornstarch
- 1 teaspoon grated lemon rind
- 24 ladyfingers
- 12 graham crackers, crushed into fine crumbs
- Hot butter or margarine
- Confectioners' sugar

In saucepan combine milk, 1 egg, granulated sugar mixed with cornstarch, and lemon rind. Stir gently over low heat for 5 minutes, or until mixture thickens. Cool at room temperature. Split 24 ladyfingers. Fill with cooled custard filling. Dip into remaining beaten egg, then into graham-cracker crumbs. Fry in hot butter for 4 minutes on each side, or until brown but not burned. Sprinkle with confectioners' sugar; serve warm. Makes 24 cakes.

Either of these pastries can be whipped up in batches as large as you care to multiply, so they're nice to keep in mind for entertainments like club teas or television coffee-and-cake. If your hospitality runs more to cocktail parties, though, Mela has something for you there, too: Chick-Pea Fritters. These mealy tidbits, used by the Spanish as a change-off from potatoes, blend beautifully with any meat course I can think of. But I have broadened their scope to include the canapé tray, where they have proven to be irresistible.

FRITURAS DE GARBANZOS
[Chick-Pea Fritters]

- 2 cups cooked chick-peas
- 1 teaspoon chopped parsley
- 1 egg
- ½ garlic clove, mashed
- 2 tablespoons all-purpose flour
- ¼ teaspoon baking powder
- 1 teaspoon salt
- Oil for deep frying

Mash together chick-peas, parsley, egg, garlic, flour, baking powder, and salt. Shape into little balls. Fry in deep hot oil (375°F. on a frying thermometer) until golden-brown and crusted. Drain. Serve warm. Makes about 1½ dozen fritters depending on size.

My Costa Brava recipes have become weekly features at our house. Fun to cook and delicious to eat, they have the added charm of novelty, especially as company dinners. Best of all, they give us and our friends, even those who've never been to Spain, a glimpse of the Costa Brava. Duty-free and good for a lifetime, there's nothing like a recipe for a travel souvenir.

SPARERIBS
—A cut of meat consisting of the lower portion of the ribs and breastbone removed from a side of fresh pig or hog. The ribs have only a small amount of meat but the succulence of the meat and fat make them good eating.

Availability and Purchasing Guide—Year round in food stores. Available fresh. Also sold pickled or cured and smoked. Canned barbecued spareribs are available.

Good quality fresh spareribs are pink in color and have a generous portion of meat between the rib bones and a thin covering of meat over the bones. Because of the amount of bone, it is necessary to allow about 1 pound of spareribs for each serving.

Storage—Remove from market paper or loosen wrapper; store unwrapped or loosely wrapped in coldest part of refrigerator.

Fresh, refrigerator shelf, raw: 3 days
Fresh, cooked; and canned, opened, refrigerator shelf: 2 to 3 days
Fresh, refrigerator frozen-food compartment, raw or cooked, prepared for freezing: 2 to 3 weeks
Fresh, freezer, raw, prepared for freezing: 3 to 4 months
Fresh, freezer, cooked, prepared for freezing: 2 to 3 months
Pickled; or cured and smoked, refrigerator shelf: 10 to 20 days
Pickled; or cured and smoked, refrigerator frozen-food compartment: 3 to 4 weeks

SPEARMINT

Pickled; or cured and smoked, freezer: 1 year
Canned, kitchen shelf: 1 year
Do not refreeze once thawed.

Nutritive Food Values—High in protein, with small amounts of calcium and iron and some phosphorus, thiamine, riboflavin, and niacin.
4 ounces, roasted, meat only cut from ribs = 312 calories
4 ounces, braised, lean and fat = 499 calories

Basic Preparation—Spareribs can be braised, roasted, or simmered. They can be broiled, but when this is done, they are usually marinated or precooked first.

To Braise—Brown spareribs (cut into servings, if desired) slowly on all sides in heavy kettle or Dutch oven. Pour off drippings. Season with salt and pepper, and herbs such as marjoram, thyme, or rosemary, if desired. Add 1 cup water, tomato juice, apple juice, bouillon, or other liquid. Cover and simmer for 45 minutes to the pound, or until tender.

To Roast—Put spareribs in a shallow roasting pan. Season with salt and pepper, and herbs, if desired. Roast in preheated moderate oven (350°F.) for 30 to 35 minutes to the pound, or until well browned and done.

To Simmer—Brown spareribs on all sides, if desired, in heavy kettle or Dutch oven. Cover completely with water, bouillon, or other liquid. (Liquid may be hot or cold.) Season with salt and pepper, and herbs, if desired. (Bay leaves, marjoram, rosemary, thyme, parsley, celery, onion, etc., may be added.) Cover and simmer for 30 minutes to the pound, or until tender.

SPICED SPARERIBS

2 pounds spareribs
2 cups beef bouillon
1 teaspoon ground allspice
2 teaspoons salt
¼ teaspoon pepper

Cut spareribs into several pieces and brown slowly on all sides. Add 1 cup bouillon and seasonings. Simmer, covered, about 1½ hours, adding remaining 1 cup bouillon as needed. Makes 4 servings.

SPICY BARBECUED SPARERIBS

4 pounds spareribs, cut into serving pieces
1 cup cider vinegar
2 tablespoons Worcestershire
1 tablespoon sugar
⅓ cup catsup
1 teaspoon each dry mustard and salt
½ teaspoon paprika
Dash of hot pepper sauce
1 garlic clove, minced

Put spareribs in shallow roasting pan and roast in preheated moderate oven (350°F.) for 1 hour. Mix remaining ingredients and simmer for 15 minutes. Broil spareribs slowly, brushing frequently with the mixture, for 30 minutes, or until ribs are done. Makes 4 to 6 servings.

CHINESE SWEET-AND-SOUR SPARERIBS

2 cups water
1½ pounds spareribs, cut into 1-inch lengths
¼ cup soy sauce
1 teaspoon salt
1 teaspoon sugar
2 tablespoons sherry
3 tablespoons each sugar and cider vinegar
2 tablespoons cornstarch
½ cup water

Heat a heavy pan, add water, ribs, soy sauce, and salt; when mixture boils, reduce heat and simmer for 1 hour. Add 1 teaspoon sugar and sherry. Turn heat high and continue to cook until the liquid is all evaporated. Blend remaining ingredients and pour slowly over ribs. Cook about 2 minutes. Place ribs on a flat dish and top with sauce. Makes 3 or 4 servings.

SPEARMINT [*Mentha spicata*, var. *viridis*]—A strong-scented perennial herb native to the temperate sections of Europe and Asia and widely naturalized in the United States. Of the dozen or so varieties of mint cultivated in the United States, spearmint is the one that is most popularly grown for home culinary use. In fact the words mint and spearmint are often used synonymously, and spearmint can be used in any recipe calling for mint.

Spearmint has dark green lance-shaped leaves and red-tinged stems. Its long pointed flower stalks bear pale purple flowers. The home gardner can easily grow spearmint in pots or in a shady damp patch and have the advantage of the fresh leaves. Either fresh or dried the leaves add a pleasant and distinctive flavor to cranberry juice, fruit cup, and such soups as pea soup; they give delicate flavor to meat ragouts or fish; they are good minced and added to cottage and cream cheese and salad dressings; with vegetables such as cabbage, carrots, celery, potatoes, and snap beans; and in jellied salads. Mint sauce, chopped mint and vinegar, is the classic accompaniment to roast lamb, as is mint jelly. Desserts such as custards, fruit compotes, and ice cream are delicious with mint flavor, and fruit beverages and jellies are a natural for its warm taste.

Availability—Fresh spearmint is not commercially available under that name although often what is sold as "mint" is actually spearmint. Dehydrated spearmint flakes are available at the spice counters of food stores. Spearmint extract and oil of spearmint are available.

SPICE—This word is applied very loosely to a great variety of vegetable products with aromatic odors and pungent flavors which are used to season foods. Such flavorings as caraway, coriander, and dill can be found on some lists of spices although generally they are classified more specifically as aromatic seeds. Bay leaves, marjoram, sage, and thyme are also spices in the broadest usage of the word, although we are more apt to think

of them as herbs. In bygone days even fragrant woods and gums—for example, frankincense, balm, and myrrh—were called spices. But nowadays, the word spice tends to be confined to the following group of products made from various parts (most often other than the seeds or leaves) of plants grown in the tropics: *allspice, red pepper,* and *whole chili peppers,* from dried fruits; *cayenne pepper,* from a ground whole plant; *cinnamon,* from bark; *cloves,* from dried flower buds; *ginger* and *turmeric,* from roots; *mace,* from the dried aril of the *nutmeg,* which itself is the kernel of a fruit; *paprika,* from dried pods; *pepper,* from a dried berry; and *saffron,* from the dried stigmas of a flower.

SPICES—NATURE'S FLAVOR MAGIC

by ETHEL M. KEATING

Nobody knows why the ancients prized spices so highly. But, for centuries, men risked their lives on long caravan treks across the Middle East, fought wars, and discovered new worlds so as to possess a few pounds of the spices available in every food store today.

Pepper, cloves, cinnamon, cassia, nutmeg, all were considered necessary for survival. Spices added zest and pungency to the ancients' food and wine; helped mask the odor of sacrifice and of "high" meat and fish. Priests needed spices for incense and anointing oils, for embalming, sacrificial rites, and funerals; doctors for medicines; lovers for potions; and spices gave delight as scent in perfumes and lotions.

The origin of the use of spices is unknown. A Chinese herbal dated 2700 B.C. speaks of cinnamon and in 2800 B.C., people flocked to the Isle of Rhodes for two Grecian delicacies—gingerbread and nougats!

Beginning some seventeen centuries before Christ, the nomadic tribes in the Arabian Desert controlled the spice industry as middlemen and their handsome profits, both from spices and taxes on spices passing through their domains, caused their country to be called *Araby Blest.* Nor would they reveal whence spices came, and kept their secret and control for more than three thousand years. Actually, spices left their East Indies homes by ship for Yemen, the place where Sheba once reigned, and Hadramaut, then made the long trip by camel-back to Macoraba. Here ownership often changed. Loaded on other camels, the pungent bags went to the then-flourishing ports of Tyre and Sidon, whence, reloaded on ships, they were carried to the cities of the Mediterranean.

The Old Testament contains frequent references to spices. In Genesis 43:11 "a little honey, spices, and myrrh, nuts, and almonds." In the thirtieth chapter of Exodus, the Lord gave Moses directions for the preparation of anointing oils, mentioning pure myrrh and cinnamon. The songs of Solomon speak of "the mountains of spices," and in Genesis after the sons of Jacob carried out their plot against Joseph, "behold, a company of Ishmaelites came from Gilead with their camels bearing spicery and balm and myrrh, going to carry it down to Egypt."

During the opulent early Christian era, spices were still used by the wealthy without restraint despite their cost. Nero lavished a year's supply of cinnamon on the funeral rites of his wife Poppaea. And in 410 A.D. Alaric, King of the Goths, demanded 3,000 pounds of pepper as part of the ransom of Rome.

As communications improved, the demand for spices enlarged. Introduced into England about 900 A.D., they were soon in such demand that any of today's common spices were worth their weight in gold. More than ever, Europeans sought ways to wrest the industry away from Arab control.

On to the Spice Islands

"If we could only find a direct route to the spice islands," men sighed. Columbus took up the search in behalf of Spain but failed. Five years later the Portuguese Vasco da Gama rounded the Cape of Good Hope, sailed up the Indian Ocean, and discovered the East Indies, the coveted treasure home of spices.

Now leadership in commerce, including the spice trade, went to seafaring Spain and Portugal; but near the close of the 16th century it was wrested away by the Dutch. Soon the English bristled under the high prices the Dutch charged them and to combat them, in 1600, one hundred and twenty-five Englishmen founded the East India Company of Gentlemen Adventurers. Company ships returned from their first voyage richly laden with 210,000 pounds of the finest Sumatra pepper. The actions of the English infuriated the Dutch, who started a war that lasted fifty years, ending with their monopoly broken and England in possession of an Empire.

Pepper

Most valuable of all spices is *pepper.* Throughout the Middle Ages, pepper was a form of wealth used in payment of dowries, taxes, rent, and tributes. In the time of Henry II, a Pepper Guild was formed and the traders were known as "pepperers." Pepper is the dried berry of a perennial vine that once grew wild in northern Sumatra but is now cultivated on large plantations in Malaysia, Ceylon, Thailand, Sumatra, Brazil, and on the Malabar coast of India. Like the grapevine, pepper climbs poles or other supports; currantlike clusters of red berries appear after two or three years and the plants usually mature anywhere from four to seven years. Dried in the sun, the berries become dark-brown to black, hard and wrinkled, and acquire flavor. Differing from other spices, pepper has no aroma to mask the flavor of food; rather, especially when freshly ground, it imparts pungency that enhances and adds zest to the dishes it is used in.

Black pepper refers to berries picked just before fully ripened, dried, cleaned, and shipped to be sold as peppercorns or ground.

White pepper, more attractive to the eye but less pungent to the taste, is prepared by removing the outer

SPICE CHART

Seafood Dishes

ALLSPICE
It is the berry of the allspice tree, and is sold either **whole** or **ground,** with a flavor which resembles a combination of cloves, cinnamon, and nutmeg. It spices many baked products, puddings, and fruits. Seasons meat, fish, and seafood, duck, sausages, and eggs. Invaluable for mincemeat, pickles, relishes, preserves, and chutneys. Special uses: potpourris and pourris and sachets.

CINNAMON
This spice comes from the bark of the cassia cinnamon tree and has a fruity sweetness and subtle warmth. **Stick** cinnamon is used as a muddler for hot spiced drinks. **Ground** cinnamon flavors cakes, breads, pies, fruits, puddings, soufflés. Seasons pork, ham, stews, casseroles. Used in pickles, preserves, ketchup, chili sauce, chutney. Scents sachets and potpourris.

CLOVES
They are the nail-shape unopened buds of clove trees, warming to the taste. **Whole** cloves stud ham, pork, pomanders; are used in spice bags for meat, stews, fruits, pickles. **Ground** cloves used in baked goods, dessert sauces, spiced fruits, meat, fish, stuffings, stews, meat sauces. Adds flavor to green beans, Harvard beets, sweet potatoes, tomatoes, and carrots.

Ginger Cookies

GINGER
It is a root spice with a strong, piquant, slightly lemony flavor. **Crystallized,** or **preserved,** ginger is a confection. **Cracked** or **whole** is used in pickles, conserves, chutneys, stewed fruits. **Ground** ginger spices gingerbread and other baked products, frostings, and fruits, as well as meat, game, poultry, fish, seafood, soups, vegetables, preserves, pickles, chutneys, conserves, relishes.

MACE
It is a lacy layer covering nutmeg seeds, with a smooth flavor more potent than nutmeg. Used in baked products, puddings, fruits, custards, candies, whipped cream. It enhances chocolate flavors particularly. Seasons sausages, meat loaves, fish and shellfish, poultry, gravies, sauces, chowders, cream soups, vegetables, jellies, pickles, preserves, relishes, and chutneys.

NUTMEG
The seed of the fruit of the nutmeg tree, it has a warm, aromatic, and slightly bitter flavor, and is available both **whole,** for last-minute grating, or **ground.** Used in hot beverages, puddings, baked goods, fruits, sauces, and whipped cream. Seasons chicken, stews, seafood, eggs, soups, salads, sauces, many vegetables, a variety of pickles, conserves, and chutneys.

Egg Dishes

Salads

Fish & Fish Sauces

PAPRIKA

It is ground from the pods of a mild pepper with a pleasant odor, an agreeable, slightly sweet taste, and bright color. Garnishes canapés and appetizers; used in and on beef, pork, veal, lamb, sausage, game, stews, goulash, fish, shellfish, poultry, egg and cheese dishes, soups, salads, vegetables lacking in color, relishes and pickles, ketchup, chili sauce, and chutneys.

BLACK PEPPER

Peppercorns are the dried berries of the pepper vine to be ground in a mill or used in spice bags. Black pepper, the whole berry ground, has a pungent taste. Used more than any other spice, it seasons appetizers, pepper cookies, meats, poultry, fish and seafood, gravies, sauces, eggs, casseroles, soups, salads, vegetables, pickles, relishes, mixed spices, and chutneys.

WHITE PEPPER

This variant comes from the same berry as black, the milder inside of ripe berries after the black hull is removed. In use it is interchangeable with black pepper, but in a little larger quantity. Its special value comes from its being white since it seasons white or light meats, sauces, vegetables, soups, and salads without the black flecks of pepper showing.

Spiced Cider

CAYENNE, RED, and WHOLE CHILI PEPPERS

These south-of-the-border favorites, all members of the capsicum family, have a piquant flavor which varies in intensity. They are used for many meat dishes, especially Mexican, sausages, dressings, gravies, sauces, casseroles, spaghetti, stews, pizzas, chicken, fish, seafood, eggs, cheese, soups, salads, vegetables, pickles, and relishes.

SAFFRON

Although not strictly a spice, it is usually classed with them. 225,000 stigmas of a crocuslike flower make a pound. It has an exotic flavor, pleasantly bitter, is used sparingly, usually sold in specialty food stores. Valued as a coloring in saffron tea, cakes, buns, rolls, biscuits, puddings, pies, and cookies, chicken and seafood dishes, rice and stuffing, curries, fish sauces, soups.

TURMERIC

Available mostly **ground**, this spice is the root of a plant of the ginger family and has a slightly bitter flavor. Used in recipes for cakes, cookies, curried meats, fish, shellfish, poultry, eggs, sauces, gravies, rice, salads, dressings. Its most common uses are in curry powders, pickles, relishes, chowchows, chutneys, and in condiments such as prepared mustard.

Spiced Fruits & Pickles

Clove-Studded Ham

Vegetables

Dessert Sauces

SPICE

coat of fully ripened berries, then grinding the inner white kernel. A pepper grinder is a necessary piece of equipment in every home, for freshly ground pepper has no flavor counterpart.

Cinnamon, Nutmeg, and Mace

When you buy a jar of cinnamon in the United States, unlike any other part of the world, you are most likely getting cassia, for no distinction is made here between the two spices although they are the products of different trees. In fact, the natives of southern China were peeling the bark from cassia trees centuries before "true cinnamon," as it is called in the trade, was known. True cinnamon is premium-priced, milder in flavor and aroma, and is the bark of a species of laurel tree that once grew wild in Ceylon but now is under cultivation.

The most aromatic of the spices, cinnamon (or cassia) was highly prized by the ancients. Its perfume was reserved for oriental women and the candles of kings.

It takes great skill to cut and peel the inner cinnamon bark which is gathered after the May and November rains. When ready for market, it is rolled in pipes or quills which resemble tight rolls of paper with neatly turned-in edges.

Pipes are used in preserving and pickling or as muddlers in hot chocolate, mulled cider or wine. Most cinnamon, however, is ground and used in sweets.

One of the most beautiful trees on earth is found in the Banda group of the Molucca Islands. The majestic *nutmeg* tree sometimes reaches a height of forty feet and has dense black-green foliage which offsets dramatic clusters of fruit resembling large apricots.

When the fruit is ripe, it splits open to reveal a pecan-shape pit covered with a waxy scarlet aril. The aril is *mace,* which is not greatly unlike nutmeg in flavor, perhaps somewhat stronger. The nutmeg is the only fruit that yields two spices. Mace is sun-dried, while nutmeg pits are subjected to several weeks of low heat to dry them until the kernels rattle within their shells. The shells are removed and the nutmegs graded for size.

The first historical mention of nutmeg is in a poem written in 1195 by Petrus d'Ebulo. He tells of the fumigation of the streets of Rome by the burning of nutmegs and other spices for the triumphal entry of Emperor Henry VI.

A century ago ladies and nurses carried little boxes in their pockets which secreted a tiny grater and a nutmeg. They used them to enhance a favorite dish or a cordial.

Spices of the East

In ancient China a courtier who wished to address his emperor was required to hold a *clove* in his mouth. For the Chinese had a predilection for garlic and the rich perfume of the clove was found to sweeten the breath.

Although the strikingly beautiful clove tree, tall, with terminal cymes of crimson flowers, is a native of the Moluccas, most cloves in our markets today come from Zanzibar or Pemba, an island in the Indian Ocean near Zanzibar. The cloves of commerce are the unopened flower buds which are hand-picked when they turn reddish in color and then are sun-dried.

The world's most costly condiment is *saffron,* from India and some Mediterranean countries. The stigma of a purple crocuslike flower, it takes 225,000 of them to make one pound. Saffron has been appreciated by connoisseurs since antiquity. King Solomon had a garden plot to supply saffron for his kitchen; and the legend about crocodile tears is attributed to saffron, for that sweet-smelling spice was said to be the only thing that could move the monster to tears. Its deep orange-yellow color has made it valuable in dyeing and it is also used in perfume.

Ginger is an unimpressive-looking plant which grows two to three feet tall and has small blue and white flowers and reedlike leaves. Its roots provide the spice. Kings of the Orient used to nibble ginger that had been boiled in honey, and in *The Book of 1001 Nights,* it is praised for its stimulating properties. In the days before central heating, English pubs and inns always had a shaker of ginger on the shelf. On cold days it was sprinkled into ale or porter, stirred with a red-hot poker, and drunk sizzling hot, thus producing inner warmth and glow. The resins in ginger provide its pungency, the oils its spicy odor; and the lighter its color, the more bite it has.

Columbus discovered a spice tree growing wild on the island of Jamaica and because of the warmth and pungency of its fruit called it a pepper, while today it is called pimento. *Allspice,* its more descriptive title, derives from its odor which resembles a bouquet of cinnamon, nutmeg, and cloves. Still growing in Jamaica and Mexico, the pimento tree soon after blossoming produces small clusters of pea-size fruit. Picked green, they are dried in the sun and after seven or eight days become shriveled, dark-brown in color, and develop a flavor that is highly aromatic.

All these, then, comprise the classic spices of which we use 100,000,000 pounds a year. This figure is even more impressive when we realize that because of their pungency only a dash is needed in any one dish and that all spices are powders and very light in weight. There are, of course, many other spices.

For one dish, curry, spices are purchased already mixed. In many parts of the world the curry recipe is a family or local secret, never entrusted to paper but transmitted only verbally. The curry powder you buy at your food store probably contains varying amounts of coriander, cinnamon, turmeric, cardamom, fennel, fenugreek, ginger, cayenne pepper, cloves, and cuminseed.

The romantic story of spices is thousands of years old, yet their use in our modern kitchens offers never-ending pleasures and novelties of taste.

ROLLED FISH FILLETS WITH SHRIMP SAUCE

6 fillets of sole or flounder
Salt and freshly ground pepper
Fresh grated nutmeg
2 tablespoons lemon juice
¾ cup dry white wine
¾ cup cooked shrimps
Shrimp Sauce

Gently flatten fillets with the flat side of a cleaver; season

SPICE

with salt, pepper, and nutmeg to taste. Sprinkle with lemon juice. Roll up and place in well-buttered baking dish. Pour wine over fillets. Cover with aluminum foil and bake in preheated hot oven (400°F.) about 15 minutes. On a broilerproof platter, place the rolled fillets; reserve liquid; cover with cooked shrimps. Top with Shrimp Sauce. If desired, around edge of platter, place mounds of Duchess potatoes. Place under broiler until nicely browned. Garnish platter with parsley sprigs and lemon wedges if desired. Makes 6 servings.

Shrimp Sauce

Blend 2 tablespoons all-purpose flour into ¼ cup melted butter; add 3 tablespoons cream, liquid from the fish dish, a dash of mace, ¼ teaspoon salt, and freshly ground pepper. Cook, stirring constantly, until thickened and smooth. Remove sauce from heat; stir in 1 egg yolk and 1 tablespoon fresh lemon juice. Cook for 1 minute.

ROAST LAMB WITH HOT CURRIED FRUIT

With a sharp knife cut 5 or 6 slits in leg of lamb; stuff each with a sliver of garlic and a small sprig of parsley. Put on rack in shallow roasting pan. Rub well with ground ginger; sprinkle with salt and freshly ground pepper. Pour juice of half a lemon over lamb. Roast uncovered in preheated slow oven (300°F.), allowing 25 minutes per pound for rare, 30 minutes per pound for medium, and 35 minutes per pound for well-done lamb. When meat has roasted for 1 hour, add juice of other half of lemon. Baste often. Place roast on heated serving platter; garnish with crisp watercress. Serve with Hot Curried Fruit.

Hot Curried Fruit

Put 8 slices of canned pineapple and 3 tablespoons pineapple juice in shallow roasting pan. Top with 4 bananas, cut into halves lengthwise and across. Melt ¼ cup butter or margarine in skillet; add ⅔ cup firmly packed brown sugar and 2 teaspoons curry powder dissolved in ⅓ cup brandy. Pour over fruit. Bake in preheated slow oven (300°F.) for 1 hour. Baste occasionally. Makes 8 servings.

JAVANESE LAMB

- 2 teaspoons ground coriander
- ½ teaspoon dried ground chili peppers
- 1 teaspoon cuminseed, pounded
- ½ teaspoon ground saffron
- 1 teaspoon ground ginger
- 2 garlic cloves, minced
- 2 teaspoons salt
- 3 pounds boneless lamb, cut into ½-inch cubes
- 1 cup cider vinegar
- ¼ cup cooking oil
- ½ cup water
- Hot cooked rice

Pound together coriander, chili peppers, cuminseed, saffron, ginger, garlic, and salt. Roll the pieces of lamb in this mixture. Place in a bowl and pour vinegar over. Marinate for 1 hour. Drain meat and discard vinegar. Heat oil in a saucepan; add meat and brown on all sides. Add water. Cover and cook over low heat for 30 minutes, or until tender. Serve hot with fluffy white rice. Makes 8 servings.

RHUBARB SAUCE FOR MEATS

- 1 quart finely chopped onion
- 1 quart diced rhubarb
- 1½ pints cider vinegar
- 4 cups firmly packed brown sugar
- ½ teaspoon each ground cinnamon, allspice, cayenne, and salt

Mix all ingredients in a large saucepan. Slowly bring to boil; simmer for 45 minutes. Pour into hot sterilized jars, and seal. Serve with beef, pork, or chicken. Makes about 4 pints.

SPICED ORANGES

Boil 6 unpeeled California oranges for 20 minutes, allowing 1 teaspoon salt to 2 quarts of water. Drain. Boil in unsalted water for 20 minutes. Drain. Cut into quarters. Pour over oranges the following syrup that has been boiled for 10 minutes:

- 2½ cups sugar
- ¼ cup light corn syrup
- ½ cup water
- 1 cup cider vinegar
- 12 whole cloves
- ½ cinnamon stick

Bake in an uncovered casserole in preheated slow oven (300°F.) for 1½ hours, or until transparent.
NOTE: These oranges are excellent with roast meats.

SPICED PRUNES IN LEMON GELATIN SALAD

- 1 pound large meaty prunes
- Water
- ½ cup firmly packed brown sugar
- 2 pieces (3 inches each) cinnamon sticks
- 1 teaspoon whole cloves with heads removed
- 1 teaspoon whole allspice
- 1 cup red wine
- Cashew nuts
- 2 packages (3 ounces each) lemon-flavored gelatin

Cover prunes with cold water and let stand overnight. Sprinkle with brown sugar and add spices that have been tied securely in a muslin bag. Simmer until plump and tender, about 30 minutes. Remove spice bag and add wine; simmer for 10 minutes longer. Let cool. Replace prune pits with cashew nuts. Dissolve gelatin in 2 cups boiling water and add 2 cups ice water. Pour small amount of gelatin into 5-cup mold brushed with oil; refrigerate until set. Arrange prunes on gelatin; pour over enough gelatin to cover; refrigerate until set; add remaining gelatin. Refrigerate. Unmold on large chilled salad plate. Garnish with greens. Makes 8 servings.

SPINACH

BUTTERED SPICED BEETS

- 8 to 10 small whole beets, cooked
- ¼ cup butter or margarine
- ½ teaspoon salt
- Freshly ground pepper
- ½ teaspoon ground cinnamon
- ¼ teaspoon ground ginger
- ¼ cup firmly packed brown sugar
- Juice of 1 lemon

Slip skins from cooked beets; dice beets. Put in pan with remaining ingredients. Heat thoroughly until flavors are well blended. Makes 4 servings.

TOASTED SPICE CAKE

- ¾ cup butter
- 2 cups firmly packed light-brown sugar
- 2 egg yolks
- 1 teaspoon vanilla extract
- 2⅓ cups sifted cake flour
- 1 teaspoon baking soda
- 1 teaspoon baking powder
- 1 teaspoon each ground cloves and cinnamon
- ¾ teaspoon salt
- 1¼ cups buttermilk
- Meringue
- ½ cup broken nut meats

Cream butter; beat in sugar, egg yolks, and vanilla. Sift cake flour with soda, baking powder, spices, and salt; add alternately to butter mixture with buttermilk. Spread in buttered pan 13 x 9 x 2 inches, and top with Meringue. Sprinkle with nuts. Bake in preheated moderate oven (350°F.) for 50 to 60 minutes. Makes 8 to 10 servings.

Meringue

Beat 2 egg whites until they hold a point when beater is raised, but not until dry. Slowly beat in 1 cup sifted light-brown sugar; continue beating until stiff and smooth.

GINGER COOKIES

- 1 cup molasses
- 1 cup shortening
- ¾ cup sugar
- 1 teaspoon baking soda
- 2 eggs, well-beaten
- 4 cups sifted all-purpose flour
- 1 tablespoon ground ginger
- 1 teaspoon ground cloves
- 1 teaspoon salt

Boil together for 3 or 4 minutes molasses, shortening, and sugar. Add baking soda and cool. Add eggs and flour sifted with spices and salt. Chill. Roll a small amount of dough at a time as thin as possible; cut with a 2-inch cookie cutter. Bake in preheated moderate oven (375°F.) for 8 to 10 minutes. Makes about 10 dozen.

SPICED CIDER

- 12 cups cider
- 12 whole cloves
- 1 cinnamon stick
- ¼ teaspoon ground nutmeg

Bring all ingredients to the boiling point. Strain, and serve hot in mugs.

SPINACH

SPINACH—An annual potherb which originated in southwestern Asia and is grown for its leafy green leaves. It was unknown to the ancient Greeks and Romans and the first written record of it is Chinese; it probably reached China around 647 A.D. It was brought to Spain by the Moors in the 8th century.

Availability—Available year round. It is grown in the South during the winter and in most other areas during spring and fall.

Spinach is sold in bulk by the pound, or washed and trimmed in transparent bags. It is available canned in assorted sizes and frozen as leaf or chopped spinach, creamed spinach, and spinach soufflé.

Purchasing Guide—Choose large, fresh, crisp dark-green leaves; these can be of the flat or crinkled varieties. Avoid decayed, crushed, wilted, insect-injured leaves.

Storage—For bulk spinach trim off the roots; wash in a sink full of warm water. The warm water sends the sand on the leaves to the bottom of the tub. Repeat washings with cold running water; lift spinach out of the water several times to free it from the sand. Drain well; store in a covered container in the refrigerator.
Fresh, refrigerator shelf, raw: 3 to 5 days
Fresh, cooked; and canned, open, refrigerator shelf: 4 to 5 days
Fresh, prepared for freezing; and frozen, refrigerator frozen-food compartment: 3 months
Fresh, prepared for freezing; and frozen, freezer: 1 year
Canned, kitchen shelf: 1 year

Nutritive Food Values—An excellent source of vitamin A, a very good source of vitamin C and iron, and a fair source of riboflavin. It is low in calories.
Fresh, 1 cup chopped (1.8 ounces) = 14 calories
Fresh; and frozen, chopped, 4 ounces, boiled and drained = 26 calories
Canned, 4 ounces, regular pack, solids and liquid = 22 calories
Canned, 4 ounces, regular pack, drained solids = 24 calories
Frozen, leaf, 4 ounces, boiled and drained = 27 calories

Basic Preparation—Rinse in cold running water. If the spinach is to be cooked, drain, and cook with the water that remains on the leaves; spinach to be used raw in salads should be drained and the leaves dried with paper towels.

To Cook—Cook in only the water that clings to the

SPINACH

leaves; cover the pan; cook for 5 to 10 minutes, until tender, stirring frequently to cook evenly; drain; season with butter or margarine, salt and pepper, and fresh lemon juice if desired. Or cook in a small amount of boiling water in an uncovered pan for about 10 minutes, until tender; drain and season.

To Freeze—Use only young tender leaves. Wash thoroughly in several changes of water. Remove tough stems. Blanch in boiling water for 1½ minutes. Chill in cold water for 4 minutes. Drain and pack into freezer containers, leaving ½-inch headspace. Seal.

SPINACH-STUFFED FISH FILLETS

- 2 medium onions, chopped
- 1 tablespoon butter or margarine
- 2 pounds frozen sole or flounder fillets, thawed
- 1 pound fresh spinach or 1 package (10 ounces) frozen spinach, cooked and drained
- 1 can (15½ ounces) meatless spaghetti sauce

Cook onions in butter until tender but not brown. Spread each fillet with cooked spinach and sprinkle with onion. Roll up and put in buttered shallow baking dish. Pour on spaghetti sauce; bake in preheated moderate oven (350°F.) about 20 minutes. Makes 4 to 6 servings.

ITALIAN EGGS FLORENTINE

- 1 package (10 ounces) frozen chopped spinach
- ¼ cup butter or margarine
- 2 tablespoons all-purpose flour
- 1 cup each milk and light cream
- 8 eggs, poached
  Salt and pepper to taste
  Grated cheese to taste

Cook spinach as directed on package. Make a white sauce with butter, flour, milk, and cream. Put spinach in greased shallow baking dish. Arrange drained eggs on top of spinach. Pour white sauce over eggs. Season with salt and pepper, and sprinkle with grated cheese. Bake in preheated hot oven (400°F.) for a few minutes, or until cheese is browned. Makes 4 servings.

GREEK SPINACH PIE

- 10 sheets (12 x 15 inches each) phyllo
- ½ cup butter, melted
- 2 packages (10 ounces each) fresh spinach
- 1 tablespoon salt
- 2 eggs
- 2 cups small curd cottage cheese
- 1 cup grated feta cheese
- 3 tablespoons parsley
- 2 green onions with tops, minced
  Salt and pepper

Cut phyllo sheets into halves and place 10 pieces in a buttered pan 7 x 11 inches. Brush each sheet of phyllo with melted butter. Wash spinach and remove stems. Cut leaves into ½-inch lengths. Sprinkle with salt and let stand for 15 minutes. Beat eggs. Add cheeses, parsley, and onion. Squeeze liquid from spinach. Fold spinach into egg mixture. Season with salt and pepper to taste. Spread mixture over phyllo sheets in pan and top with remaining 10 pieces of phyllo, brushing each sheet with remaining melted butter. Bake in preheated moderate oven (350°F.) for 40 minutes. Cut into squares and serve hot. Makes 6 servings.

BAKED SPINACH RING WITH EGGS

- 2 packages (10 ounces each) frozen chopped spinach
- 3 eggs, beaten
- ¼ cup heavy cream
- ¼ cup melted butter or margarine
- 1½ teaspoons seasoned salt
- ¼ teaspoon pepper
- 1 teaspoon instant minced onion
- ½ teaspoon monosodium glutamate (optional)
- 1½ cups soft bread crumbs or cubes
  Creamed Eggs Supreme

Cook and drain spinach. Whirl in electric blender or chop very fine. Mix with next 8 ingredients and pour into well-greased 6-cup ring mold. Set in pan of hot water and bake in preheated moderate oven (350°F.) for 1 hour, or until firm. Unmold on hot platter; fill center with Creamed Eggs Supreme. Makes 6 servings.

Creamed Eggs Supreme

Melt ¼ cup butter or margarine; blend in ¼ cup all-purpose flour. Add 1 teaspoon Worcestershire, 1½ cups milk, and ½ cup heavy cream. Cook, stirring constantly, until thickened. Add a dash of hot pepper sauce, 2 tablespoons chopped parsley, 1 chopped pimiento, and 8 hard-cooked eggs cut into chunks. Heat. Season to taste.

SAG PANEER

An Indian accompaniment for meats, made with spinach and cottage cheese

- ¼ cup butter or margarine
- ½ teaspoon ground turmeric
- 1 teaspoon ground coriander
- 1 teaspoon salt
- 2 packages (10 ounces each) frozen chopped spinach
- ⅔ cup creamy cottage cheese
- 1 tablespoon dairy sour cream

Melt butter; add turmeric, coriander, and salt. Cook, covered, over low heat for 5 minutes, stirring occasionally. Add spinach. Cook, covered, over moderate heat until spinach is completely thawed. Beat together cottage cheese and sour cream. Stir in spinach. Cook, stirring constantly, until cheese has completely blended with spinach. Serve very hot. Makes 6 servings.

CREAMED SPINACH

- 2 pounds spinach
- 2 tablespoons butter or margarine
- 1 tablespoon all-purpose flour
- Dash of garlic powder
- Salt and pepper to taste
- ¼ cup milk or light cream

Wash spinach and cook, without adding water, until tender; drain and chop. Melt butter; blend in flour, garlic powder, and salt and pepper. Add milk and cook, stirring constantly, until thickened. Add spinach and heat well. Makes 4 to 6 servings.

GERMAN SPINACH SALAD

- 1 pound small fresh spinach leaves
- ½ cup mayonnaise
- ½ cup dairy sour cream
- 6 anchovies, minced
- 1½ tablespoons chopped green-onion tops
- 1½ tablespoons minced parsley
- 1½ tablespoons cider vinegar
- 1½ tablespoons lemon juice
- ½ garlic clove, minced
- Cheddar-cheese cubes or garlic croutons

Wash and dry spinach. Mix remaining ingredients except cheese and add to spinach. Mix lightly; garnish with cheese. Makes 4 servings.

SPINACH AND CABBAGE SALAD

- 1 small head red cabbage
- 2 pounds fresh spinach
- 3 hard-cooked eggs
- 1 cup French, sour-cream, or Roquefort-cheese dressing
- 2 tablespoons grated onion

Trim cabbage and cut into halves, removing the core. Shred cabbage finely. Wash spinach and trim stems. Tear leaves into bite-size pieces. Toss cabbage with spinach and top with chopped eggs. Beat salad dressing with grated onion. Chill salad until ready to serve. Pour salad dressing over greens and toss lightly just before serving. Makes 8 to 10 servings.

WILTED RAW SPINACH

- 2 tablespoons bacon fat or butter
- 2 tablespoons all-purpose flour
- 1 small onion, minced
- 1 cup water
- ½ teaspoon dry mustard
- 2 tablespoons cider vinegar
- ¾ pound fresh spinach, cleaned, drained, and chopped
- Salt and pepper

Melt bacon fat. Stir in flour and onion. Gradually stir in water, mustard, and vinegar. Cook over low heat, stirring constantly, until smooth and thickened. Pour over spinach. Mix well, and season to taste. Serve at once. Makes 4 servings.

RAW-SPINACH, TOMATO AND BACON SALAD

- 1 bag (10 ounces) fresh spinach, washed, cleaned and coarsely chopped
- 4 slices bacon, crisply cooked and crumbled
- 2 large tomatoes, cut in wedges
- 1 small onion, grated
- ½ cup salad oil
- ¼ cup cider vinegar
- ½ teaspoon salt
- ¼ teaspoon pepper

Combine first 4 ingredients in large bowl. Combine remaining ingredients and toss with spinach mixture just before serving. Makes 6 to 8 servings.

SPONGECAKE

SPONGECAKE—A light airy cake with a delicate flavor and texture which is leavened with air incorporated into beaten egg whites. The egg yolks are beaten separately with sugar and folded into the whites. Flour and salt are then carefully folded into batter. Shortening is not generally used in this cake. The cake is turned in an ungreased pan, usually one with a removable bottom, and baked until the top is lightly browned and springs back when touched. It is cooled in its inverted pan. When the cake is cool, it is loosened with a sharp knife or spatula and removed from the pan.

Spongecake is a very old cake, found in the cooking of many nations. In France it is called *génoise* and in Italy *genovese*, since it is said to have originated in the city of Genoa. Old English and Scandinavian cooking also knew the spongecake, as did Jewish cooking. The reason why this cake appears in so many different places is a simple one: it dates back to days when yeast was the only leavening agent known, and since it was unsatisfactory for cakes, they had to be leavened by natural means such as egg whites beaten full of air. Electric beaters have made this task much easier.

Spongecake has many virtues as a cake. It is light and easily digestible, and lends itself admirably to frostings and fillings and to use as the base for *petits fours*. One of the simplest and best ways of serving a spongecake is to fill and frost it with well-flavored whipped cream.

Caloric Values
1/12 of 10-inch cake (2.3 ounces) = 196 calories

SPONGECAKE

- 1½ cups egg whites (9 to 10 whites)
- ½ teaspoon salt
- 1 teaspoon cream of tartar
- 1⅓ cups sifted granulated sugar
- Grated rind of 1 orange or 1 teaspoon orange extract
- 1⅓ cups sifted cake flour
- ⅔ cup egg yolks (8 or 9 yolks)
- Confectioners' sugar

Beat egg whites until frothy; add salt and cream of tartar gradually, beating constantly. Continue beating until stiff but not dry. Gradually add granulated sugar, beating constantly until all sugar is used and mixture does not run or slip when bowl is stood on edge. Blend in orange rind. Sift flour onto mixture gradually, folding carefully and gently until well blended after each addition. Beat egg yolks until thick and lemon-colored, and gradually fold into first mixture. Pour into ungreased 10-inch tube pan and bake in preheated slow oven (325°F.) for 1¼ hours. Invert cake on rack and let stand until cold before removing from pan. To decorate, dust sifted confectioners' sugar through the holes in a fancy paper doily placed on the top of the cake; then carefully remove doily.

HOT-WATER SPONGECAKE

- 5 eggs (at room temperature)
- 1½ cups sugar
- 2 cups sifted cake flour
- 2 teaspoons baking powder
- ¼ teaspoon salt
- 1 teaspoon vanilla extract
- ½ cup boiling water
- Confectioners' sugar

Beat eggs with rotary beater until very light; gradually beat in sugar. Add dry ingredients slowly, stirring constantly. Stir in vanilla and boiling water. Pour into a medium Turk's-head pan (fluted cake pan with a central tube). Bake in preheated slow oven (325°F.) for 1 hour. Allow spongecake to stand for 1 hour, or until it has cooled. Remove it from the pan and dust with sifted confectioners' sugar, or frost as desired.

SPOON—This is the oldest and simplest of all eating utensils. Spoons may have many refinements, but basically a spoon is an oval or concave bowl which is fixed to a handle. Throughout many years of use, shapes for various uses have been developed; tea, coffee, sugar, cereal, soup, fruit, dessert, cream soup, thin soup, and serving—each has its own type of spoon.

The earliest spoons were made of wood. As man developed skills in the working of materials he found about him, he developed more elaborate spoons. The early Egyptian ones were elaborately carved of ivory and wood, or made of various metals, finely wrought. The handles were often in the shape of men, women, or animals, and were frequently adorned with lotus blossoms. The spoon was the mark of class in medieval society. Each person had to bring his own eating utensils to the table and children were given a set when they were old enough to eat with company. So to be born with a silver spoon in one's mouth meant that one's family was well-to-do.

In the early days of this country spoons were made of wood, then of pewter and later of silver. The simple colonial patterns of New England were among the best silver spoons made anywhere. In the 19th century, many people collected souvenir spoons upon which memorable scenes of places visited were engraved. The habit still persists.

SPREADS

SPOON BREAD—A famous Southern specialty, this is a baked dish made from white or yellow cornmeal, milk, eggs, and shortening. It is served with a spoon.

The history of spoon bread goes back to the first days of the Virginia Colony when the settlers adapted one of the Indian methods of preparing the native white cornmeal. The Indian's *Suppawn* was a simple porridgelike dish, cooked in pots. The English colonists, recalling the quick breads and porridges eaten in their homeland, refined the dish by adding milk and eggs. Some unknown cook left this mixture in the oven by mistake. Spoon bread was the result.

Spoon bread, and other batter breads made from corn, were especially suited to the colonial way of life. The poorer settlers at first relied more on quick-cooking hoecakes and ashcakes, which could be cooked over a fire rather than in an oven. During the 17th and 18th centuries refinements were introduced which "remain in staunch Favour today among all Classes of Virginians." The batter breads, with their richer ingredients and need of an oven, were developed during this period.

Americans have always eaten many more "quick" breads than have Europeans, largely because of the availability of cheap fuel to make home-baking possible. In continental Europe, conditions demanded that the housewife buy her breads from the village baker or at least take them to him to bake. But in the American South, organized around a central plantation kitchen, spoon bread and its countless relatives could be enjoyed by all.

SPRAT—One of the smallest of the herrings, *Clupea sprattus*, five inches is its normal maximum length. Sprats are caught in abundance in many parts of Europe and extensively eaten there fresh and smoked, both under their own and other names. For example, a sprat is also called a Norwegian sardine or anchovy. In the United States the term sprat is applied to the young of the common herring and to many other small fishes. Sprats are imported canned, under that title, from Denmark and France and are available in specialty food stores and in the gourmet-food sections of many food stores.

SPREADS—Whether crunchy or smooth, hot or cold, these sandwich spreads are sure to delight all.

NUT BUTTER

Finely chop equal amounts of almonds, pecans, filberts and walnuts. For each 2 cups chopped nuts, cream ½ cup butter with 1 teaspoon curry powder (optional). Add nuts, then stir in ½ cup mayonnaise. Season to taste with salt. Store covered in refrigerator. Will keep 2 to 3 weeks. Makes about 2½ cups.

SPREADS

CRUNCHY PEANUT-BUTTER FILLING

2 packages (3 ounces each) cream cheese, softened
⅔ cup crunchy peanut butter
¼ cup milk
⅓ cup sweet-pickle relish
¼ cup chopped pimiento-stuffed olives

Combine cheese, peanut butter and milk and mix until creamy. Add remaining ingredients and mix well. Store covered in refrigerator. Will keep 2 weeks. Makes about 2 cups.

BOLOGNA-SALAD FILLING

2 cups finely chopped bologna
1 cup finely chopped celery
⅓ cup chopped sweet pickle
½ cup mayonnaise

Mix all ingredients. Store covered in refrigerator. Will keep 5 to 7 days. Makes about 3 cups.

POT-CHEESE AND SALAMI FILLING

1 pound pot-style cottage cheese
¼ pound hard salami, cut in small pieces
⅓ cup finely chopped dill pickle
2 tablespoons finely chopped green onion
½ cup mayonnaise

Mix all ingredients. Store covered in refrigerator. Will keep 1 week. Makes 3 cups.

CREAM-CHEESE AND LIVERWURST FILLING

1 package (8 ounces) cream cheese, softened
¾ pound liverwurst
1 can (3 or 4 ounces) chopped mushrooms, drained
1 tablespoon instant minced onion
2 teaspoons Worcestershire
⅛ teaspoon pepper
¼ cup undiluted evaporated milk

Mash together cream cheese and liverwurst. Add remaining ingredients and mix well. Store covered in refrigerator. Will keep 1 week. Makes 3 cups.

CHEESE-PIMIENTO-OLIVE FILLING

2 cups coarsely shredded sharp Cheddar cheese
½ cup mayonnaise
1 tablespoon minced onion
½ cup chopped black olives
1 jar (4 ounces) pimiento, chopped

Let cheese stand at room temperature about 15 minutes, then add mayonnaise and beat until smooth. Add remaining ingredients and mix well. Store covered in refrigerator. Will keep 2 weeks. Makes about 2 cups.

EGG-HAM-SALAD FILLING

6 hard-cooked eggs, coarsely chopped
1 cup diced cooked ham
1 cup chopped celery
½ cup coarsely chopped sweet pickle
¼ cup chopped pimiento-stuffed olives
⅓ cup mayonnaise
Salt and pepper to taste

Combine all ingredients and mix lightly. Store covered in refrigerator. Will keep 4 to 5 days. Makes about 2½ cups.

CREAM-CHEESE AND RAISIN FILLING

1 package (8 ounces) cream cheese, softened
1 tablespoon grated lemon rind
1 tablespoon chili sauce
¾ cup seedless raisins
½ cup chopped pimiento-stuffed olives
1 cup finely shredded carrot

Beat cream cheese with lemon rind and chili sauce. Add remaining ingredients and mix well. Store covered in refrigerator. Will keep 1 week. Makes 2 cups.

SAVORY CORNED-BEEF FILLING

1 can (12 ounces) corned beef
¾ cup chopped celery
¼ cup sweet-pickle relish
1 teaspoon onion powder
⅛ teaspoon garlic salt
⅛ teaspoon black pepper
⅓ cup mayonnaise

Break up corned beef with fork. Add remaining ingredients and mix well. Store covered in refrigerator. Will keep 1 week. Makes 2½ cups.

HAM-CHEESE FILLING

1 cup finely chopped cooked ham
1 cup finely chopped process American cheese
⅓ cup chopped sweet pickle
½ teaspoon onion powder
⅓ cup mayonnaise

Mix all ingredients together. Store covered in refrigerator. Will keep 1 week. Makes 2 cups.

SARDINE-OLIVE FILLING

2 cans (3¾ ounces each) sardines in oil, drained
2 hard-cooked eggs, mashed
½ cup chopped pimiento-stuffed olives
3 tablespoons mayonnaise to moisten (about)
1 tablespoon lemon juice

Mix all ingredients. Store covered in refrigerator. Will keep 1 week. Makes 1½ cups.

HOT SPREADS FOR BREADS

Butter- or mayonnaise-based spreads that bake into the bread

Choose a spread from the list below and use in any of the following ways:

1. Cut crusty French or Italian bread crosswise in ½-inch slices. Spread each slice with chosen mixture, put loaf back together and wrap in foil. Bake in preheated hot oven (425°F.) 15 minutes, then fold back foil and bake 15 minutes, or until bread is browned and crisp. If preferred, bread can be cut in half lengthwise, spread with mixture and cut in slices. Heat as above.
2. Slice finger, Parker House or other rolls 3 or 4 times from top almost to bottom, making slices ¼ inch to ½ inch apart. Spread small amount of chosen mixture between slices and bake in preheated hot oven (425°F.) 15 minutes, or until browned and bubbly.
3. Separate halves of split hot-dog, hamburger or dinner rolls. Spread each half with chosen mixture and bake in preheated hot oven (425°F.) 15 minutes, or until browned and bubbly.
4. Spread thin layer of chosen mixture on slices of white, whole-wheat, rye or other sliced bread. Cut in fingers, triangles or other shapes and bake in preheated hot oven (425°F.) 8 minutes, or until browned.

OVEN SPREADS

To ½ cup (1 stick) butter or margarine, softened, add any one of the following:
 ½ cup each chopped parsley and green onion or chives
 Crushed dried celery leaves, marjoram, sage or poultry seasoning, and onion powder to taste
 Seasoned salt and seasoned pepper to taste
 ⅓ cup chopped chutney
 Mashed anchovy fillets and grated Parmesan cheese to taste
 Crushed dried salad herbs to taste
 2 tablespoons chopped capers
 ½ cup crushed canned onion rings
 Bacon-flavor bits to taste
 ½ cup each chopped watercress and green onion
 ½ cup softened blue cheese and 1 tablespoon parsley flakes
 ½ cup grated Parmesan cheese; dried parsley, garlic salt and oregano to taste
 Lemon-pepper marinade to taste

To 1 cup (2 sticks) butter or margarine, softened, add either of the following:
 1 can (8 ounces) crushed pineapple, well drained, and ½ cup flaked coconut
 1 envelope (1⅜ ounces) onion-soup mix

To ½ cup mayonnaise, add any one of the following:
 ½ cup finely diced Swiss or Gruyere cheese and a dash of cayenne
 ½ cup grated Parmesan cheese and 1 tablespoon parsley flakes
 ½ cup shredded Cheddar cheese and 1 tablespoon parsley flakes
 ¼ cup mustard relish
 ¼ cup barbecue sauce
 1 teaspoon instant chicken-bouillon granules and 1 tablespoon parsley flakes
 (Bottled tartar sauce can also be used as a spread.)

Breads brushed with melted butter, sprinkled with seasoning and baked

Choose an ingredient or ingredients from the list below and use in any of the following ways:
1. Select any ready-sliced bread and cut off crusts. Cut bread in fingers, triangles or cookie-cutter shapes. Brush with melted sweet or salted butter, or margarine, and sprinkle with chosen ingredient. Bake in preheated slow oven (300°F.) 10 to 15 minutes, or until edges just begin to brown. (Baking time will vary with thickness of bread.)
2. Separate halves of split hot-dog, hamburger or soft dinner rolls, brush with melted butter or margarine and sprinkle with chosen ingredient. Bake in preheated slow oven (300°F.) 10 to 15 minutes, or longer if necessary to brown edges.
3. Trim bread slices and cut bread in shapes with cookie cutter. Brush with melted butter or margarine and arrange chosen ingredient artistically on each shape. Combinations of ingredients, such as freeze-dried chives and fresh-onion rings, or chopped parsley and fresh green onion, can be used, if desired. Bake in preheated slow oven (300°F.) 10 to 15 minutes.

OVEN SPRINKLES

To 1 stick (½ cup) butter or margarine, softened, add:
 Sesame seed
 Poppy seed
 Dillseed
 Caraway seed
 Kosher salt
 Grated Parmesan cheese
 Lemon-pepper marinade
 Curry powder and flaked coconut
 Seasoned salt and seasoned pepper
 Finely chopped or sliced pimiento-stuffed olives
 Coarsely ground black pepper
 Fresh-onion rings (sprinkle with paprika after baking)
 Bacon-flavor bits
 Chopped or strips of pimiento
 Freeze-dried chopped chives
 Chopped fresh parsley
 Chopped fresh green onion

BROILER SNACKS

Spreads that pop under the broiler for a hot, bubbly snack

ENGLISH-MUFFIN SPREADS

Split 3 muffins, toast and spread each half with any one of the following. Put under broiler until browned and bubbly.

½ recipe pineapple-coconut filling. Good with ham.

Combine ½ cup applesauce; 2 tablespoons butter or margarine, softened; and ¼ cup firmly packed brown sugar.

Soften and beat together 1 package (3 ounces) cream cheese and 2 tablespoons butter or margarine. After broiling, top with dollop of guava, strawberry or other preferred jelly.

Beat together ½ cup crunchy peanut butter; ¼ cup butter or margarine, softened; and ⅓ cup firmly packed light-brown sugar.

PARTY-RYE ROUNDS

Spread any one of the following on 20 slices of party-rye bread. Put under broiler a few seconds, or just until bubbling. Serve hot.

Combine 1 cup shredded (or grated) Parmesan cheese; ½ cup mayonnaise; 1 medium onion, grated; dash of cayenne.

Combine ½ cup mayonnaise, 1 cup shredded Cheddar cheese, 2 tablespoons finely chopped green onion and dash of hot pepper sauce.

Combine ½ cup mayonnaise, 1 cup diced Swiss or Gruyère cheese and 2 tablespoons dried parsley.

Combine ½ cup mayonnaise, 1 cup crumbled soft blue cheese and ½ cup sliced pimiento-stuffed olives.

SPRITZ—A cookie with a high butter content that is forced out of a special spritz tube. The name comes from the German and it means "to squirt." The spritz cookie dough is squirted out of the cookie press, in interesting patterns, onto an ungreased cookie sheet.

SPRITZ COOKIES

½ cup soft butter or margarine
½ cup shortening
⅔ cup sugar
3 egg yolks
1 teaspoon almond extract
2¼ cups sifted all-purpose flour

Cream butter, shortening, and sugar until light. Beat in egg yolks and flavoring. Add flour, and blend. Fill cookie press and shape fancy cookies on chilled ungreased cookie sheets. Bake in preheated moderate oven (375°F.) for 10 to 12 minutes. Makes 4 to 5 dozen.

CHOCOLATE SPRITZ COOKIES

1 cup soft butter
¾ cup sugar
3 egg yolks
2 squares (2 ounces) unsweetened chocolate, melted
1 teaspoon vanilla extract
2½ cups sifted all-purpose flour
¼ teaspoon salt
Colored tiny candies, colored sugar, bits of candied cherries

Cream butter and sugar; add egg yolks and beat until light. Blend in chocolate and vanilla. Add flour and salt; mix well. Force through cookie press. Decorate. Bake in preheated hot oven (400°F.) for 7 to 10 minutes. Store airtight. Will ship well if not too thin. Makes about 6 dozen.

SPROUTS—*From Seed to Sprout to Salad in Less Than a Week*

by Gay E. Courter

Can you imagine growing your own vegetables on your kitchen counter, then harvesting and cooking your produce in less than a week? I had always wanted a little garden—minus the five *W*'s of weeding, watering, waiting, worrying and WORK. My little bean-sprout patch grows in three to five days and has never failed yet. For me the sprouts are a source of wonder and satisfaction, while my family enjoys eating this versatile vegetable.

I am not a health-food faddist or a far-out gourmet, but I'm always looking for simple nutritious dishes and new ways to stretch that shrinking dollar. The little bean sprout develops from dried beans. One of the most expensive is the mung bean, but one pound makes about thirty servings.

The incredible bean sprout is not only economical, but one of the most nutritious foods available. Something wondrous happens as the little seed swells and sprouts, releasing dormant energy and vitamins. The Chinese first recorded the use of sprouts in 2939 B.C. and most people are familiar with this vegetable only in Chinese dishes. Recently sprouts have been discovered by nutritionists, who have found them to be as rich as tomatoes and grapefruit in vitamin C and to contain enough proteins and other vitamins to be classed as a "complete food." Many of the sprout proteins are predigested, for they are converted to amino acids during the sprouting, and the starches are converted to sugar, making the sprouts a quick-energy food. These facts about sprouts vary with the type of seed sprouted, but the nutritional value has been demonstrated to me by numerous studies. I refuse to claim that sprouts are a "miracle food," good for every ill, from scurvy to lack of virility. Sprouts are best described as a delicious addition to salads, soups and casseroles, and as an excellent fresh vegetable. Canned sprouts are colorless, odorless and tasteless in comparison to fresh.

Our favorite sprout recipe takes less than five minutes to prepare. I quickly sauté the sprouts—alone or combined with green pepper, onion or chives—in hot oil. When they are hot (about 3 minutes), season with salt, soy sauce, gravy or broth and serve. The taste is nutty, the texture crisp; best recommendation of all, no child has yet left them on his plate untouched.

A long list of seeds sprout with excellent results. Many are available in the dry-bean section of the supermarket and are very reasonable in price. Others, such as mung, wheat and alfalfa, are sold at health-food stores, farmers' supply stores and by mail order. The most popular seeds for taste and the easiest are mung, soy, lentil, alfalfa and wheat. Other suitable and delicious sprouts may be grown from barley, buckwheat, fava, lima, pinto, corn, dill, flax, fenugreek, garbanzos, lettuce, millet, pumpkin, peanuts, onions, oats, red beet, safflower and sunflower. Don't buy seeds treated with certain chemicals, such as fungicides. Buy untreated seeds (the package gives this information). Organically grown seeds are often recommended, but it is inexpensive and fun to experiment with the different characteristics and tastes of various sprouts.

There are many methods of growing sprouts. The following is my choice for its simplicity and for its use of ordinary kitchen equipment. I highly recommend that beginners use the mung bean, for its universal taste appeal and reliability.

Dry mung beans are recommended for beginners because they're reliable and have a pleasing taste.

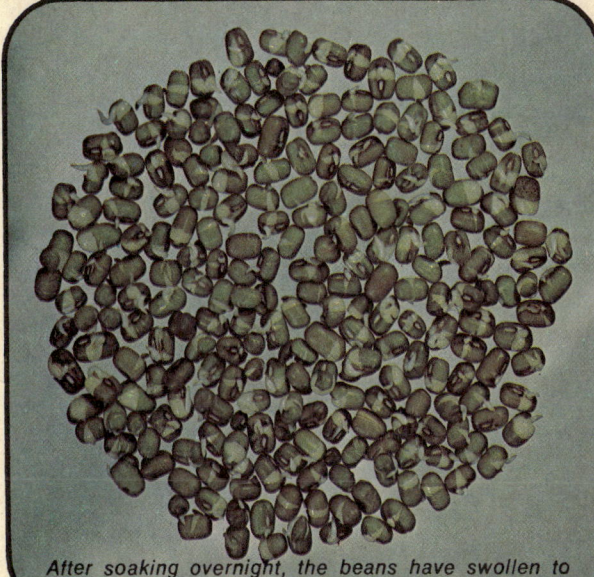

After soaking overnight, the beans have swollen to twice their size; husks are breaking away.

The next day the sprouts are nearly 1" long. One more day and they'll be ready for eating.

DAY 1. Rinse ½ cup dry beans (or desired amount) several times in strainer. Soak beans in warm water (4 parts water to 1 part beans—½ cup dry beans in 2 cups water). Let stand in warm place 8 hours or overnight.

DAY 2. Rinse beans again in strainer. (Beans will have at least doubled in bulk.) Place in container that allows for expansion of about 8 times swelled amount (1 cup swelled beans in 2-quart container). Container should be earthenware, porcelain enamel or opaque glass. It must be nonmetallic and opaque. Ideal containers include unglazed crocks, bean pot, crockery canister, cookie jar, or a mixing bowl covered with a dinner plate. (It's important that the container be unglazed, since the lead sulfate used for glazing can cause lead poisoning.) Drain excess moisture. Soak 3 sheets of paper towel in water and lay on top of beans. Cover and put aside at room temperature. In about 4 hours, moisten towels.

DAY 3. Already you will notice considerable growth and the outer shell will be falling off. Fill container with warm water to about one inch above sprouts. Cover, turn upside down and drain thoroughly. Gently stir with hands or wooden spoon so that bottom sprouts move toward top. Moisten paper towels and cover. Later in the day, moisten towels.

DAY 4. Repeat procedure for Day 3 if necessary.

DAY 5. Repeat procedure for Day 3 if necessary.

SPROUTS

Mung, soy, garden peas and lentils are ready to serve when the sprout is 1 to 1½ inches long. Rye, wheat and alfalfa are ready when the sprout is about the same length as the seed. Sunflower seeds are best when they are less than 3/8 inch long. Don't be afraid of the whiskers that appear on the sprout rootlet. They are the feeder roots looking for nourishment. The whole sprout—seed, root, stem and outer shell—is edible, but some people prefer to rinse away the discarded shell.

When the sprouts are the proper length (there really is no set rule; experiment to taste), they may be refrigerated by placing them in a plastic bag along with a moist paper towel. Many of the vitamins, especially vitamin C, increase after 3 to 4 days of refrigeration. Sprouts refrigerate successfully for 8 to 10 days, but may also be frozen for up to 3 months. They become rich in chlorophyll if placed in the sun a few hours before serving.

The secret of successful sprouting is to keep the sprouts warm and moist. If they sit in water, they will rot. If they look dry, rinse and freshen with water more frequently. This may be necessary in hot weather. Drain thoroughly. If a bad odor is emitted, some beans are rotting. Eliminate them and freshen with water.

There are many other acceptable methods of sprouting. One is by using Beales Famous Seed Sprouter, which is unglazed. It can be ordered from Frederic B. Sadtler, Inc., P.O. Box 323, Fort Washington, Pa. 19034. Sadtler also sells many varieties of beans and seeds for sprouting, including a sample package containing fifteen varieties of seeds to test for preference.

Beans and seeds can also be ordered from El Molino Mills, 1839 West Valley Blvd., Alhambra, Calif. 91803. When you take into account that the weights of these seeds increase six to eight times after sprouting and that larger quantities come cheaper, the price of sprouts is ridiculously low. Also low, by the way, is caloric content.

WAYS TO USE SPROUTS

Soups—add just before serving. Rye sprouts taste like wild rice!

Casseroles—add just before serving.

Salads—tossed, fruit, three-bean, Waldorf. Let the sprouts get their first tiny primary green leaves and toss with any salad.

In omelets, soufflés, scrambled eggs.

Grind sprouts in meat grinder and add to the final kneading of breads, or stir into muffin, waffle and pancake batter.

Eat rye and wheat sprouts as a snack, like peanuts.

In sandwich spreads as a crunchy replacement for celery.

Stewed with tomatoes.

Marinated and served raw.

As a vegetable, steamed, sautéed or baked.

Most sprouts should never be cooked more than 5 to 8 minutes, or the taste, texture and nutritional value may be lost. Soybeans may need an extra 10 minutes of steaming.

SPROUT SOUP

1½ quarts seasoned chicken or beef broth
2 cups bean sprouts
3 eggs, well beaten
3 tablespoons minced parsley

Heat broth. Add sprouts and simmer 3 minutes. Remove from heat and stir in eggs. Garnish with parsley. Makes about 2 quarts.

SPROUT SUEY

2 tablespoons oil or bacon fat
1 pound pork or beef, cut in ½-inch dice
1 cup thinly sliced onion strips
2 teaspoons salt
½ teaspoon pepper
1½ cups diced celery
¾ cup diced green pepper
3 cups mung or soy sprouts
1 cup boiling water
1 tablespoon soy sauce
2 tablespoons all-purpose flour
1 tablespoon cold water
Hot cooked rice

Heat oil in skillet. Add meat and cook slowly about 30 minutes. Add next 6 ingredients and 1 cup boiling water. Simmer, covered, 10 minutes. Make paste of soy sauce, flour and cold water. Stir into mixture and cook until thick. Serve with rice. Makes 6 servings.

EGGS FOO YONG

6 eggs
1 teaspoon salt
2 tablespoons chopped green pepper
½ cup chopped onion
2 cups bean sprouts, well drained

Beat eggs until frothy. Add remaining ingredients and mix well. Generously grease skillet, pour in ½ cup egg mixture and brown on both sides. Repeat until all of mixture is used. Makes 4 to 6 servings.

SAUTÉED PORK SLICES

¾ pound fresh pork, cut in thin slices
1 tablespoon vegetable oil
1 cup coarsely chopped onion
12 fresh or dried mushrooms, cut in strips
1 cup chopped celery
2 green peppers, diced
¼ cup soy sauce
1 to 2 cups bean sprouts
½ can (6 ounce size) water chestnuts, sliced
1 teaspoon ground ginger
Water
2 tablespoons cornstarch

Sauté pork in oil in skillet 10 minutes, or until thoroughly cooked. Add onion and mushrooms and stir-fry a few minutes. Add celery and peppers and stir-fry a few minutes. Add next 4 ingredients and ½ cup water. Bring to boil and thicken with the cornstarch blended with 2 tablespoons water (do not overcook; all vegetables should be crisp and crunchy). Makes 6 servings.

CREOLE SPROUTS

- 1 tablespoon vegetable oil
- ⅓ cup minced onion
- ½ cup diced celery
- 1 can (1 pound) stewed tomatoes
- 1 bay leaf
- ½ teaspoon salt
- 2 cups bean sprouts

Heat oil in skillet, add onion and celery and sauté until golden brown. Add next 3 ingredients, bring to boil and simmer, uncovered, 10 minutes. Remove bay leaf. Steam sprouts in covered saucepan about 5 minutes. Add to first mixture and heat 5 minutes. Makes 4 servings.

SHRIMPS AND VEGETABLES

- 2 tablespoons soy sauce
- ½ teaspoon salt
- 1 teaspoon ground ginger
- 1 tablespoon sherry
- 1 pound raw shrimps, shelled and cleaned
- 3 tablespoons vegetable oil
- 1 cup chopped onion
- ¾ cup chopped celery
- 1 can (6 ounces) water chestnuts, sliced
- 2 to 3 cups bean sprouts
- 1 tablespoon cornstarch
- 1 cup broth or water

Mix first 4 ingredients and sprinkle on shrimps. Heat 1 tablespoon oil in skillet, add shrimps and sauté about 7 minutes. Remove from skillet. Put remaining 2 tablespoons oil in skillet, add onion and celery and sauté about 5 minutes. Add shrimps, water chestnuts and bean sprouts. Mix cornstarch and broth and stir into mixture. Cook, stirring, until thickened. Cover and simmer about 3 minutes. Makes 6 to 8 servings.

SPROUTED-WHEAT BALLS

- 2 cups sprouted wheat
- 1 cup almonds, walnuts or pecans
- 1 large onion
- 1 cup milk
- 1¼ cups fine dry bread crumbs
- 1 teaspoon salt
- 2 tablespoons vegetable oil
- Parsley

Force first 3 ingredients through coarse blade of food chopper. Stir in milk, then add next 3 ingredients and mix well. Let stand 10 minutes to allow crumbs to absorb liquid, then shape in 1¼-inch balls. Put on greased cookie sheet and bake in preheated hot oven (400°F.) about 15 minutes. Or sauté in greased skillet until golden brown. Garnish with parsley. Good with meat gravy or cream sauce. Makes about 3½ dozen.

BEAN-SPROUT SALAD

- 3 cups bean sprouts
- 1 can (1 pound) cut green beans, drained
- 1 can (1 pound) wax beans, drained
- 1 can (1 pound) red kidney beans, drained and rinsed, or 1 can (1 pound) chick-peas, drained
- ¾ cup cider vinegar
- ½ cup salad oil
- ¾ cup sugar
- 2 tablespoons soy sauce
- 2 teaspoons dry mustard
- 1 cup chopped onion
- Salt and pepper to taste

Put sprouts and beans in large bowl. Mix remaining ingredients and pour over beans. Toss well, cover and marinate 3 to 4 hours in refrigerator. Makes 10 to 12 servings.

SPUMONI—Italian molded ice cream with an outer layer of custard containing chopped almonds and an inner filling made with heavy cream, sugar, cherries, and candied orange peel.

SPUMONI

- 2 cups milk
- 5 egg yolks, slightly beaten
- ⅛ teaspoon salt
- 1 cup sugar
- 1 teaspoon vanilla extract
- 1 cup heavy cream
- 8 maraschino cherries, finely chopped
- 2 tablespoons minced candied orange peel
- 8 slivered blanched almonds
- 2 tablespoons brandy

Turn refrigerator control to coldest setting. In top part of double boiler mix milk, egg yolks, salt, and ¾ cup sugar. Cook over simmering water, stirring constantly, until mixture is thickened and coats a metal spoon. Cool; add vanilla. Pour into refrigerator tray and freeze until almost firm. Line a 2-quart melon mold with the mixture. Whip cream until stiff; fold in remaining ¼ cup sugar, cherries, peel, almonds, and brandy. Fill center of mold, cover, and freeze in freezer or freezing compartment of refrigerator until firm. Unmold on serving plate and cut into wedges. To loosen spumoni from the mold, put a cloth wrung out of hot water on the bottom of mold. Makes 6 to 8 servings.

SQUAB—A young pigeon which has not been allowed to fly. Squabs weigh about one pound and are eaten as a delicacy. They were especially prized in Victorian and Edwardian days, when chickens were not the commercially produced, weight- and quality-controlled birds they are today. In those days, the cook never could be quite sure that even a young chicken would be tender. But squabs were, and this is why they were used for festive dinner parties.

SQUASH

Availability and Purchasing Guide—Available all year in gourmet food stores and specialty stores. They are more plentiful and less costly during the summer months. Frozen squabs are also available in food specialty stores.
Squabs should be plump and firm in appearance.

Storage—Refrigerator shelf, raw: 2 to 3 days
Refrigerator shelf, cooked: 4 to 5 days
Frozen, refrigerator frozen-food compartment: 1 to 2 months
Frozen, freezer: 6 to 8 months

Nutritive Food Values—Good source of protein, with some phosphorus and a small amount of calcium.
Meat and skin, 4 ounces = 333 calories
Meat only, 4 ounces = 161 calories

Basic Preparation—Squabs can be split and broiled, stuffed and roasted, sautéed, or stewed. They need long, slow cooking and should be served well done. Squabs should be eaten with the fingers as it is impossible to cut off all the meat with a knife and fork.

To Roast—If frozen, thaw squab. Season inside and out with salt and pepper. Stuff, if desired, just before cooking, allowing ¼ cup stuffing for each squab. Skewer neck and body openings. Turn back wings. Brush with melted butter and roast on a rack in preheated hot oven (400°F.) for 45 minutes to 1 hour, or until drumstick moves easily in the joint. Brush with more melted butter occasionally during roasting.

To Broil—Wash, dry, and split squabs. Or have butcher split them. Put skin side down on a rack in a broiler pan. Brush with melted butter. Season with salt and pepper. Broil 7 to 9 inches from heat for 30 minutes, or until tender, turning squab once during this time. Brush with more butter during cooking.

To Sauté—Cut squab into quarters and bread pieces or dip into flour. Season with salt and pepper. Sauté in shallow fat until brown and then continue cooking over low heat for 15 to 20 minutes, or until squab is tender.

To Freeze—Eviscerate, wash, and pat dry. Do not stuff before freezing. Wrap in moisture-vaporproof wrapping, excluding as much air as possible. Seal.

ROAST STUFFED SQUABS

1 onion, chopped fine
Butter or margarine
1 cup fine, soft stale-bread crumbs
1 cup chopped cooked ham
½ cup pine nuts
¼ cup chopped parsley
½ teaspoon dried thyme
4 squabs (about 1 pound each)
4 pieces of fat bacon
¼ cup white wine

Sauté onion in 6 tablespoons butter until golden. Mix with next 5 ingredients. Stuff birds with the mixture, close openings with poultry pins and lace with twine. Put, breast sides up, on rack in shallow roasting pan. Cover the breast of each squab with a piece of bacon. Melt ¼ cup butter and mix with wine. Roast in preheated slow oven (325°F.) for 1 hour and 15 minutes, basting frequently with the butter-wine mixture. Remove bacon during last 15 minutes of roasting. Makes 4 servings.

SQUASH
—A gourd fruit native to the Western Hemisphere, belonging to the genus *Cucurbita*. The Indians called it *askutasquash*, meaning "green thing eaten green" and grew it in Peru as long as 2,000 years ago.

The two main types of squash are summer and winter squash. There are many varieties of each, differing in shape, size, and color:

SUMMER SQUASH—Small, quick growing, with thin skins and light-colored flesh. They are marketed before the rinds and seeds harden. The varieties most common in our food stores are:

Scallop, Cymling, or Pattypan—Diskshape, with a scalloped edge. The skin is smooth or slightly worted, pale green when young, and turns white as it matures. It is best harvested when half grown or 3 to 4 inches across.

Cocozelle—Cylindrical, with smooth skin slightly ribbed with alternate stripes of dark green and yellow. Similar to zucchini. Best when 6 to 8 inches long and 2 inches in diameter.

Caserta—Also cylindrical but thicker than cocozelle at the tip. The skin has alternate stripes of light and dark green. Best when 6 to 7 inches long and 1 to 1½ inches thick.

Chayote—A pear-shape squash about the size of an acorn squash, light green in color. It has one soft seed in the center. When prepared for cooking, it is cut up unpeeled, without removing the edible seed.

Yellow Crookneck—A squash with a curved neck, larger at the top than the base. The worted skin is light yellow in young squash, turning to a deep yellow when mature. It is best when still light yellow and about half grown. Grows to be 8 to 10 inches long and 3 inches thick.

Yellow Straightneck—Similar to the Crookneck except that the neck is straight and it grows to be much larger, 20 inches long and 4 inches thick when mature.

Zucchini—Sometimes called Vegetable Marrow or Italian Marrow. It is cylindrical but larger at the base. The skin has a lacy pattern of green and yellow that concentrates to give the appearance of stripes. It grows to be 10 to 12 inches long and 2 to 3 inches thick.

WINTER SQUASH—Winter squash has a hard, coarse rough rind that is dark green or orange in color. There are many types of winter squash. The most common varieties in our food stores are:

Acorn, Table Queen, or Des Moines—Acorn-shape and grows to be 5 to 8 inches long and 4 to 5 inches thick. It has a thin, smooth, hard shell which is widely ribbed, and is dark green but changes to orange during storage. The flesh is pale orange and there is a large seed cavity.

Buttercup—Has a turbanlike formation at the blossom end. It grows to be 4 to 5 inches long and 6 to 8 inches thick, with a turban 2 to 3 inches thick. The hard skin is dark green with faint gray pockmarks and stripes and the turban is light gray. The dry sweet flesh is orange in color.

Butternut—Cylindrical in shape with a bulblike base. The skin is smooth and hard and is a light brown or dark yellow color. It grows to be 9 to 12 inches long; at the bulbous end it is often 5 inches in diameter.

Warren Turban—Drum-shape with a turbanlike formation at the blossom end. It grows to be 8 to 10 inches long and 12 to 15 inches in diameter. The hard worted skin is bright orange, the blossom end slightly striped, and the turban a bluish color.

Hubbard—Globe-shape with a thick tapered neck that is somewhat smaller at the blossom end. It grows to be 9 to 12 inches in diameter. The skin may be bronze-green, blue-gray, or orange-red in color; it is hard, worted, and ridged. The flesh is yellowish orange and has a sweet taste.

Sugar or Pie Pumpkin—Green or orange rind with ridges, round or oval-shape, with stem at the top. The flesh is bright orange with many seeds in the center of the pumpkin.

Availability—The varieties of summer squash listed are found in some markets all year round with the peak season May to July.

Among the winter squash, acorn and butternut are available year round, and the other varieties are in food stores from August to December, with the peak season from October to December.

Canned puréed squash is available, as is frozen zucchini and winter squash.

Purchasing Guide—When buying summer squash, look for young squash with fresh tender rinds, free from blemishes, and fairly heavy for their size.

Look for winter squash with a hard rind that is free from blemishes. It should be heavy for its size.

Storage—Purchase summer squash in small quantities and store immediately in the vegetable compartment of the refrigerator.

Place winter squash so that they do not touch in a fairly dry, well-ventilated room with temperatures between 50°F. and 55°F.

Summer squash, fresh, refrigerator shelf or vegetable compartment, raw: 3 to 14 days

Winter squash, fresh, kitchen shelf: 1 to 4 weeks
Fresh, refrigerator shelf, cooked: 4 to 5 days
Fresh, prepared for freezing; and frozen, refrigerator frozen-food compartment: 2 to 3 months
Fresh, prepared for freezing: and frozen, freezer: 1 year
Canned, kitchen shelf: 1 year

Nutritive Food Values—Summer squash provides vitamin C, vitamin A, and niacin. Since summer squash is low in calories and sodium, it may be used frequently in a sodium-restricted diet, reducing, or other special diets.

Winter squash is an excellent source of vitamin A, and has fair vitamin C, riboflavin, and iron.

Summer squash, crookneck and straightneck, boiled and drained, ½ cup diced (3.6 ounces) = 15 calories
Summer squash, scallop, boiled and drained, ½ cup mashed = 16 calories
Summer squash, cocozelle and zucchini, boiled and drained, ½ cup slices (2.7 ounces) = 9 calories
Winter squash, acorn, ½ cup boiled (4.1 ounces) = 39 calories
Winter squash, acorn, ½ cup baked = 56 calories
Winter squash, butternut, 4 ounces, boiled = 46 calories
Winter squash, butternut, 4 ounces, baked = 77 calories
Winter squash, Hubbard, ½ cup boiled (4.2 ounces) = 35 calories
Winter squash, Hubbard, ½ cup baked (3.6 ounces) = 51 calories
Winter squash, frozen, heated ½ cup (4.2 ounces) = 46 calories

Basic Preparation, Summer Squash—Wash, but do not pare; remove the stem and blossom ends. Leave whole or cut into ¾-inch slices or cubes.

To Cook—Cook, covered, in a small amount of boiling salted water (2 to 4 tablespoons) for 10 to 15 minutes, or until tender. Uncover and boil rapidly for a few minutes longer to evaporate excess liquid. Season with salt, pepper, and butter or margarine. A garlic clove or a bouillon cube may be added during cooking, if desired.

To Freeze—Use young tender squash with small seeds. Cut squash after washing into ½-inch slices. Blanch in boiling water for 3½ minutes. Chill in cold water for 5 minutes. Drain. Pack into containers, leaving ½-inch headspace. Seal.

Basic Preparation, Winter Squash—Wash; cut small squash such as acorn or butternut into halves; cut larger squash into individual servings; remove the seeds and stringy portions.

To Bake—Dot cut portions with butter or brush with bacon or ham drippings; season with salt and pepper; place in a covered baking dish or wrap in foil. Bake in preheated hot oven (400°F.) for 30 to 60 minutes, or until tender; time varies according to size and type of squash. Remove the cover and unwrap during the last 15 minutes of baking.

Squash may also be baked, uncovered, in a shallow greased pan, cut side down for the first half of the baking period to allow it to steam. Turn up, brush with butter, and season. Continue baking until tender. Allow longer time for baking when using this method.

To Mash Baked Squash—Prepare and bake as directed above. When tender, cool slightly and scrape out pulp. Mash pulp, using a potato masher, electric mixer, or blender. Season with salt, pepper, butter, and brown sugar if you wish. Mix well and reheat before serving.

To Freeze—Use firm squash. Cut into cubes and remove seeds. Cook, covered, in water to cover and until squash is tender. Remove rind and mash squash. Cool quickly and pack into containers, leaving ½-inch headspace.

If desired, bake squash as above and pack halves or quarters in plastic bags and seal, or wrap in foil. Freeze until firm.

1 — Butternut
2 — Hubbard
3 — Scallop
4 — Sugar or Pie Pumpkin
5 — Acorn
6 — Summer
7 — Zucchini

SUMMER SQUASH

SQUASH MANDARIN

- 2 pounds summer squash
- Salt
- 1 tablespoon butter or margarine
- 1 can (8 ounces) mandarin oranges
- 2 teaspoons light-brown sugar
- ¼ teaspoon ground nutmeg
- ¼ cup toasted slivered almonds

Wash squash. Cut, unpeeled, into crosswise slices. Cook in small amount of boiling salted water until just tender; drain and add butter. Keep warm. Pour syrup from oranges into saucepan, add sugar, and bring to boil. Add nutmeg and orange segments. Pour over squash and sprinkle with nuts. Makes 6 servings.

BAKED SUMMER SQUASH

- 1 small onion, minced
- 3 tablespoons butter or margarine
- 3 hard-cooked eggs, chopped
- 3 summer squash, diced
- 2 eggs, well beaten
- ⅓ cup light cream
- ¼ cup soft bread crumbs

Sauté onion in butter; add hard-cooked eggs and squash. Put mixture in well-greased 1-quart casserole. Mix beaten eggs with cream and pour over casserole. Sprinkle top with bread crumbs. Bake in preheated moderate oven (350°F.) about 30 minutes. Makes 6 servings.

CHEESE-STUFFED SQUASH

- 3 medium cymling squashes
- 2 onions, minced
- ½ teaspoon each dried thyme and sage
- ½ teaspoon salt
- ⅛ teaspoon pepper
- ¼ cup butter or margarine
- 2 celery stalks, minced
- 1 ripe tomato, peeled and diced
- 1½ cups soft stale bread crumbs
- 1 cup shredded Cheddar cheese

Wash squashes, cut into halves crosswise, and scoop out seeds. Cover with boiling water in skillet or kettle and simmer for 5 minutes; drain. Cook onion and seasonings in butter for 3 to 4 minutes. Add celery and tomato. Heat well and stir in crumbs and cheese. Stuff squashes. Put squashes in shallow baking pan and cover bottom of pan with boiling water. Bake in preheated moderate oven (350°F.) for 30 minutes, or until squashes are tender. Makes 6 servings.

SQUASH

WINTER SQUASH

SCALLOPED HUBBARD SQUASH

- 1 onion, chopped
- 1 green pepper, chopped
- 3 tablespoons butter or margarine
- 3½ cups mashed cooked Hubbard squash or 2 boxes (12 ounces each) thawed frozen squash
- Salt and pepper
- ½ cup crushed cornflakes

Cook onion and green pepper in butter until tender. Add squash and season with salt and pepper to taste. Put in greased shallow baking dish and sprinkle with cornflake crumbs. Bake in preheated hot oven (400°F.) about 30 minutes. Makes 4 servings.

SQUASH CASSEROLE

- 2 cups mashed cooked Hubbard squash
- ¼ cup butter or margarine
- 3 tablespoons firmly packed brown sugar
- 1 tablespoon prepared mustard
- 1 egg, slightly beaten
- Salt and pepper to taste
- ¼ cup crushed cornflakes

Mix squash with 2 tablespoons each melted butter and brown sugar, mustard, and egg; season with salt and pepper. Put in greased shallow baking dish. Mix cornflakes with remaining 2 tablespoons melted butter and 1 tablespoon brown sugar; sprinkle over top. Bake in preheated moderate oven (350°F.) for 20 minutes, or until heated through. Makes 6 servings.

ANISE SQUASH PIE

- ¾ cup sugar
- 1 tablespoon all-purpose flour
- ½ teaspoon salt
- ¼ teaspoon ground ginger
- 1½ teaspoons crushed aniseed
- ¾ teaspoon lemon juice
- 3 eggs
- 1½ cups mashed cooked winter squash
- 1 cup milk
- Pastry for 1-crust 9-inch pie

Combine first 6 ingredients in mixing bowl. Beat in eggs. Stir in squash and milk. Turn into 9-inch pie pan lined with pastry. Bake in preheated hot oven (400°F.) for 40 to 50 minutes, or until center of pie is firm. Cool before serving. Makes 6 to 8 servings.

BAKED ACORN SQUASH WITH WHIPPED POTATO ROSETTES

- 3 medium-size acorn squashes
- 3 tablespoons melted butter or margarine
- Salt and pepper to taste
- 3 cups seasoned mashed potatoes
- 1 egg, well beaten

Cut squash into halves and place, cut side up, in a baking pan. Pour ½ inch of boiling water into pan, cover, and oven-steam in preheated hot oven (400°F.) for 40 minutes, or until just tender. Drain water. Brush squash with butter and sprinkle with salt and pepper. Whip potatoes and egg together. Be sure there are no lumps. Force through pastry bag into hollows of squash, using star-shape tip to form rosettes. Or, potatoes can be spooned lightly into squash. Bake in preheated hot oven (400°F.) for 20 minutes, or until thoroughly heated and lightly browned. Makes 6 servings.

SQUID—This odd many-armed salt-water creature belongs to the Cephalopoda, the highest class of mollusks, along with the cuttlefish and octopus. Squids are found all over the world; they are much used in Mediterranean countries and in Japan. Squid has a group of ten long muscular arms around the front of its head with suckers at the ends, like hands. Squids have a bag of inklike fluid inside which they eject (like working a siphon) when danger is near. The ink clouds the water and protects them.

Availability and Purchasing Guide—Fresh squid is available year round in fish markets in large cities. It should have a sweet fresh odor.

Frozen squid is available; also canned, dried, and salted squid can be found in oriental markets and specialty stores.

Storage—Wrap fresh squid in moisture-proof paper or place in tightly covered dish in coldest part of refrigerator.
Fresh, refrigerator shelf: 1 to 2 days
Canned, kitchen shelf: 1 year
Canned, refrigerator shelf, opened: 3 to 4 days
Dried, refrigerator shelf: 2 to 3 months

Nutritive Food Values—High in protein and phosphorus, with some calcium and traces of thiamine and riboflavin. 4 ounces, raw = 95 calories.

Basic Preparation—To clean squid, hold body in one hand and grasp head and tentacles in the other. Gently but firmly pull head end from body in one piece. Cut off tentacles to use; discard head and remaining portions pulled from body. Pull out from the body the rudimentary shell, like a piece of transparent plastic. Rinse body and tentacles. Skin can be peeled off or not as you prefer. Cut squid into rings or small pieces or leave whole for stuffing.

To Fry—Cut tentacles into small pieces. Roll pieces in flour. Dip pieces into beaten egg and then into crumbs or into a batter. Fry in deep hot fat or oil (375°F. on a frying thermometer), or sauté in shallow cooking oil until golden brown. Drain on absorbent paper and add salt and pepper to taste.

To Bake—Soak cleaned squid in milk to cover. Drain; roll in dry bread crumbs and put in a well-greased shallow baking dish. Season with salt and pepper and dot with butter or margarine. Bake in preheated extremely hot oven (500°F.) for 12 minutes. Serve with tartar sauce or a spicy tomato sauce.

SQUID, ITALIAN STYLE

- 1½ pounds small squids
- ½ cup olive oil
- 1 garlic clove, sliced
- Few parsley sprigs
- ½ teaspoon salt
- 2 anchovy fillets, chopped
- 1 tiny piece hot dried red pepper
- 1 cup dry white wine
- ½ cup water

Skin squid, remove insides; wash squid well and cut into pieces. Lightly brown garlic in olive oil. Add remaining ingredients except wine and water. Sauté squid in oil until opaque. Add wine and simmer until most of wine is evaporated. Add water and simmer for a few minutes longer, until squid is done to your taste; do not overcook.

SQUIRREL—A widely distributed, largely arboreal rodent of the family Sciuridae. Two kinds of squirrels are found in the United States and occasionally eaten as food, particularly in some rural sections of the southern states. These are the red and gray squirrels. The gray squirrel is fatter and the texture and flavor of its meat are superior to that of the red. The flesh of squirrel is light red or pink in color and has a pleasing flavor. The slight gamy taste present in most game meats is not so pronounced in squirrel. Young ones can be fried or broiled the same as rabbits. Only the oldest and toughest animals require parboiling to make them tender.

FRICASSEED SQUIRREL

- 1 gray squirrel, cleaned and disjointed
- ½ teaspoon salt
- ⅛ teaspoon pepper
- ½ cup all-purpose flour
- 3 slices of bacon, diced
- 1 small onion, sliced
- 1½ teaspoons lemon juice
- ⅓ cup broth or water

Cut squirrel into 6 or 7 pieces. Rub with salt and pepper and roll in flour. Fry slowly with bacon until browned. Add remaining ingredients, cover, and simmer for 1 hour, or until tender, adding more broth or water if necessary. Makes 4 servings.

STARCH—A carbohydrate found in certain grains, vegetables, and roots which is reduced to a white powder or to granules by a complicated chemical process. Starch has no odor or flavor. It acts as a stiffener of liquids, so that in cooking it is used as a thickener. Starches used for thickening are mixed into a cold liquid or beaten egg, to make a slurry, or mixed with sugar, before being stirred into a hot liquid. The heat makes the softened starch granules swell, thus stiffening the mixture. Or, to make a roux, the starch is stirred into melted fat (butter, oil, etc.) over low heat before hot liquid is added. Starch also absorbs a certain amount of moisture without caking too much; it is added to confectioners' sugar and to baking powder to control moisture which otherwise would be totally absorbed by the sugar or baking powder ingredients, making them impossibly hard.

The best known culinary starches are made from corn, rice, potatoes, arrowroot, and cassava, manioc or tapioca. Some starches are precooked as in instant puddings, pie fillings, and sauce mixes. They require little or no cooking to thicken.

For various kinds of cooking, such as the thickening of sauces and the making of puddings, starches produce better results than flour. They thicken into a softer, more gelatinous, and clearer substance, and they cook more quickly, without the raw taste of flour that has not been sufficiently cooked. Foods like lemon juice should be added after the starch solution has thickened and little or no further cooking is required.

To substitute a starch for flour as a thickening agent, 2 tablespoons flour = 1 tablespoon cornstarch, rice starch, potato starch, or arrowroot.

Mix starch with a little cool water to a smooth paste. Stir gradually into hot liquid. Cook, stirring constantly, until liquid has thickened and is clear.

Some starches are used to stiffen clothes; sometimes they are packed in pressurized cans as spray starches.

STEAK—A slice of meat cut from the fleshy part of the carcass of an animal or a cross-section slice of a large fish. When the word steak is used without further specification it generally refers to a beefsteak. However, there are ham steaks, lamb steaks, salmon steaks, etc.

Ground beef, shaped into a patty for cooking, is also called steak, for example: hamburger steak, Salisbury steak.

Steak cuts are usually broiled or grilled. For additional information see entries under the specific meats and fishes.

STEAKS, CHARCOAL BROILED

by PHILIP S. BROWN

We Americans dearly love steak and our annual consumption of it is a matter of awe and amazement to the rest of the world. Even the English, from whom we got our passion for beefsteaks, think we overdo it a bit, but maybe there is a tiny touch of envy mingled with their scorn. Still, it was the English who started it all with their famous beefsteak clubs. Far and away the most famous of them all was the Sublime Society of Steaks, which was founded by the celebrated theater manager John Rich in 1735, and continued until 1867. In addition to great figures from the literary and theatrical worlds, its membership included brilliant men from all walks of life, even some members of the royal family. In truly democratic

STEAK

fashion all members were on an equal footing; nevertheless, I suspect that membership in The Club was a status symbol of the times.

The French, who had not yet become Kings of the Kitchen, seem to have adopted this English culinary discovery early in the 19th century. Today, of course, travelers in France are everywhere offered the ubiquitous *entrecôte*, as well as *filets* and *aloyaux* (sirloin steaks). But it was the Americans who, in the last century, really took the steak to the family heart. Not at the clubs, not at restaurants serving *haute cuisine*, but in the well-to-do American home, steak was eaten morning, noon, or night, or all three. Steak and eggs was a standard breakfast dish, along with fried potatoes, toast, bacon, and frequently a piece of pie. The trenchermen of the day thought nothing of sitting down, at noon, to a 2-inch, 3-pound T-bone or sirloin steak, then returning home to a family meal of steak and onions.

It has been in this century, however, that steaks have really come into their own. As living conditions have improved, more and more families could afford to splurge on a steak, and the demand grew. Perhaps the greatest impetus given to steak-eating was the discovery that cooking them over glowing coals (the original way of broiling) was still the best. Restaurants began boasting of their charcoal-broiled steaks and before long smart wives figured out that their husbands could do just as good a job in their own backyards. And so they can, if they follow a few simple rules.

Although most of us, including me, mean beefsteak when we say "steak," there are steaks from other animals and fish that are marvelous. The general rules applying to the broiling of beefsteaks apply, with a few slight variations. Veal, pork, ham, lamb, and mutton are all superb, as are fish steaks of various kinds. It's fun to experiment and any of these will be a welcome change, in the unlikely event that you find beefsteaks monotonous.

The Size of Steaks

Steaks vary tremendously in size, shape, tenderness, and beauty. Your steaks should preferably be government-graded Choice at least, and in the case of some less tender cuts (rump, round, flank, and so on), Choice or Prime.

Generally speaking, steaks should be cut no thinner than 1 inch, as it's nearly impossible to control the degree of rareness in a thinner one. Steaks which must be well done, like pork, may be thinner, of course. Personally, I prefer steaks from 1½ to 2½ inches thick as that's the way to grill them with that crisp brown crackling of the fat and a little crust on the outside, so that each slice is a lovely juicy pink framed in appetizing brown. For boneless cuts, allow at least ½ pound for each diner; 10 to 12 ounces of meat with the bone in. It's a good idea to trim off some of the surplus fat, thus preventing too much flaring with attendant dousing. If you have one of the new slant-grill barbecues, this is no longer a problem, as the fat runs down the grill and not into the fire. While most articles on the subject recommend turning steaks with tongs or a spatula, I find the fork much easier and the resultant holes in the meat close up as soon as the heat reaches them, which is immediately.

How do you know when the steak is done? The easiest way for a novice charcoal cook is to make a slit in the meat with a very sharp-pointed knife and take a peek inside. Here again all the vital juices will not spurt out and the cut will soon be sealed. After a little practice, **you should be able to tell by the "feel" of the meat,** the way professional chefs do. Press down on the meat with the back of a fork and just wiggle it a little. As the meat cooks it becomes "tighter" and you'll get less reaction to the movement of the fork. As I said, this method requires some practice, but it's a nice professional touch and doesn't impair the appearance of the meat.

How to Start a Charcoal Fire

There are innumerable ways of starting a charcoal fire, and your way is undoubtedly the best for you. The most important thing about fires for steaks is to keep them small. Charcoal is an expensive fuel but a little goes a long way. In general, 12 to 18 briquettes are plenty to cook any steak, although more may be needed if many steaks are being broiled on a large grill area. After igniting, they should be allowed to burn until covered with a thin layer of gray ash; the temperature at the grill level should be around 300°F. for most steaks: this is a medium fire. Most grills in use today have grates or fireboxes which can be raised or lowered for heat control; if yours is fixed in one position, be sure that the fire's right before starting to cook.

As for the grill itself, it can be as simple or elaborate as you like. An old oven grate on two stacks of bricks will produce superb results if the cook knows what he's doing. So use whatever equipment suits you, but understand what you're trying to do. I have cooked steaks on improvised wire-mesh grills, on propane-heated tiles, on electric grills with ceramic "charcoal," and practically every other kind known to man. A couple of minutes devoted to learning the capabilities of the grill will result in perfect steaks every time, and under almost any sort of conditions.

If your steak is 1½ inches thick or more, it should be at room temperature before cooking; if it's thinner than that, better keep it in the refrigerator until just before grilling. A 2-inch steak will take about 3 hours to warm up to 70°F., so if you buy it in the morning, don't refrigerate it; just leave it out. Also remember that the temperature of the air will make a big difference in the time required to cook over an open fire. If there's a cool breeze blowing, not as much heat will reach your steak on the grill, and the top side will not retain its heat as well. If it's a hot summer night, your steaks will cook considerably faster. So consider all these factors, then step up confidently and grill that perfect steak.

BEEFSTEAKS

TENDERLOIN

Tenderloin or *filet* steaks, cut from the long narrow muscle which runs along the backbone in the loin area, cost a pretty penny. Don't let that always stop you, however.

Remember that they are boneless and are usually "stretched" with a rich sauce, so they are not always the most expensive meal. Classically the tenderloin is divided into several sections: the Chateaubriand, near the large end; the *filet* steak, a little farther down; the *tournedos*, still smaller, which is the piece of tenderloin found in a T-bone steak; and the *filet mignon,* which is cut from the very smallest part of the tenderloin. Today the terms *filet mignon* and *tournedos* are used to cover just about any steak cut from the tenderloin, while Chateaubriand usually implies a tenderloin steak with Chateaubriand Sauce. Steaks from the tenderloin are usually cut from 1 to 2 inches thick, but those from the larger end may be cut even thicker, if desired. As they are very lean, larding (weaving strips of fat through the meat) or barding (covering the outside of the meat with a sheet of fat) is usually in order.

CHATEAUBRIAND STEAK

There are a number of stories about what the original Chateaubriand steak was. If you want to go quietly crazy, try to prove which is the right one. Here's the one I prefer, and even though it's seldom seen today it's still a superb idea. A thick slice, 2½ to 3 inches, from the large end of the tenderloin is required. Insert the point of a sharp knife halfway down the outside and move it back and forth to make a pocket. Heat 3 or 4 chopped shallots in beef fat or butter in a skillet, and fill the cavity with this mixture; close the opening with a skewer or toothpicks, or sew it up. Broil for 8 to 10 minutes on a side over a medium fire; it should be quite rare but cooked through. Serve with Béarnaise Sauce or with maître d'hôtel butter. Carve into fairly thin slightly diagonal slices.

A later way with Chateaubriand (at least I think it was later!) was to place the steak between two lesser steaks, then broil it until the outer pieces of meat were black. They were then discarded and the succulent steak within was served with a rich sauce—what glorious extravagance!

A Chateaubriand steak in most modern restaurants is a thick slice of tenderloin, larded with beef fat or bacon, and broiled to the desired degree of doneness (*à point,* as the French say), then served up with Chateaubriand Sauce. This steak should be at least 2 inches thick, and preferably a little thicker. It should be sliced diagonally across the grain, then the sauce poured over the slices. It's a fine luxurious dish for an outdoor party, and each steak will serve at least two, probably more.

Chateaubriand Sauce

Cook together 1 cup brown gravy or sauce Espagnole and 1 cup white wine until very thick. Add ½ cup butter, 3 tablespoons fresh lemon juice, 1 tablespoon minced parsley, and salt and pepper to taste. Beat well and serve when the butter is melted. Makes about 1 cup.

TOURNEDOS BÉARNAISE

A *tournedos* is cut from the *filet* after it has been surrounded with a layer of pounded beef fat and tied well. The steak should preferably be cut 1½ to 2 inches thick, and grilled over a medium charcoal fire for about 5 minutes on a side (for rare, that is; allow 7 to 8 minutes on a side for medium, longer if you want to spoil it completely). When done; sprinkle with salt and pepper, pepper, and serve with Béarnaise Sauce.

Béarnaise Sauce

In a skillet put 2 tablespoons white wine, 1 tablespoon tarragon vinegar, 2 teaspoons chopped fresh tarragon (or 1 teaspoon dried tarragon), 2 teaspoons chopped shallot or onion, and ¼ teaspoon freshly ground black pepper. Bring to a boil and cook rapidly until almost all the liquid disappears. Melt ½ cup butter in a small saucepan, but don't let it brown. In the top of a blender put 3 egg yolks, ½ teaspoon salt, a dash of cayenne, and the wine-tarragon-shallot mixture. Cover and flick the motor on and off high speed. Remove cover, turn motor on high, and gradually add the hot butter, partially covering blender to prevent spattering. Sauce will thicken and become smooth quickly and you'll have ¾ cup Béarnaise Sauce.

TOURNEDOS WITH TIVOLI SAUCE

After grilling tournedos as directed in Tournedos Béarnaise, cover with Tivoli Sauce and top with a delicately browned mushroom cap. Sprinkle with paprika.

Tivoli Sauce

Dice ¼ pound mushrooms and brown with 1 carrot, diced, and 1 shallot, minced, in 2 tablespoons butter or margarine. Add 2 teaspoons paprika, 1 cup dairy sour cream and salt to taste. Simmer very gently until heated through. Do not allow to boil. Makes about 1¼ cups.

TOURNEDOS ROSSINI

This is very rich and very good. The garnishings will be made ready in the kitchen before the meat is cooked. After grilling the *tournedos,* as directed in Tournedos Béarnaise, place each one on a round of fried toast, top with a slice of *foie gras* and one of truffle, and pour over Bordelaise Sauce or Madeira Sauce.

Bordelaise Sauce

Cook 2 tablespoons minced shallots or green onions in 2 tablepoons butter. Add ¾ cup red wine and simmer until the liquid is reduced to half. Add 1 can (8 ounces) beef gravy or sauce Espagnole, 2 tablespoons each fresh lemon juice and minced parsley, and salt and cayenne to taste. Heat, add sliced poached beef marrow if you like, and serve. Makes 2 cups.

Madeira Sauce

Heat 1 can (8 ounces) beef gravy or sauce Espagnole with 2 beef bouillon cubes. Add ¼ cup Madeira, heat, and serve. Makes about 1¼ cups.

Tournedos with Tivoli Sauce, Noodles and Tossed Salad

SIRLOIN

The sirloin lies just toward the front of the beast from the rump and round, and to me is one of the most flavorsome of steaks. The whole sirloin contains the large end of the tenderloin, as well as the "top sirloin" and the "sirloin tip." It has a fairly large percentage of bone as well. Frequently the boneless top sirloin is sold separately, but you'll have to dig a little deeper to pay for it. Prime or Choice meat should be selected for these steaks, and they should be cut not less than 1½ inches thick, preferably thicker. Some butchers differentiate between various whole sirloin cuts, depending upon the size and shape of the bone; "wedge bone" and "pinbone" are the usual categories.

WHOLE THICK SIRLOIN FOR A LARGE PARTY

This is my idea of the perfect party steak. Have a whole sirloin cut 2 to 3 inches thick, some of the excess fat removed, and the fat around the edge slashed prettily. Grill over a medium fire for 10 to 15 minutes on a side. If you like a "charred" surface, let the fire flare up around the steak when it is almost done, but remember not to get it really black—the flavor of the fat will be spoiled. Place on a carving board and remove the bone for easier carving. Sprinkle with salt and pepper, top with a goodly hunk of butter, and carve into slices when the butter has melted. The resultant blend of beef juice and butter is really all the sauce you need here. The meat should be carved into slices not more than ½ inch thick, all the way across so that each diner gets some of the top sirloin and some of the tenderloin. The dainty feeders will be happy with a slice or two, while the real trenchermen can indulge in their happy gluttony. Although baked potatoes may seem pedestrian, they are just right with this steak. Serve them simply with butter, salt, and fresh pepper. For a salad, try lettuce with lots of chopped green pepper.

STEAK

LOIN-STRIP STEAK

This cut is also known as strip steak, shell steak, *contre-filet,* New York cut, or Kansas City cut. It is the strip of loin, usually sold boneless, which is left when the tenderloin is removed from the short loin. A 2- to 2½-inch steak should serve two comfortably, with maybe a little snack left over for breakfast. Grill over a medium fire for 8 to 10 minutes on a side (4 or 5 minutes for a thinner steak) and serve at once. If you're serving individual strip steaks, a good idea, I think, is to roll a bar of butter in finely chopped parsley until it is heavily coated; as the steaks are served, put a slice of this on top of each one, to melt and mingle with the meat juices. There are many sauces that are good with these steaks—Bordelaise or Béarnaise, maître d'hôtel butter, or Wine-Shallot Sauce.

Wine-Shallot Sauce

Sauté 1 cup chopped shallots or green onions in ¼ cup butter until soft. Add 1 cup white wine, 2 tablespoons wine vinegar, 1 teaspoon salt, and some freshly ground black pepper, and cook for 5 minutes. Cut in ½ cup butter, cook until melted, and serve the sauce at once.

TOP SIRLOIN STEAK

The top sirloin is really the large end of the loin strip, and is almost always sold boneless. It's a fine steak for serving to several people, sliced and served with butter sauce. Have it cut 2 to 3 inches thick and broil as usual, from 10 to 12 minutes on a side. While it's cooking, prepare the platter or serving board by liberally strewing or spreading it with butter. When the sizzling steak is laid upon this unctuous bed and carved, the melted butter and meat juices will mingle into a harmonious sauce, which is spooned over the meat slices as it is served. You'll want crusty bread to sop up the juices, and perhaps a casserole of corn, tomatoes, and okra.

PORTERHOUSE, T-BONE, AND CLUB STEAKS

These steaks are all cut from the short loin and it's often hard to tell where one ends and the next one begins. The porterhouse comes from the large end and has more tenderloin; the club steak is from the small end and has no tenderloin; the T-bone lies in between. Porterhouse and T-bone steaks should be cut at least 2 inches thick, while the club should be 1 to 1½ inches. They are cooked in the usual manner and I think they're best as is, with salt, pepper, and butter. To carve them, remove the T-shape bone and slice across, so that each serving has a piece of the tenderloin and a piece of the loin strip.

STEAK WITH ONIONS

One of the great American dishes is steak smothered in onions, and I defy anyone to best it. Traditionally, this is a good size T-bone, not too thick. Before you cook it, peel and slice 4 to 5 large onions, and cook them very slowly in plenty of butter in a covered skillet, stirring occasionally. They should be golden with little flecks of brown. Grill the steak quickly, put it on a hot platter, and engulf it with the onions. Add salt and pepper and tie into it, eating some onions with each forkful of meat. Such luxury! With it have hard rolls, and ripe tomatoes stuffed with chopped celery and green pepper.

RIB STEAKS

Rib steaks, known in France as *entrecôtes,* can be very good indeed. The ones from the smaller end of the rib are frequently served as "club" steaks. Actually they are next-door neighbors on the hoof and are definite look-alikes. To my notion, a proper rib steak should be at least 1 bone thick (about 1½ inches), and preferably should have a little extra on each side of the bone. The Spencer or "eye of the rib" steaks have the bone, coarser meat, and fat removed. These should be cut 1 to 2 inches thick and treated like tenderloin.

ENTRECÔTE BERCY

This is an old French classic, still very much in evidence in that country today. Grill the rib steak over a brisk fire, having first sprinkled it with salt and pepper. While it's cooking, heat a platter on the grill and mix 3 tablespoons butter (as it melts) with lots of chopped parsley, chervil, and shallots. Cream them well together and when the steak is done, turn it in the sauce. Put another piece of butter on top and sprinkle with more chopped parsley. Serve with noodles dressed with butter and grated Parmesan, and with green beans vinaigrette.

RUMP

For some reason or other, rump steaks are not very widely used in this country, at least not for grilling. Choice-grade rump steak is well worth seeking out. It will need marinating or tenderizing before grilling.

MARINATED RUMP STEAK

In bottom of a dish pour enough olive oil to cover it; about ¼ cup for each steak should do it. Add 1 finely chopped garlic clove and the juice of ½ fresh lemon for each steak, and let 1½-inch rump steaks stand in this for 12 to 24 hours, turning them every once in a while. Add more oil if too much is absorbed. Grill in the usual manner, and add salt and pepper when they are just done. Garnish with sliced sautéed mushrooms: for each steak slice ½ pound mushrooms; sauté slowly in plenty of butter until tender. Serve roasted corn, too, and have cherry tomatoes and other raw vegetables for nibbling.

STEAK

FLANK STEAKS

Personally, I think this one of the finest flavors of any steak, bar none. It has the added advantage of being inexpensive, boneless, and easy to cook. Most flank steaks sold in this country are braised endlessly; a great pity, to my notion. Next time you have one, try broiling it.

LONDON BROIL

The steak should be of Choice or Prime grade. Have the membrane on the outside pulled off, but do not have the meat scored. In its raw state it will have a maximum thickness of about 1 inch or a little less, but during the cooking it will contract and become considerably more compact and thicker. Have the meat rather cold, brush with a little oil or melted butter, and grill over a hot fire for 3 or 4 minutes on a side: it must be rare to be good. The only trick involved in preparing this excellent steak is in the carving, and that's very easy if you have a sharp knife. Put the cooked steak on a carving board and, starting at the thick end, slice across the grain into very diagonal slices. The knife is held at a very acute angle to the meat, about 25 degrees or less. Thus the slices will be 3 to 4 inches wide, each with a lovely brown frame around the juicy red interior. Salt and pepper are the only sauce needed for the enhancement of this fine steak. A 1½- to 2-pound flank steak will serve 3 or 4 persons. Anything is good with flank steak, but there's nothing better, perhaps, than asparagus and a baked potato.

MINUTE STEAK

These are thin steaks cut from the strip, the sirloin, or the ribs. They won't really cook in a minute, but they don't take very long. They usually weigh 6 to 9 ounces. They should be quite cold before cooking over a good hot fire for about 2 minutes on a side.

DEVILED MINUTE STEAKS

For 4 steaks have ready 1½ to 2 cups toasted buttered crumbs and about ½ cup butter. Grill the steaks quickly, undercooking them a little, then spread them with butter and roll in the crumbs, pressing the crumbs in firmly. Replace them on the grill just long enough for the crumbs to be brown and crisp, about 1 minute. Serve with Sauce Diable. Makes 4 servings.

Sauce Diable

Cook 3 tablespoons minced shallots in the same amount of butter until wilted. Add ¼ cup fresh lemon juice or cider vinegar, 2 teaspoons each Worcestershire and prepared mustard, a dash of hot pepper sauce, and 1 can (8 ounces) beef gravy or sauce Espagnole. Heat well and serve.

ROUND STEAK

TERIYAKI

Have a 1-inch-thick piece of top round sliced into very thin strips ¼ to ½ inch thick. Marinate in the following mixture: combine ½ cup soy sauce, ½ cup cooking oil, 2 teaspoons sugar, ½ cup fresh orange juice, 1 teaspoon grated fresh gingerroot (or ground ginger if you can't get the fresh), and 1 pressed garlic clove. Let the meat strips remain in this for 1 hour, then weave them back and forth on bamboo or metal skewers. Grill them very quickly over a fairly hot fire, about 30 seconds on a side. Let each guest cook his own.

SKIRT STEAKS

You don't see these too often in markets (I suspect the butchers take them home). If from top-grade beef, they are delicious, and have a flavor and texture all their own. They may be simply grilled, like a London Broil.

MARINATED SKIRT STEAK

Make a marinade of ½ cup each: soy sauce, sherry, and oil; add 2 tablespoons grated fresh gingerroot or 2 crushed garlic cloves. Marinate the skirt steak in this mixture for 1 to 2 hours, turning frequently. Broil quickly over a hot fire until nicely browned on the outside and rare within, about 3 minutes on a side. Carve like flank steak. Save any marinade for next time. Fried rice is good with this.

GROUND BEEF

Perhaps the most popular meat in America is the hamburger (oh, all right, maybe the hot dog is!), and tons of them are consumed every day. As with almost everything else, there are two schools of thought (at least) about forming the meat into patties. One group admonished you to be sure not to handle the meat any more than you can help; form it loosely. The other, to which I belong, believes that the patties should be compact and firmly pressed together. For charcoal grilling this is especially true. A loosely made patty will be apt to disintegrate when you turn it. Lean round, shoulder, rump, or sirloin all make fine hamburgers, but it should be lean. The grill should be greased or the patties brushed with butter, or both, to lessen the danger of sticking. Here again, they're much better if not cooked too much; when well done, they're dry and tasteless.

HAMBURGER SANDWICHES

Form ground beef into thin cakes about ½ inch thick. Put a slice of onion, of Cheddar cheese, a layer of chopped ripe olives, deviled ham, herb butter, or whatever pleases you on one cake and top with another, pressing firmly together around the edges. Brush with butter and grill quickly over a brisk fire just long enough to warm the filling through. These may be eaten as is, or on toast, or between slices of buttered bread.

OTHER STEAKS

VEAL STEAKS

Young white veal is the real rarity these days, and when you're lucky enough to find it you'll probably roast it or have veal scaloppine or something similar. As it's very lean, it's not the most successful meat for grilling over charcoal, but it can be done well. Most veal steaks are cut from the leg (round), but a porterhouse is very good, too.

MARINATED VEAL STEAK

Have a 1-inch-thick steak cut from the leg, and remove the outside skin. In a shallow dish put ½ cup olive oil and 2 crushed garlic cloves and let the steak marinate in this for several hours, turning occasionally. Broil over a low fire for 7 to 9 minutes on each side. No further basting should be necessary, as the meat will have absorbed enough of the oil to moisten it. Serve with fettuccine and a zucchini and tomato casserole.

PORK STEAKS

Pork is wonderful on the charcoal grill, and the smell of it cooking will stimulate the most jaded appetite. It must be cooked until well done, so a fairly slow fire is in order, but it should develop a slightly charred crust to be perfect. Pork steaks are usually cut from the leg, but a steak from a boneless shoulder butt is also excellent and economical.

PORK SHOULDER STEAK TERIYAKI

For several people buy a pork shoulder butt, boneless or bone-in, and have it cut into 1-inch slices. You should get 6 or 7 steaks from an average piece. Marinate in the sauce you make for Teriyaki to which you have added an extra crushed garlic clove. (There's a very good bottled Teriyaki Sauce now on the market, from Japan.) Turn the meat in the marinade about 1 hour. Broil over a brisk fire for 2 minutes on each side; lower heat and cook for 8 to 10 minutes more on each side. This has a real oriental flavor.

HAM STEAKS

Most smoked hams steaks are too thin for proper grilling. They should be 1 to 1½ inches thick from the center of the ham. Those ½-inch ones, so widely sold, used to be known as "breakfast slices" in the good old days, and one made a nice morning snack along with 2 or 3 fried eggs and some fried potatoes. Alas, those days of free-wheeling eating are long gone, but still there are few things better than a fine ham steak, grilled to perfection over charcoal. Cooking time depends upon how the ham has been processed: a "tenderized" but not fully cooked ham steak, 1 inch thick, will take about 15 minutes on a side over a slow fire; a 2-inch one will take 25 to 30 minutes on a side. An "old-fashioned" ham steak will take about the same length of time. Fully cooked ham steaks need only browning and warming through, so a hotter fire can be used. The fat at the edges should be gashed to prevent curling. Steak may be brushed with butter before broiling, but that isn't really necessary, as ham has plenty of fat.

FRESH HAM STEAK

This should be cut about 1½ inches thick, and the fat around the edge should be slashed in several places to prevent the steak from curling up. Brush it lightly with butter and place it on the grill letting it cook slowly. After 10 minutes, turn and cook on the other side, then turn again and give it 5 to 10 minutes more. It should be thoroughly cooked but not dried out in the middle. The fat around the edge will be a crisp dark brown, and the surface of the meat itself a little lighter in color. Salt and pepper are the only adornment needed to make this perfect.

DEVILED HAM STEAK

Cover a 1½-inch ham steak with a good coating of English mustard. (Combine 1 tablespoon dry mustard, ¼ teaspoon salt, and enough cider vinegar to make a thin paste.) Grill over a low fire, turning fairly often; it should take 40 to 45 minutes. Make a mixture of mustard and honey (1 teaspoon mustard to 2 tablespoons honey); about 5 minutes before the steak is done, brush both sides with it. Turn the ham several times so that a glaze will form. Remove to a hot platter and slice into medium-thin diagonal slices. Serve with corn bread and coleslaw.

LAMB STEAKS

Lamb or mutton steaks are usually cut from the leg, sometimes from the shoulder. If properly cooked and seasoned, they're among the best meats for charcoal grilling. I think they should be on the rare side, pink at least; like beefsteaks, they become dry and uninteresting when overcooked. They should be cut from 1 to 1½ inches thick. If you need several, buy a whole leg and have the butcher cut the steaks out for you; use the rest for lamb stew or *shashlik*.

GARLIC LAMB STEAKS

Lamb loves garlic and steaks are no exception. Crush a clove of it and let it rest in ½ cup olive oil. Tie some celery leaves, a bunch of parsley, and a good sprig of rosemary or marjoram together in a fagot, and use this to brush the oil on the steaks while they are cooking. Cook the steaks over a brisk fire, from 3 to 6 minutes on a side, basting them with the garlic oil. Season.

FISH STEAKS

There are any number of good-size fish which provide fine steaks for the outdoor cook. Salmon, halibut, and

STEAM

swordfish are the most widely used, but dolphin (the mahimahi of the islands), white sea bass, and albacore are also popular in coastal regions. The main trick to remember is to have the grill and fish both well oiled to prevent sticking. Fish steaks do not take as long as meat to cook, and should be carefully watched so that they don't dry out too much. A 1-inch steak will take about 7 minutes to cook; a 1½-inch steak, 12 minutes; and a 2-inch one about 15 minutes over a moderate fire. They are done when they flake easily and have lost their translucent look. Brush the steaks while they're cooking with melted butter to which lemon juice has been added.

LIVER STEAKS

A properly cooked liver steak, crisply brown on the outside and pink and juicy in the middle, is truly a delight. Have the liver (calf's, lamb, or beef) sliced about 1½ inches thick. Butter the outside well and grill over a moderate fire until done to your liking, 7 to 10 minutes on a side. Test by making an incision with a small sharp knife and looking inside. Serve the liver steaks with butter and lemon, or with Béarnaise Sauce. Broiled tomatoes are almost a must here, and crisply fried potatoes are good, too.

TURKEY STEAKS

These are a real conversation piece, and can be very good indeed. They're fun and worth a try, I think. Have your butcher cut a frozen young turkey into 1-inch slices (across the bird) on his power saw, from where the wings join the body to the leg joint. (The butcher will probably shake his head at such goings on, but smile sweetly and say nothing.) Or slice a boneless turkey roll; you can find one at most markets. A good-size bird should provide 8 steaks; the ends can be cooked and used for other things. Lay the frozen slices in a large flat pan and let them thaw in a mixture of white wine and melted butter or oil, and use the mixture as a baste when they're cooking. If the slices are too big, divide each into 2 through the section of breastbone. Grill them over a moderate fire 20 to 30 minutes on a side, turning occasionally and basting frequently, until well done.

STEAM, TO—In culinary language the phrase refers to a method of cooking by exposure to the vapor of boiling water. The food must be above the liquid and never in it. The container is closed during cooking to let the steam accumulate. Steaming is one of the methods used to cook rice, fish, dried fruits, vegetables, breads, puddings, etc. As a cooking technique it has the great advantage of retaining a high proportion of the original flavor and texture of the food so prepared because the nutrients are not dissolved in the cooking liquid as is the case with boiling or poaching. Steaming does have some disadvantages in that it is a more time-consuming way of cooking and the food cannot be browned.

Steaming is the principle used in pressure cooking in which the lid is sealed and the steam accumulates, building up pressure and cooking foods more quickly. There are also available vegetable steamers which resemble two saucepans, one over the other. There are holes in the top one for the steam to enter and cook the vegetable. Steaming can also be done in a double boiler or in an ordinary colander if it fits down inside the kettle and can be covered tightly to prevent steam from escaping. When steaming in vegetable steamers or double boilers, make sure the water is boiling before the top part is placed over the water—not in the water. All steamers and double boilers must have tight-fitting lids and water must be kept boiling during the entire cooking time. If water must be added, it must be boiling water to keep the temperature of the water high.

When steaming fish, the fish should be wrapped in cheesecloth, allowing the long ends of the cheesecloth to hang out on either side of the pan. When the fish is cooked it can be removed by lifting out by the long ends of cheesecloth. A fish steamer should have a rack which holds the fish above the level of boiling water.

To steam pudding or brown bread it is necessary to put the mixture into a well-greased pudding mold and top it with a tight-fitting lid. The mold should be only two-thirds full. Set the mold on a rack in a kettle. Add boiling water to cover halfway up the sides of the mold. Cover the kettle and keep water boiling for the required length of time, replacing evaporated water with more boiling water. Puddings may also be steamed in a pressure cooker. When the pudding is done, remove the lid and allow it to stand for 10 minutes. Then unmold; if cooled slightly, it will not crack. Puddings cannot be steamed successfully in the top of a double boiler since steam cannot circulate completely around the mold.

STERILIZE—To heat foods or utensils to a high enough temperature to kill harmful microorganisms. The simplest and most successful method is to boil the food or utensil at least 15 minutes in alkali-free water; more time may be required, depending on the consistency of the food and the size of the containers, for the entire contents must reach the required temperature. Sterilizing by dry heat has also been tried and is still used to some extent, but heat transfer is more rapid in water than in air, therefore sterilization in the home oven requires a longer time with a greater possible change in the food itself. Spores of some types of microorganisms are so heat-resistant that processing long enough to kill them would result in changes in the taste and nutritive values of the food. Chemical sterilization has also been tried, and salting and meat curing may be considered early examples of this kind of process, but other types of chemicals present great hazards even in sterilizing utensils, as residues of the chemical would produce undesirable effects. Sterilization through radiation is as yet a costly process, but this way may be the method of the future. Some food items such as packaged cereals and wheat which are to be stored are successfully sterilized by being passed through an electronic oven. This process takes a much shorter time than any other method. Freezing does not produce sterilization; many organisms simply pass into a dormant stage when frozen. It is for this reason that blanching is necessary before freezing most nonacid foods.

In the home kitchen, sterilizing is chiefly used in preparing canning jars or bottles for a baby's formula. With home equipment it is probably impossible to obtain complete sterilization, but it is possible to reduce organisms to a safe level. To prepare jars or bottles, scrub them with soap and water and rinse well. Immerse the jars in warm water and bring to a boil, keeping the boiling temperature constant. The jars must be completely covered with water throughout. Handle the boiled jars with tongs that have also been boiled. Drain jars upside down on a rack. When cool, turn jars or bottles right side up and fill as soon as possible, or cap with lids that have been sterilized as well.

Processing filled jars or cans is another example of the same procedure. Industry and medicine have developed various techniques for sterilization of materials and instruments. These techniques have been scientifically worked out so that it is possible to have complete sterilization. The nearest approach to this in the home kitchen is the pressure canner.

STEW—As a culinary method stewing is the process of long slow cooking of food in liquid in a covered pot. Any dish prepared in this way may be called a stew, although most often the word is reserved for dishes containing meat and one or more vegetables.

CHICKEN STEW

- 1 stewing chicken (about 5 pounds), cut into pieces
- ½ cup rendered chicken fat or clarified butter
- 1 celery stalk, chopped
- 1 onion, chopped
- 1 carrot, chopped
  Water
- 2 teaspoons salt
- ¼ cup all-purpose flour
- ½ cup heavy cream
- 2 egg yolks
  Chopped parsley

Brown chicken pieces in ¼ cup rendered chicken fat. Put into a heavy pot and add vegetables and water just to cover. Season. Simmer until chicken is just tender, about 1½ hours, depending upon the bird. (Don't let it get dry and stringy.) Remove meat to a hot dish, strain broth, and simmer to reduce to 3 cups. Cook remaining ¼ cup rendered chicken fat and flour together for 2 minutes, add broth, and stir until smooth. Add chicken. Beat cream and egg yolks together. Stir in small amount of hot mixture. Gradually stir into hot mixture left in kettle. Heat, but do not boil. Garnish with parsley and serve with rice or mashed potatoes. Makes 4 to 6 servings.

BEEF STEW

- 2 pounds beef chuck, cubed
- 3 tablespoons all-purpose flour
- 3 tablespoons shortening
  Salt
- ¼ teaspoon pepper
- 6 cups water
- 12 small white onions, peeled
- 2 cups diced peeled yellow turnip
- 6 carrots, scraped and cut into chunks
- 4 raw medium potatoes, peeled and cut into quarters
- ½ cup cooked peas

Dredge meat with flour and brown on all sides in shortening in kettle. Add 2 teaspoons salt, pepper, and water. Bring to boil, cover, and simmer for 1½ hours, or until meat is almost tender. Add remaining ingredients except peas and simmer for 45 minutes, or until vegetables are tender. Season, and sprinkle with peas. Makes 6 servings.

LAMB STEW

- 2½ pounds boneless lamb shoulder
  Onions
  Raw potatoes
- 2 celery stalks, chopped
- 1 garlic clove, sliced
- 1 teaspoon salt
  Pepper
  Water
- 4 white turnips (optional)
- 6 small carrots

Cut lamb into 1½- or 2-inch cubes and put in a heavy pot with 1 large onion, chopped and 1 raw large potato, chopped, celery, garlic, salt, and a grinding or two of pepper. Add enough water to cover meat and vegetables by ½ inch. Bring to boil, skim, and reduce heat. Simmer for 45 minutes, or until potato is mushy. Remove meat. Pour liquid through strainer and force as much of the vegetables through as possible. Combine with meat, and correct seasoning. Meanwhile peel 18 small onions but leave whole. If medium onions are used, cut them into large dice. Cut 2 or 3 raw large potatoes into uniform cubes, or into balls using a French vegetable cutter. Do the same with turnips, if you like their assertive flavor. Scrape carrots and cut into 1-inch pieces, or use small scraped whole French carrots. Put vegetables on top of meat and cover. Add enough water or stock just to cover the vegetables, and simmer until the vegetables are tender. Makes 4 to 6 servings.

Brown Lamb Stew

Follow recipe above. Dredge lamb lightly with flour and brown on all sides in 2 tablespoons fat or cooking oil. Proceed as directed.

Creamy Veal Stew with Mushrooms

STOCK

CREAMY VEAL STEW WITH MUSHROOMS

 2½ pounds boneless veal, cubed
  4 cups water
  1 onion stuck with 3 cloves
 1½ teaspoons salt
  1 bay leaf
  1 carrot, chopped
 18 small white onions
  1 pound small mushrooms
  1 teaspoon lemon juice
  2 egg yolks
 ½ cup heavy cream
   Minced parsley

Put first 6 ingredients in kettle, cover, and simmer about 1¼ hours. Remove meat; strain broth over onions; cook until tender. Add mushrooms; cook for 10 minutes. Strain off broth; reduce to one third its volume. Return vegetables and meat to broth; reheat. Mix lemon juice, egg yolks, and cream; stir in ½ cup of hot broth. Add to sauce; heat, stirring, until slightly thickened. Sprinkle with parsley. Makes 4 to 6 servings.

STIR-FRYING—A term generally referring to the sautéeing of foods in a wok, or in a flat-bottomed skillet. To stir-fry (1) cut ingredients into small pieces, preferably slicing on an angle; (2) heat oil in wok or skillet over moderate to high temperature and add ingredients; (3) stir constantly for several minutes until the surface of the ingredients is cooked; (4) reduce heat, and continue stirring lightly until cooked to taste. Stir-frying has become a popular method for cooking vegetables. *See* Chinese Cookery, Volume 4.

STIR, TO—As a culinary term this phrase means to agitate one or several food ingredients with a rotary motion, using a spoon or a whisk, to make them smooth and prevent them from sticking. Batters and dough of all kinds are stirred to get uniform smooth mixtures. Sauces are stirred during cooking to prevent lumps and scorching on the bottom. Diced and sliced foods being browned or sautéed are stirred occasionally during cooking to prevent scorching and sticking.

The word "stir" involves one of the most important techniques in cooking. To stir constantly means just that. Do not leave the mixture for one second or the resulting product will suffer. To stir occasionally means to stir every few minutes, usually to allow thick food mixtures to cook more evenly. When cooking a sauce it is very important to stir with a rotary motion which cleans the sides and a small part of the bottom of the utensil but it is also important to scrape the entire bottom of the utensil. This is done by pretending to write the figure 8 on the bottom of the pan.

STOCK—A liquid food made by cooking ingredients slowly for a long time so that all the essential flavor and nutrients of the ingredients are dissolved in the liquid. The solid particles remaining are discarded and the liquid may be further concentrated or clarified according to the way it is to be used. Stock is used as a basis, or *fonds,* in the preparation of soups, sauces, and gravies.

The word stock is sometimes used for the liquid in

STOCK

which a food has been cooked, but this is an inaccurate usage. When the purpose of cooking is to prepare a food to be served, it will be cooked just until done. The liquid which remains, which is properly called a broth, may be used for sauces, gravies, or soups; in fact, since it contains many nutrients, it is healthful to use it so. When making stock, however, the food is cooked past the point at which it is done; it is cooked until it is shapeless and almost tasteless since all the nutrient value is in the stock.

Fish, poultry, meat, game, vegetables—all may be used to make stock and the resulting product is designated accordingly. Also there is brown stock which is usually made from beef and veal as well as vegetables. The ingredients are roasted or browned before being cooked in liquid in order to give the stock a rich brown color. White stock is made from chicken, veal and fish and the ingredients are not browned.

If stock is to be used as a basis for aspics, calf's feet and other veal bones should be added as they are rich in gelatin. Good stock vegetables are carrots, onions, and celery. Parsley and other leaf herbs are possible additions, but remember to use strong-flavored herbs with care as the flavor will be highly concentrated at the end. While it is possible to make stock with the bones of roast meat or poultry, the flavor will not be as good as if some uncooked meat or poultry is added.

BROWN STOCK
[Bouillon or Beef Stock]

- 1 to 2 pounds cracked marrow bones
- 6 pounds beef shin or other soup meat
- 3 quarts cold water
- 8 peppercorns, slightly crushed
- 6 whole cloves
- 1 bay leaf
- ⅛ teaspoon each dried thyme and marjoram
- Few parsley sprigs
- 1 carrot, diced
- 1 turnip, quartered
- 1 small onion, diced
- 1 celery stalk, cut into 1-inch pieces
- 1 tablespoon salt

Scrape the marrow from the marrow bones and melt in a large kettle. Remove the lean meat from the shin and cut into 1-inch cubes. Brown half the meat cubes in the marrow. Add remaining meat and bones and water. Bring to boil and skim off scum. Add remaining ingredients and simmer, covered, for 3 hours. Skim occasionally. Strain stock through a fine sieve. Cool quickly and refrigerate.

To Clear*—When cold, loosen cake of fat on stock with the edge of a knife. Lift off fat. The small quantity of fat which remains can be removed by passing a cloth wrung out of hot water around the edge of bowl and over top of stock. Makes about 2½ quarts.

To Clarify—Taste stock after removing fat. Add seasoning as desired. For each quart add 1 egg white, beaten slightly and mixed with 2 teaspoons cold water. Add broken egg shell. Bring to a boil and boil for 2 minutes, stirring constantly. Let stand for 20 minutes over very low heat. Strain through a fine strainer lined with a double thickness of cheesecloth.

* If stock is to be refrigerated for any length of time, leave fat on as this excludes air and preserves the stock. If stock is to be frozen, the fat should be removed.

CHICKEN STOCK

- 1 stewing chicken (about 5 pounds)
- Extra chicken necks if available
- 2 quarts cold water
- 2 leeks
- 1 bay leaf
- 10 parsley sprigs
- 2 celery stalks, cut into pieces
- 1 thyme sprig
- 2 whole cloves
- 1 medium carrot, quartered
- 1 small white turnip, peeled and quartered
- 1 large onion, peeled and quartered
- 8 peppercorns, crushed slightly
- 1 small parsnip, halved
- 2 teaspoons salt

Put chicken with necks in a large kettle. Add water, bring slowly to a boil, and skim off scum. When clear and free of scum, add remaining ingredients. Bring again to a boil and simmer, covered, about 3 hours. Remove chicken and strain mixture through cheesecloth. Cool quickly and refrigerate. To clear and clarify, see Brown Stock. Makes about 1¾ quarts.

FISH STOCK

- 2 pounds any white-meated fish with bones and trimmings
- 2 quarts cold water
- 1 medium onion, thinly sliced
- 12 white peppercorns, crushed slightly
- 1 teaspoon salt
- 1 large bay leaf
- 1 large thyme sprig
- 10 parsley sprigs
- 1 medium carrot, thinly sliced
- 2 whole cloves

Bring all ingredients to a boil, lower heat, and simmer, covered, about 1 hour. Strain through a fine sieve, cool quickly, and refrigerate. Makes about 1¾ quarts.

WHITE OR VEAL STOCK

- 4 pounds veal knuckle
- Neck of 1 chicken
- 4 quarts cold water
- 2 medium onions, quartered
- 2 medium carrots, cut into 1-inch pieces
- 1 medium turnip, peeled and quartered
- 1 celery stalk, cut into 1-inch pieces
- 12 parsley sprigs
- 1 thyme sprig
- 2 bay leaves
- 4 whole cloves
- 12 peppercorns, crushed slightly
- 1 tablespoon salt
- 1 garlic clove

Cut up the meat from the veal knuckle and break the bones into small pieces. Put in a large kettle with chicken neck. Add water, cover, and let stand in a cool place for 1 hour. Put over low heat and bring slowly to a boil, skimming as the scum rises to the surface. Simmer until clear. Then add remaining ingredients. Bring again to a boil, skim again, and when clear, cover and simmer for 4 to 4½ hours, skimming occasionally as fat and scum rise. Remove from heat and strain through cheesecloth. Cool quickly and refrigerate. To clear and clarify, see Brown Stock. Makes about 3½ quarts.

VEGETABLE STOCK

- ¼ cup butter or margarine
- 2 medium onions, diced
- 3 medium carrots, diced
- 1 medium turnip, diced
- 1 celery stalk, diced
- 1 small head of lettuce, diced
- 2 large tomatoes, peeled and quartered
- 1 bay leaf
- 8 parsley sprigs
- 1 thyme sprig
- 8 peppercorns, crushed slightly
- 1 garlic clove
- 2 whole cloves
- 2 vegetable bouillon cubes
- 1½ quarts boiling water
- 1 teaspoon monosodium glutamate (optional)

Heat butter in kettle. Add next 5 ingredients and cook very slowly, covered, about 25 minutes, stirring frequently. Add remaining ingredients except monosodium glutamate. Simmer, covered, about 1½ hours, skimming as scum rises to the top. Strain through cheesecloth. Add monosodium glutamate. Cool quickly and store in the refrigerator. Makes about 1½ quarts.

STOLLEN—A sweet, fruit-filled yeast bread baked in the form of a folded-over roll, like a large Parkerhouse roll. Some cooks put a layer of sugar and cinnamon between the cake layers. The baked loaf is usually frosted and decorated with slivered almonds and with candied cherries. Stollen is traditionally served in Germany for Christmas breakfast. Often thin slices are served with coffee or a glass of wine to guests or callers during the holiday season, as fruitcake is served in England.

STOLLEN

- ¼ cup water*
- 1 package active dry yeast or 1 cake compressed yeast
- ½ cup milk
- 6 tablespoons sugar
- 1 teaspoon salt
- 3 tablespoons soft butter or margarine
- 2¾ to 3 cups all-purpose flour
- 1 egg
- ½ cup chopped blanched almonds
- ¼ cup each finely cut citron and candied cherries
- 1 teaspoon grated lemon rind
- ½ teaspoon ground cinnamon
  Frosting
  Whole candied cherries
  Slivered blanched almonds

*Use very warm water (105°F. to 115°F.) for dry yeast; use lukewarm (80°F. to 90°F.) for compressed. Sprinkle dry yeast or crumble cake into water. Scald milk and pour into large mixing bowl. Add ¼ cup sugar, salt, and 2 tablespoons butter. Cool until just warm. Stir in 1 cup flour. Mix in dissolved yeast. Add egg and beat hard. Stir in 1½ cups flour, chopped almonds, citron, cut cherries, and lemon rind. Sprinkle 2 tablespoons flour on board. Turn dough out and knead adding more flour as needed to make a soft dough. Knead until smooth and satiny, about 5 minutes. Shape into a smooth ball and put in lightly greased bowl. Cover and let rise until doubled, about 2¼ hours. Punch down. Cover and let rest for 5 to 10 minutes. With palms of hands press dough into oval shape about ½ inch thick. Spread half of oval with remaining 1 tablespoon butter. Mix remaining 2 tablespoons sugar and cinnamon and sprinkle on butter. Fold unspread half lengthwise over sugar and cinnamon, making edges even. Lift to lightly greased baking sheet and curve the ends slightly. Press down the folded edge. This helps the loaf to keep its shape as it rises and bakes. Cover and let rise until doubled, about 1¼ hours. Bake in preheated moderate oven (350°F.) for 30 to 35 minutes. Remove to cake rack to cool. Pour Frosting over loaf, letting it drip down the sides. Decorate with whole cherries and slivered almonds.

Frosting

Mix ¾ cup confectioners' sugar and 1 tablespoon milk or cream to make a smooth thick frosting that will just pour.

STRAIN, TO—As a culinary term the phrase is used to describe the process of pouring food, usually a liquid, through the holes of a sieve or through a cloth to remove lumps or undesirable particles or to clarify the liquid.

Soup stocks are strained after cooking to remove bits of bone and pieces of flavoring vegetables and meats, and to make the stock clear and smooth for both soups and sauces. Tea made from loose tea must be strained before drinking to remove the tea leaves. At times sauces are strained before serving to remove any lumps that may have formed during cooking. In jelly making, the fruit juice must be strained through several thicknesses of cheesecloth without pressing to produce clear jewellike jelly.

At times the term can also mean to press a soft or cooked food through the holes of a sieve. Applesauce, cooked fruits, and vegetables are often strained. Strained foods are a part of many special diets and many infant diets. Today a large variety of foods are available already strained. An electric blender can do much to prepare this type of food quickly and with a minimum of waste.

STRAWBERRY COOKBOOK

STRAWBERRY—A juicy edible fruit produced by various plants native to the temperate zones of the Old and New World. Strawberries belong to the genus *Fragaria,* a member of the Rose family. The fruits vary in size and even in color; there are whitish or yellowish fruits as well as the much more common red ones. Some strawberries are cultivated, other wild; the wild strawberries are perhaps the most fragrant of all fruits.

Although strawberries have been cultivated to a limited extent in European gardens since the early 14th century, for the most part Europeans ate the wild strawberry, called the Alpine strawberry, *Fragaria vesca,* which was a native of northern Italy. It is this fruit that was mentioned by the Roman writers Virgil, Ovid, and Pliny. To this day, Frenchmen and Italians prefer these tiny, incredibly delicious wild berries to all others. The French call them *fraises des bois,* "Strawberries of the woods," and they serve them simply, with a squeeze of lemon or orange juice and a bit of sugar.

We can thank 18th and 19th century French, English, and American horticulturists for the cultivated species we know today. They are a result of the crossbreeding of a wild strawberry of the eastern seaboard, the Virginia strawberry, *F. virginiana,* which was taken to Europe in the 17th century, with a kind of strawberry found in Chile, *F. chiloensis,* taken to Europe in the early 18th century. In the mid-19th century descendants of these hybrids, reimported into the United States, began being further developed and cultivated on a large scale.

Strawberries have long been eaten plain, or with wine, or with cream. Made into preserves, they are one of the most popular of all jams. Strawberry shortcake is a beloved classic of the strawberry season. But there are other older uses, too, dating from the days before the white people came to this continent. The Indians, and folk people everywhere, made delicious beverages out of the berries. Strawberry wine was a favorite, and the Iroquois' strawberry drink, made with crushed strawberries and water, is still drunk by these Indians today. Roger Williams reports another early use of the berry: "The Indians bruise them in a Morter, and mixe them with meale and make Strawberry bread."

Availability—Fresh strawberries are now available almost all year round in large cities. Peak months are May and June.

Frozen strawberries, packed in water or syrup, sliced or whole, are available, as are a limited quantity of canned strawberries. Strawberry jam, preserves, syrup, gelatin dessert, and pie filling are also available.

Purchasing Guide—Select fresh berries that are bright, fresh, plump, well shaped, and solid in color. The caps should be attached.

Storage—Sort berries and refrigerate unwrapped. Do not wash until ready to use. Fresh berries are very perishable and should be used as soon as possible.
Fresh, refrigerator shelf: 3 days
Canned, kitchen shelf: 1 year
Canned, refrigerator shelf, open: 4 to 5 days
Fresh, prepared for freezing; and frozen, refrigerator frozen-food compartment: 2 to 3 months
Fresh, prepared for freezing; and frozen, freezer: 1 year

Nutritive Food Values—An excellent source of vitamin C. They also contain iron and other minerals.
Fresh, 1 cup (5.1 ounces) raw and unsweetened = 53 calories
Canned, 4 ounces, water pack = 25 calories
Frozen, whole, 4 ounces, syrup pack = 105 calories
Frozen, sliced, 5 ounces, syrup pack = 175 calories

Basic Preparation—Wash gently before using. Do not allow berries to soak in water. Remove hulls.

To Freeze—Select firm ripe berries. Wash quickly in cold water. Prepare berries as desired—whole, halved, sliced, or crushed. Pack as desired in syrup, in sugar, or unsweetened, or freeze in loose pack.

In syrup: Fill containers with berries to within ½ inch of the top. Fill with a cold syrup of 4 cups water to 4¾ cups sugar.

In sugar: Mix 1 cup sugar with each 4 cups berries until juice is released and sugar is almost dissolved. Pack in containers, allowing ½-inch headspace.

Unsweetened: Fill containers with berries to within ½ inch of the top. Add an ascorbic-acid solution of 4 cups water and 1 teaspoon ascorbic acid.

Loose pack: Put berries in a single layer on a cookie sheet. Put in freezer and freeze until hard. Pour berries into containers, allowing no headspace. Seal.

SALADS

JELLIED CHEESE AND STRAWBERRY SALAD

1 envelope unflavored gelatin
¼ cup cold water
2 cups (1 pound) creamed cottage cheese
¾ teaspoon salt
⅛ teaspoon paprika
Dash of cayenne
½ cup milk
Salad greens
1 quart strawberries
Fresh mint

Soften gelatin in cold water; dissolve over hot water. Mash cheese. Stir in seasonings, milk, and gelatin. Turn into 6 individual molds and chill until firm. Unmold on greens. Wash and hull berries and arrange around salad molds. Garnish with mint sprigs. Makes 6 servings.

STRAWBERRY

AVOCADO RING WITH STRAWBERRIES

- 2 boxes (3 ounces each) lime- or lemon-flavored gelatin
- ½ teaspoon salt
- 2 cups hot water
- 1½ cups cold water
- 2 tablespoons lemon juice
- 2 very ripe avocados, peeled, pitted, and mashed
- ⅓ cup mayonnaise
- 3 cups sliced fresh strawberries (reserve ½ cup for Dressing)
- Salad greens
- Honey-Cream Dressing

Dissolve gelatin and salt in hot water. Add cold water and chill until slightly thickened. Pour lemon juice over avocados. Stir avocados and mayonnaise into gelatin, blending well. Pour into 5-cup ring mold and chill until firm. Unmold ring on greens and fill with 2½ cups berries. Serve with Honey-Cream Dressing. Makes 6 to 8 servings.

Honey-Cream Dressing

Mix ½ cup each dairy sour cream and mayonnaise, 1 tablespoon honey, and ½ cup reserved sliced berries.

FROZEN STRAWBERRY DESSERT SALAD

- 1 envelope unflavored gelatin
- ¼ cup water
- 1 can (13¼ ounces) pineapple tidbits
- 1 tablespoon lemon juice
- ⅛ teaspoon each salt and ground ginger
- 2 tablespoons honey
- 1 pint strawberries, sliced
- ½ cup heavy cream, whipped
- ½ cup mayonnaise
- Salad greens
- Whole strawberries
- Watercress (optional)

Soften gelatin in water and dissolve over hot water. Add pineapple and syrup, lemon juice, salt, ginger and honey and mix well. Add sliced strawberries and chill until slightly thickened. Mix cream and mayonnaise and fold into fruit mixture. Pour into 9 x 5 x 3-inch loaf pan (pan will be about half full) and freeze until firm. Turn out on board and slice in 8 to 10 slices. For each serving, put 2 slices on greens. Garnish with whole strawberries, and watercress, if desired. If salad is frozen solid, let stand at room temperature about ½ hour after slicing. Makes 4 or 5 servings.

CAKES

CHOCOLATE-GLAZED STRAWBERRY ICE CREAM CAKE

- 2 squares (2 ounces) semisweet chocolate
- 1 square (1 ounce) unsweetened chocolate
- ½ cup heavy cream, whipped
- Instant coffee or cream sherry
- 1 pint fresh strawberries
- ½ package (½-gallon size) vanilla ice cream
- 2 tablespoons sliced almonds, toasted

Combine chocolates, melt over hot water and set aside. Flavor whipped cream with instant coffee to taste. Wash and hull berries. Cut ice cream in 2 rectangles about 7 x 5 inches. Rewrap one and return to freezer for later use. Place other on chilled serving platter. Pour all chocolate on top and spread quickly to cover top and sides. Cover top with whipped cream, sprinkle with almonds and put back in freezer until serving time. Just before serving, cover top with berries and put remainder around cake. Cut in squares. Makes 6 servings.

INDIVIDUAL STRAWBERRY SHORTCAKES

- ½ cup butter or margarine, softened
- ¼ cup sugar
- 1¼ cups all-purpose flour
- 1 quart vanilla ice cream
- 2 packages (1 pound each) frozen sliced strawberries, just thawed

Mix butter and sugar with pastry blender or fork. Add flour and mix until crumbly. Then, with hands, mix gently until dough is formed. Roll ¼ inch thick on lightly floured board and cut in 16 rounds with 2½-inch cookie cutter. Put on baking sheet and prick several times with fork. Bake in preheated slow oven (325°F.) 20 minutes, or until lightly browned. Cool. To serve, put ice cream and berries between and on top of rounds, allowing 2 for each serving. Makes 8 servings.

STRAWBERRY REFRIGERATOR CAKE

- 7 or 8 whole ladyfingers
- 1 package (6 ounces) or 2 packages (3 ounces each) strawberry-flavor gelatin
- 2 cups boiling water
- 1½ cups crushed strawberries
- 1 tablespoon lemon juice
- ½ cup sugar
- ⅛ teaspoon salt
- 2 cups heavy cream
- Whipped cream
- Whole strawberries

Put a 3-inch strip of waxed paper around inside of 8- or 9-inch springform cake pan. Split ladyfingers and cut tips from one end so halves will stand. Arrange, rounded end up, around edge of pan. Add 2 cups boiling water to gelatin and stir until dissolved. Mix next 4 ingredients and add to gelatin. Chill until mixture begins to set, then whip cream and fold into gelatin mixture. Carefully spoon into lined pan and chill until firm (at least 5 hours or overnight). Remove sides of pan and put cake on serving plate. Decorate with whipped cream and whole strawberries. Makes 10 or more servings.

STRAWBERRY

STRAWBERRY CAKE ROLL

- 1 cup sifted cake flour
- 1 teaspoon baking powder
- ¼ teaspoon salt
- 3 eggs
- 1 teaspoon vanilla extract
- 1 cup granulated sugar
- ¼ cup water
- ¼ cup sifted confectioners' sugar
- 1 cup sliced fresh strawberries
- 1 pint strawberry ice cream, softened
- 1 package (1 pound) frozen sliced strawberries
- 2 tablespoons brandy (optional)

Sift flour, baking powder, and salt. Beat eggs with vanilla until fluffy and light colored. Gradually beat in granulated sugar. Stir in water. Fold in sifted dry ingredients carefully but thoroughly. Turn into baking pan 1 x 10 x 15 inches lined with wax paper. Bake in preheated moderate oven (350°F.) for 15 minutes, or until done. Sift confectioners' sugar evenly onto smooth dish towel. Turn hot cake out on towel and carefully peel off paper. Roll up cake from end, jelly-roll fashion; cool. Add fresh strawberries to ice cream. Unroll cake and spread with ice cream mixture; reroll, wrap in foil, and freeze. Thaw for 10 minutes before serving. When ready to serve, thaw strawberries and mix with brandy. Serve as sauce on sliced roll. Makes 8 servings.

SOUR-CREAM CHEESECAKE WITH STRAWBERRIES

- 1 pound soft cream cheese
  Granulated sugar
- 3 eggs
- ¼ teaspoon salt
- ½ teaspoon almond extract
- 1 cup dairy sour cream
- ½ teaspoon vanilla extract
- 1 pint strawberries, washed and hulled
  Confectioners' sugar

Beat cream cheese until smooth. Gradually beat in ⅔ cup granulated sugar. Beat in eggs, one at a time. Blend in salt and almond extract; beat until thick and lemon-colored. Pour into greased 9-inch piepan. Bake in preheated moderate oven (350°F.) 30 minutes. Remove; cool 20 minutes. Mix sour cream with 1 tablespoon granulated sugar and vanilla. Beat until smooth. Pour over cooled cake; return to preheated moderate oven (350°F.) and bake 10 minutes. Cool and decorate with strawberries dipped in confectioners' sugar. Makes 6 servings.

PIES AND TARTS

STRAWBERRY SNOWBANK PIE

- 1 quart strawberries
- 1 baked 9-inch pastry shell
- 1¼ cups sugar
- ½ cup water
- ½ teaspoon cream of tartar
  Dash of salt
- 2 egg whites
- ½ teaspoon vanilla extract

Wash and hull strawberries; arrange in pastry shell, putting prettiest berries in center. Mix sugar, water, and cream of tartar in saucepan. Cover and bring to boil. Uncover and cook until syrup spins long threads (240°F. on a candy thermometer). Add salt to egg whites and beat until stiff. Gradually pour syrup onto whites, beating constantly, until mixture forms stiff peaks. Add flavoring and pile on pie, leaving center uncovered. Cool, but do not refrigerate. Makes 6 to 8 servings.

STRAWBERRY-ALMOND-CHEESE TART

- 6 tablespoons soft butter or margarine
- 2 tablespoons sugar
- 1 egg yolk
- ¼ cup finely chopped blanched almonds
- 1 cup all-purpose flour
- 1 package (3 ounces) cream cheese
- 1 tablespoon light cream
- 1 teaspoon vanilla extract
- 1 pint strawberries, washed and hulled
  Strawberry Glaze
  Toasted slivered blanched almonds

To make pastry, cream butter with sugar until light and fluffy. Add egg yolk, chopped almonds and flour. Shape in a ball with hands. Chill. Roll out to a 9-inch round; press on bottom and sides of loose-bottomed tart pan. Bake in preheated moderate oven (350°F.) 30 to 35 minutes, or until golden brown. Cool. To make filling, beat cream cheese with cream and vanilla until smooth. Spread on bottom of tart shell. Decorate tart with whole or sliced berries. Pour chilled Glaze over. Decorate with toasted almonds. Makes 8 servings.

Strawberry Glaze

Mix 2 cups sliced strawberries with ½ cup sugar and 1 tablespoon lemon juice. Crush and press through sieve. Mixture should measure 1⅓ cups. Add 2 tablespoons cornstarch, blended with a small amount of water, to berry mixture. Bring to a boil, stirring constantly. Simmer until thick and clear. Cool.

Strawberry Devonshire Tart and Fondant-Dipped Strawberries

STRAWBERRY

STRAWBERRY DEVONSHIRE TART

Pastry Shell
1 package (3 ounces) cream cheese, softened
3 tablespoons dairy sour cream
1 to 1½ quarts strawberries
Water
1 cup sugar
3 tablespoons cornstarch
Red food coloring

Make Pastry Shell and cool. Beat cream cheese until fluffy, add sour cream and beat until smooth. Spread on bottom of shell and refrigerate. Wash and hull strawberries. Mash enough uneven ones to make 1 cup. Force through sieve and add water to make 1 cup. Mix sugar and cornstarch. Add ½ cup water and sieved berries. Cook over medium heat, stirring, until mixture is clear and thickened, then boil about 1 minute. Stir to cool slightly and add a little red food coloring if necessary. Fill shell with remaining berries, tips up, and pour cooked mixture over top. Chill 1 hour. Makes 6 to 8 servings.

Pastry Shell

1 cup all-purpose flour
1 tablespoon sugar
6 tablespoons butter, at room temperature, but not soft
1 egg yolk
1 tablespoon ice water

Combine flour and sugar, then work in butter with fingertips. Add egg yolk and ice water and work with fingers until dough holds together (work well but don't overwork). Pat into flat round, wrap and chill until firm enough to roll. Then roll between sheets of waxed paper to fit a 9-inch loose-bottomed tart pan. Remove top paper and turn pastry over pan, centering. Let pastry slip down into pan and gently pull off paper. Use fingertips to press pastry into pan; even off rim and chill shell. Bake in preheated moderate oven (375°F.), pricking dough with fork whenever it begins to bubble (this helps to keep shell flat), about 15 minutes, or until lightly browned.

MERINGUE

MERINGUE RING WITH STRAWBERRY ICE CREAM AND STRAWBERRIES

2 pints fresh strawberries
Confectioners' sugar
Butter
2 tablespoons sliced pistachio nuts
5 egg whites at room temperature
¼ teaspoon salt
½ teaspoon cream of tartar
1¾ cups granulated sugar
1 quart strawberry ice cream

Wash and hull berries. Reserve a few whole ones for decoration and slice remainder. Sweeten with confectioners' sugar to taste. Preheat oven to hot (425°F.). Butter a 6-cup ring mold well and sprinkle nuts on bottom; set aside. Beat egg whites with salt and cream of tartar until foamy. Gradually add granulated sugar and beat until stiff glossy peaks form. Spoon into mold and smooth top with spatula. Tap mold a few times against counter to eliminate air bubbles. Put on rack set in center of oven. Turn off heat and leave in oven overnight (do not open oven). Just before serving, unmold on serving platter and fill center with ice cream. Decorate with reserved whole berries and serve with sliced berries. Makes 8 servings.

OTHER DESSERTS

STRAWBERRY-ALMOND ROLL

1 package (10 ounces) frozen strawberries, thawed
8 tablespoons sugar
Water
1 teaspoon unflavored gelatin
Red food coloring
3 tablespoons chopped blanched almonds
¼ teaspoon almond extract
½ cup heavy cream, whipped

Turn refrigerator control to coldest setting. Force berries through sieve. Add 5 tablespoons sugar and water to make 2 cups. Sprinkle gelatin on 1 tablespoon cold water, and let stand for 5 minutes. Dissolve over hot water. Stir into berry mixture. Pour into refrigerator tray and freeze until mushy. Add small amount of red food coloring. Beat well, and turn into a 28-ounce can. (It will not fill can.) Put in freezer or freezing compartment of refrigerator until almost firm. Push mixture against sides of can, leaving center hollow. Add remaining 3 tablespoons sugar, nuts, and flavoring to whipped cream and pour into center of mold. Cover with wax paper; freeze. To serve, run a spatula around inside of can; wrap in hot cloth until dessert slides out. Cut into slices. Makes 4 servings.

STRAWBERRY ICE CREAM

1 quart strawberries (or more to taste)
¾ cup sugar
¼ teaspoon salt
2 cups light cream

Wash and hull berries. Mash well and stir in sugar. Let stand for 20 minutes. Then force through a sieve to remove seeds. Mix with salt and cream and pour into container of crank freezer. Freeze with ice and salt until firm. Makes 1½ quarts.
NOTE: Two packages (10½ ounces each) frozen sliced strawberries, thawed, can be substituted for the fresh in the above recipe. Stir in ½ cup sugar and force through sieve. Proceed as directed above.

STRAWBERRY PARFAIT

- 1 quart strawberries, washed, hulled and sliced
- ¾ cup sugar
- ¼ cup water
- 2 egg yolks
- 1 tablespoon lemon juice
- 1 cup heavy cream, whipped

Crush 2 cups strawberries well and set aside. Mix ½ cup sugar and the water in a saucepan. Bring to a boil and simmer 5 minutes. Beat egg yolks in top of double boiler; gradually stir in sugar syrup. Cook over simmering water, stirring constantly, until thick and lemon-colored. Remove from heat. Continue beating until cool. Add crushed strawberries, lemon juice and whipped cream. Pour into refrigerator tray; freeze until firm. Serve with remaining sliced strawberries sweetened with remaining sugar. Makes 4 to 6 servings.

STRAWBERRY BLANCMANGE

- 1 quart strawberries, washed and hulled
- 1 cup sugar
- 2 tablespoons lemon juice
- 2 envelopes unflavored gelatin
- ¼ cup cold water
- 2 cups heavy cream, whipped

Reserve 1 cup berries for decorating. Add sugar and lemon juice to remaining berries; crush and stir until sugar is dissolved. Soften gelatin in cold water. Dissolve over low heat and add to strawberry mixture. Chill until thickened but not firm. Fold into whipped cream and pour into 2-quart mold, rinsed in cold water. Chill until set, 3 to 4 hours. Unmold and decorate with reserved berries, sliced. Serves 8.

BAKED STRAWBERRY PUDDING

- 1 quart strawberries, washed and hulled
- 5 eggs, separated
- Sugar
- 1 cup fine, dry bread crumbs
- 1 teaspoon grated lemon rind
- ½ cup heavy cream, whipped

Slice 1 cup berries and reserve; crush remainder and drain thoroughly. Beat egg yolks until thick. Gradually add ¾ cup sugar and beat until light and fluffy. Add bread crumbs, lemon rind and crushed berries. Fold in stiffly beaten egg whites. Pour into buttered and sugared 2-quart casserole. Bake in moderate oven (375°F.) 35 minutes, or until firm. Serve warm or cold with a sauce of sliced berries mixed with whipped cream. Makes 6 to 8 servings.

STRAWBERRY RICE PUDDING

- 2 cups milk
- ½ cup raw rice
- ½ teaspoon salt
- ¼ cup rum
- 1 pint strawberries, sliced
- 1 envelope unflavored gelatin
- ¼ cup water
- 3 egg yolks
- ½ cup sugar
- ½ teaspoon vanilla extract
- 1 cup heavy cream, whipped
- 1 pint strawberries, halved

Scald 1⅓ cups milk in top part of double boiler. Add rice and salt and cook, covered, over boiling water until rice is soft. Depending on the quality of the rice used, this may take up to 1 hour. Stir rice occasionally. If rice dries out before getting soft, add more milk. Pour rum over sliced strawberries and chill. Soften gelatin in water. Beat egg yolks with sugar and add remaining ⅔ cup milk. Cook over simmering, not boiling, water until mixture coats spoon. Stir constantly. Add gelatin and blend until gelatin is completely dissolved. Add gelatin-custard mixture to rice and mix thoroughly. Add vanilla. Chill until mixture is slightly thickened. Fold in sliced strawberries and whipped cream. Chill. Pile into sherbet glasses; garnish with berry halves. Makes 6 to 8 servings.

CHEESE-CREAM HEART WITH STRAWBERRIES

- 1 package (8 ounces) cream cheese, softened
- 1 cup creamed cottage cheese
- 2 tablespoons honey
- ½ cup heavy cream
- 1 envelope unflavored gelatin
- 1 quart strawberries, washed
- Green leaves (optional)
- Sugar

Beat cream cheese and cottage cheese with honey until smooth. Gradually add cream, beating until thick. Soften gelatin in ¼ cup water and dissolve over low heat. Add to cheese mixture, blending well. Pour into lightly oiled 1-quart heart-shaped (or other shape) mold. Chill until firm. Unmold in serving dish and decorate with whole strawberries, and green leaves, if desired. Serve sugar separately. Makes 6 to 8 servings.

FONDANT-DIPPED STRAWBERRIES

- 1¼ cups water
- 2 cups sugar
- ⅛ teaspoon salt
- 2 tablespoons white corn syrup
- 1 quart strawberries

Combine first 4 ingredients in saucepan. Heat, stirring constantly, until sugar dissolves. Then boil without stirring until a small amount of mixture forms a soft ball when

STRUDEL

dropped into cold water (238°F. on a candy thermometer). If crystals form on side of pan, remove with fork covered with damp cloth. Pour onto cold wet platter; cool to lukewarm. Beat with fork until white and creamy; knead until smooth. Store in covered jar; let ripen overnight. Melt over hot water. Dip washed and drained berries into fondant; let stand until cool. Serve within a short time.

STRAWBERRIES ALEXANDRA

- 1 ripe pineapple
- ¼ cup brandy or rum
- Sugar
- 3 cups fresh strawberries, washed and hulled
- ½ cup pitted canned apricots, drained
- 1 cup heavy cream, whipped and sweetened to taste

Slice and peel pineapple. Cut 4 of the best slices in half and sprinkle with 2 tablespoons brandy and sugar to taste. Chill. Dice remaining pineapple. Reserve 1 cup of the best berries for decorating. Cut remaining berries in quarters and add to diced pineapple. Sweeten to taste; chill. Purée apricots in blender or force through food mill. Add ¼ cup sugar and cook until mixture is thick and shiny, stirring constantly. Add remaining 2 tablespoons brandy and chill. To serve, pile diced fruit in center of serving dish. Surround with whole strawberries and half-slices of pineapple. Cover center fruit with whipped cream. Drizzle apricot purée over pineapple and berries. Makes 6 to 8 servings.

SNOW PUDDING WITH STRAWBERRY SAUCE

- 1 envelope unflavored gelatin
- ¼ cup cold water
- ¾ cup sugar
- ⅛ teaspoon salt
- 1 cup boiling water
- Grated rind of 1 lemon
- ¼ cup lemon juice
- 3 egg whites
- Strawberry Sauce
- Toasted sliced almonds

Soften gelatin in cold water. Add ½ cup sugar, salt and boiling water; stir to dissolve gelatin and sugar. Add rind and juice and chill until partially set. Beat egg whites until almost stiff; gradually add remaining ¼ cup sugar, beating until stiff. Add gelatin mixture and beat until well blended. Chill until firm. Using large serving spoon, mound in glass serving bowl, drizzle sauce on top and sprinkle with nuts. Makes 6 to 8 servings.

Strawberry Sauce

Wash, hull and slice 1 pint strawberries and purée in blender or by hand. In top part of double boiler, mix 3 egg yolks, 3 tablespoons sugar, ¼ cup water and strawberry purée. Cook, stirring, over hot water until thickened and foamy. Flavor with ½ teaspoon strawberry extract; chill. If too pale, tint with a few drops of red food coloring, if desired.

STRAWBERRIES WITH RASPBERRY PUREÉ

- 2 to 3 pints strawberries
- Cointreau
- 1 package (10 ounces) frozen raspberries

Wash and hull strawberries. Sprinkle with 2 tablespoons Cointreau for each pint of berries and let stand 1 to 2 hours. Thaw raspberries slightly, then whirl in blender set at high about ½ minute. (Or force through food mill.) Strain through fine sieve to remove seeds and serve as sauce for strawberries. Makes 6 to 8 servings.

SAUCES AND BEVERAGES

STRAWBERRY HARD SAUCE

Cream ⅔ cup soft butter or margarine and gradually beat in 2 cups sifted confectioners' sugar. When thoroughly blended, stir in 1 cup sliced fresh strawberries. Makes 8 servings.

STRAWBERRY VELVET SAUCE

Thaw 1 package (10½ ounces) frozen sliced strawberries. Put berries in container of electric blender and whirl for a few seconds. On low speed, gradually add ½ cup heavy cream, whirling until thick and smooth. Makes about 1½ cups.

STRAWBERRY-ORANGE COOLER

- 1 cup orange juice
- 1 package (10 ounces) frozen strawberries, partially thawed
- 2 scoops strawberry ice cream

Put first 2 ingredients in container of electric blender. Turn motor on high. Turn off and add ice cream. Cover, then run motor until blended. Makes 2 generous servings.

STRAWBERRY ICE-CREAM SODA

Into a large glass put ⅓ cup frozen or sweetened crushed fresh strawberries, 3 tablespoons milk, and a large scoop of strawberry ice cream. Almost fill glass with chilled carbonated water. Stir.

STRUDEL—A pastry consisting of many layers of paper-thin dough which encases a sweet or savory filling. Strudel is one of the glories of Austrian, Hungarian, and Czechoslovakian baking, and the cooks of those countries produce their crisp, transparent strudel dough in a trice, as a daily food.

Strudel dough resembles *filo*, the equally thin sheets of pastry dough used in much Greek and Turkish cookery. A certain amount of skill is required to make good strudel. But it is not at all impossible to acquire this skill, and the persevering cook will see that her third and subsequent efforts are far superior to her first and second ones.

STRUDEL DOUGH

1½ cups sifted all-purpose flour
¼ teaspoon salt
1 egg, well beaten
⅓ to ½ cup lukewarm water
Filling

Sift flour with salt into a mound on a board. Mix egg with ⅓ cup water. Make a depression in the center of the flour. Pour in liquid and stir with a fork until a soft dough is formed. It may be necessary to add a little more water until entire flour is used. Knead dough on a lightly floured board until it no longer sticks but becomes smooth and elastic. Cover the dough with a bowl and let stand for 20 to 30 minutes.

Cover a table top with a sheet or other cloth. Sprinkle the cloth lightly with flour. Roll out the dough as thin as possible on the cloth. Brush the dough with melted butter to keep the surface from drying. At this point the dough is stretched with the hands until it is about 1 yard square. The dough should be brushed occasionally with melted butter during the stretching process. To avoid making holes with the fingernails put the hands under the sheet of dough palms down, clench the fists, and stretch the dough with the knuckles. When the dough is stretched, cut off the thick outer edge. This dough when stretched can be used for patching the sheet of dough if there are any holes. Fill the dough as specified under each filling.

When ready to roll the strudel, lift one edge of the cloth to allow the dough to roll over itself. Continue rolling until a long roll is shaped. Roll onto a greased cookie sheet and shape into a horseshoe. Brush with melted butter and sprinkle lightly with water. Bake in preheated hot oven (400°F.) for 20 minutes. Brush with additional butter. Then lower heat and continue baking in moderate oven (350°F.) for an additional 10 minutes, or until deep brown. Remove from oven and cool. Sprinkle with confectioners' sugar. Makes 10 to 12 servings.

CHERRY STRUDEL

8 cups fresh cherries, pitted (An equivalent would be about 6 cups canned pitted dark cherries, drained, with enough juice to make a thick filling)
Strudel Dough
Melted butter
1 cup blanched almonds, ground finely
½ cup sugar
Grated rind of 1 lemon
¾ cup fine dry bread crumbs

Cook fresh cherries until slightly wilted and cooked. Spread cooked cherries over the surface of the dough which has been brushed with melted butter. Combine remaining ingredients and sprinkle them over the cherries. Roll as directed in Strudel Dough recipe and bake as directed. Makes 8 to 10 servings.

APPLE STRUDEL

8 cups chopped peeled cored tart apples
Strudel Dough
½ cup chopped blanched almonds
1½ cups seedless raisins
1 tablespoon grated lemon rind
1 cup sugar
⅓ cup dry bread crumbs
3 tablespoons melted butter

Sprinkle apples over the entire surface of Strudel Dough. Sprinkle with almonds and raisins. Mix lemon rind with sugar, bread crumbs, and melted butter. Sprinkle mixture over the apples. Roll up as instructed in Strudel Dough recipe and bake as directed. Makes 8 to 10 servings.

CHEESE STRUDEL

¼ cup soft butter or margarine
2 cups (1 pound) cottage cheese
4 egg yolks
1 whole egg
⅓ cup sugar
1 teaspoon vanilla extract
Strudel Dough
1 egg, well beaten

Combine all ingredients except Strudel Dough and beaten egg. Brush the entire dough with beaten egg. Put filling in one line down one side of the dough. Roll as directed in Strudel Dough recipe and bake as directed. Makes 8 to 10 servings.

MOHN [POPPY-SEED] STRUDEL

2 cups ground poppy seeds
½ cup milk
½ cup honey
½ cup sugar
½ cup seedless raisins
Rind and juice of 1 lemon
Strudel Dough
Melted butter

Mix poppy seeds with milk. Add next 4 ingredients. Brush dough with melted butter. Put filling in one line at one side of the dough. Roll as directed in Strudel Dough recipe and bake as directed. Makes about 10 servings.

STUFF, TO—As a culinary term, the phrase refers to filling the hollow of a food with a mixture of other foods. Tomatoes, green peppers, squash, etc., are hollowed and stuffed with meat, bread stuffing, vegetables, etc. Poultry is often stuffed. Some meats such as flank steak, breast of veal, sparerib racks, thick chops, frankfurters, hamburgers, etc., are stuffed. Stuffings can be simple, as single pieces of fruit or vegetables, or can be very complicated, as a forcemeat stuffing.

STUFFING

STUFFING—A savory mixture of foods used to fill fish, poultry, meat, and vegetables. Stuffings, which are also called dressings, keep up the shape of the food that is being stuffed.

Stuffings need not always be used as fillings. They make excellent protein extenders and can be served as a vegetable or bread substitute with almost any meat or fish. Both the stuffing and meat benefit in flavor when roasted or baked together. However, some stuffings are designed only for baking in casseroles and are served as meat accompaniments. Almost any stuffing, whether left from filling a bird or made to serve separately, can be baked in a covered casserole in preheated moderate oven (350°F.) about 30 minutes. For a moister stuffing, add a little broth or water to casserole before baking.

Bread, rice, corn bread, potatoes, corn, ground meat, wild rice, sauerkraut, and macaroni can be used as a base for a stuffing. They are seasoned with salt, spices, herbs, and chopped vegetables. Some fat is added to the stuffing such as butter, sausage, bacon, cheese, drippings, etc. Olives, clams, chestnuts, oysters, nuts, mushrooms, apples, prunes, mint, shrimps, pickles, anchovies, etc., may also be added for flavor and texture. Eggs or broth are put in if a moist stuffing is desired.

Many stuffing mixes in different flavors are available. Some are range-top and need not be baked at all. They can be served with broiled or panfried fish, meat or poultry as well as with baked or roasted meats. During the holiday season unsliced stuffing bread is generally available. Other times, use day-old firm-type bread with or without crusts removed. Whole-grain breads can be used.
Fine fresh-bread crumbs can be made in the blender. Remove crusts and break bread in pieces. Whirl a few pieces at a time in blender until fine crumbs are formed.
Fine dry-bread crumbs can be made from toasted French or firm-type bread. Break up and whirl in blender.
Coarse crumbs or tiny bread cubes can be made from sliced bread. Trim off crusts, then cut fine lengthwise fingers. Stack together and, with a scraping motion, cut in very fine cubes or crumbs.

Stuffings and their ingredients and flavorings are to a large degree a matter of personal taste, but the general rule to remember about stuffings is that rich meats and fish require simple or fruity stuffings and that plain lean meats and fish gain succulence from a rich stuffing. Whatever the kind of stuffing, it should be well seasoned.

Another rule to remember is that all stuffings expand greatly during cooking and that they will burst the meat, fish, or vegetable if they don't have enough room to expand. Excess stuffing should be baked separately; 1 cup stuffing for each pound of meat or fish is ample.

Stuff poultry only just before cooking.

The onion, shallots, or garlic that may be used in a stuffing should always be slightly sautéed in hot butter before being added to the stuffing.

Never use raw pork in a stuffing since it will not cook through. Before being added, raw pork or sausage meat should always be panfried until it loses its raw color.

Some frozen already stuffed poultry is sold. Do not attempt this at home. The extremely low temperatures required are not possible in home freezers.

STUFFINGS FOR FISH

VEGETABLE STUFFING

- 2 carrots, shredded
- 2 tablespoons minced parsley
- 2 pimientos, minced
- 2 green onions with tops, chopped
- ⅓ cup melted butter or margarine
- 6 slices bread, crusts removed and cubed
- Salt and pepper to taste

Mix all ingredients. Use as stuffing for fish. Makes about 3 cups.

CRAB-MEAT STUFFING

- 1 can (7½ ounces) crab meat, drained and flaked
- 2 eggs, slightly beaten
- ¼ cup butter or margarine
- ½ cup minced onion
- ¾ cup finely chopped celery
- 1 to 2 teaspoons minced fresh dill or ¼ teaspoon lightly crushed dillweed or 1 tablespoon brandy or sherry
- 1 cup fine fresh-bread crumbs
- Salt and white pepper

Combine first 2 ingredients in mixing bowl. Melt butter in skillet, add onion and celery and sauté a few minutes; cool. Add to crab mixture with dill and bread crumbs. Mix well and season to taste with salt and pepper. Good as stuffing for fish, 4 small green peppers, 4 to 6 tomatoes or a small roasting chicken. Makes about 2½ cups.

PIQUANT STUFFING

- 1 tablespoon grated onion
- 2 cups soft stale-bread cubes
- ⅓ cup melted butter or margarine
- Juice of ½ lemon
- Few parsley sprigs, chopped
- ½ teaspoon celery salt
- 2 teaspoons capers
- Salt and pepper to taste

Cook onion and crumbs in butter until crumbs are lightly browned. Mix with remaining ingredients. Use as stuffing for fish. Makes 2 cups.

Cucumber Stuffing

Use recipe for Piquant Stuffing; reduce bread cubes to 1½ cups and add 1 cup drained chopped cucumber.

Pickle Stuffing

Use recipe for Piquant Stuffing; add ¼ cup finely chopped sweet or dill pickles.

STUFFINGS FOR MEAT

MINT STUFFING

- 1 small onion, chopped
- ¼ cup chopped celery and leaves
- ¼ cup butter or margarine
- ½ cup chopped fresh mint leaves or 1 tablespoon dried mint
- 3 cups soft stale-bread cubes

Cook onion and celery in butter for 5 minutes. Mix with remaining ingredients. Use to stuff shoulder of lamb. Makes about 3 cups.

SAUERKRAUT STUFFING

- 1 can (1 pound 11 ounces) sauerkraut, drained
- 2 tablespoons firmly packed brown sugar
- 1 garlic clove, minced
- 1 large onion, chopped
- 1 tart apple, peeled, cored, and chopped
- ¼ cup dry currants
- 1 cup chopped water chestnuts
- ⅛ teaspoon dried thyme
- Salt and pepper to taste

Chop sauerkraut. Add remaining ingredients and mix thoroughly. Use as stuffing for spareribs. Makes about 5 cups.

Stuffed Spareribs

Put stuffing in bottom of baking dish and cover with spareribs cut into serving pieces. Bake in preheated slow oven (325°F.) for 1½ to 2 hours, turning ribs occasionally to brown evenly on all sides.

CASSEROLE ALMOND-PRUNE STUFFING

- ½ cup chopped blanched almonds
- 1 cup pitted ready-to-eat prunes, cut up
- 2 medium red-skinned apples, cored and chopped
- 2 cups very small fresh white-bread cubes
- ½ teaspoon dried marjoram
- ⅛ teaspoon white pepper
- ¼ cup butter or margarine
- ⅔ cup beef broth
- 2 tablespoons sherry (optional)
- ¼ cup fine fresh-bread crumbs

Combine first 6 ingredients in mixing bowl and toss to mix. Put in lightly greased shallow 5- to 6-cup baking dish. In small saucepan, melt butter; add beef broth and sherry and heat. Pour over mixture in baking dish. Sprinkle with bread crumbs. Cover and bake in preheated moderate oven (375°F.) 20 minutes. Uncover and bake 15 minutes longer. Good with pork, ham, goose or duckling. Makes 4 to 6 servings.

SAUSAGE AND SWEET-POTATO STUFFING

- ½ pound pork-sausage meat
- 1 medium onion, minced
- ½ cup diced celery
- ¼ teaspoon poultry seasoning
- ½ teaspoon salt
- Dash of pepper
- 1½ cups soft stale-bread cubes
- 2 cups mashed cooked sweet potatoes

Cook sausage, breaking up with fork, until half done. Add next 5 ingredients and cook, stirring, until sausage is cooked. Add bread cubes and sweet potatoes and mix well. Use as stuffing for pork or poultry. Makes about 4 cups.

CURRIED PEACH-BREAD STUFFING

- ½ cup finely chopped celery
- ½ cup finely chopped onion
- ¼ cup butter or margarine
- 1 teaspoon curry powder
- 1 quart firm-type bread cut in ½-inch cubes
- ⅔ cup seedless raisins
- 1 cup diced canned peaches
- Peach syrup
- Salt to taste

Sauté celery and onion in butter until tender. Stir in curry powder. Toss with bread cubes. Plump raisins in hot water a few minutes, then drain. Add to bread mixture along with peaches. Sprinkle with ¼ cup peach syrup and toss. Season with salt. Add a little more peach syrup if moister dressing is desired. Bake in casserole and serve with pork or lamb. Use as a stuffing for poultry. Makes about 5 cups.

HERB-SEASONED-CROUTON STUFFING

- ⅔ cup butter or margarine
- 2 cups chopped onion
- 2 cups chopped celery with tops
- 2 cups chicken broth
- 1 package (7 ounces) herb-seasoned stuffing croutons

Melt butter in large skillet. Add next 2 ingredients and sauté, stirring, 5 minutes. Add chicken broth and heat. Pour over croutons and toss to mix. Good as stuffing for lamb shoulder. Makes about 6 cups.

STUFFING

STUFFINGS FOR VEGETABLES

MEXICAN-CORN STUFFING

- 1 small onion, minced
- ¼ cup chopped green pepper
- 2 tablespoons butter or margarine
- 2 pimientos, diced
- 1½ cups drained canned whole-kernel corn
- ¼ teaspoon sugar
- Dash of cayenne
- Salt to taste

Cook onion and pepper in butter for 5 minutes. Mix with remaining ingredients. Use as stuffing for baked tomatoes, eggplant, or squash. Makes about 1¾ cups.

ITALIAN CHEESE STUFFING

- 1 cup cooked rice
- ¼ cup melted butter or margarine
- 3 tablespoons grated Parmesan cheese
- Few parsley sprigs, chopped
- ⅓ cup finely diced Mozzarella cheese
- Salt and pepper to taste

Mix all ingredients. Use as stuffing for baked tomatoes. Also good in fish. Makes about 1¼ cups.

TURKISH MEAT-AND-RICE STUFFING

- 1 pound ground raw fatty lamb or beef
- 1 medium onion, chopped
- ¼ cup raw rice
- 1 teaspoon each chopped fresh mint and dill or crumbled dried herbs to taste
- 1 tablespoon tomato sauce
- Salt and pepper to taste

Mix all ingredients well and use as stuffing for eggplant, zucchini, green peppers, or tomatoes. Makes about 2½ cups.
NOTE: When stuffing these vegetables, cut off a slice from end of eggplant and zucchini, or top of green pepper and tomato. Scoop out insides, and stuff vegetables. Replace cut-off slice, fasten with toothpicks, and cook upright in covered saucepan with 2 tablespoons butter and 1 cup water. Allow 30 to 40 minutes cooking time.

PIEDMONT STUFFING

- 12 large mushroom stems
- 4 anchovies, minced
- 1 medium onion, minced
- 1 tablespoon chopped parsley
- 2 tablespoons olive oil
- ¼ cup fine dry bread crumbs
- 1 egg, beaten
- Salt and pepper to taste

Chop mushroom stems. Cook anchovies, onion, and parsley in oil for 5 minutes. Add mushroom stems and cook for 5 minutes longer. Remove from heat and cool. Add remaining ingredients. Use as stuffing for mushrooms.

Stuffed Mushrooms

Stuff 12 large mushroom caps with Piedmont Stuffing. Arrange stuffed caps in shallow pan and add ½ cup olive oil. Bake in preheated moderate oven (350°F.) about 20 minutes, basting occasionally with oil in pan.

STUFFINGS FOR POULTRY

BREAD STUFFING

- 1 cup butter or margarine
- 1 cup minced onions
- 1 tablespoon poultry seasoning
- 1½ teaspoons salt
- ¾ teaspoon pepper
- ⅓ cup chopped parsley
- ¾ cup chopped celery leaves
- 2½ quarts soft stale-bread crumbs or cubes

Melt butter in skillet and add all ingredients except crumbs. Cook for 5 minutes. Add crumbs. Use as stuffing for turkey. Makes about 9 cups.
NOTE: Add 2 beaten eggs with crumbs if desired.

Oyster Bread Stuffing

Follow recipe above. Add 2 cups (1 pint) shucked small oysters, drained and chopped, to butter with other ingredients. Makes about 10 cups.

Chestnut Bread Stuffing

Follow recipe for Bread Stuffing, reducing crumbs to 2 quarts. Add 1 pound Italian chestnuts, cooked, shelled, and chopped, to stuffing with bread crumbs. Makes about 10 cups.

MUSHROOM AND WILD RICE STUFFING

- ¼ pound mushrooms, chopped
- 1 small onion, chopped
- 2 tablespoons butter or margarine
- 1 cup wild rice, cooked (or 2 cups canned rice)
- Salt, pepper, and ground nutmeg

Cook mushrooms and onion in butter for 5 minutes. Add to rice. Season to taste with salt, pepper, and nutmeg. Use as stuffing for chicken or Rock Cornish hen. Makes 3 cups.

STUFFING

CHESTNUT AND SAUSAGE STUFFING

- 4 dozen Italian chestnuts
- 2 tablespoons butter or margarine
- 1 small onion, minced
- ½ pound sausage meat
- 2 teaspoons salt
- ¼ teaspoon pepper
- ⅛ teaspoon poultry seasoning
- 1 tablespoon minced parsley
- 1 cup soft-stale bread crumbs or cubes

Cook and shell chestnuts. Mash half of chestnuts and leave remainder whole. Melt butter in saucepan, add onion, and cook for 3 minutes. Add sausage meat. Cook, stirring constantly, for 5 minutes. Add mashed chestnuts and mix well. Add seasonings and crumbs. Stir in whole chestnuts. Use as stuffing for chicken. Makes 4 cups.

GIBLET-BUTTERNUT STUFFING

Wash giblets; cook neck, heart, and gizzard about 2 hours in boiling salted water with a small onion and a few celery leaves. Add liver during last 15 minutes. Drain, and reserve stock. Chop heart, gizzard, and liver. Melt 1 cup butter or margarine, add 1 cup each chopped onion, celery, and butternuts, and sauté for 5 minutes. Add 1 tablespoon poultry seasoning, 1½ teaspoons salt, ¾ teaspoon pepper, and chopped giblets. Mix with 4 quarts soft stale bread cubes. Stuff neck and cavity. Enough to stuff a 16- to 20-pound turkey.

SAGE AND ONION STUFFING

- 1 cup butter or margarine
- 1 tablespoon dried sage
- 1½ teaspoons salt
- ¾ teaspoon pepper
- ⅓ cup chopped parsley
- ¾ cup chopped celery and leaves
- 2 cups chopped boiled onions
- 2½ quarts soft stale-bread crumbs or cubes

Melt butter in skillet. Add all ingredients except last two. Cook for 5 minutes. Add onions and crumbs. Use as stuffing for turkey. Makes about 11 cups.

CREAMY BRAZIL-NUT STUFFING

- ¾ pound shelled Brazil nuts
- 1¼ cups butter or margarine
- 2 quarts tiny bread cubes
- 1 or 2 fresh sage leaves
- Heavy cream
- Salt and pepper

Cut nuts into small chunks. Brown lightly in ¼ cup butter. Dry out breadcrumbs in slow oven (300°F.) a few minutes. Brown in remaining butter. Mix nuts, bread, and sage. Add cream to moisten and salt and pepper to taste. Use as stuffing for turkey. Makes about 8 cups.
NOTE: If fresh sage is not available, add a tiny pinch dried sage.

CRISP WALNUT-STUFFING BALLS

- 4 cups soft stale coarsely crumbled white bread crumbs
- 1 cup chopped walnuts
- ½ cup chopped celery
- ½ cup chopped parsley
- ¼ cup finely chopped onion
- ½ cup butter or margarine
- ½ teaspoon salt
- ½ teaspoon poultry seasoning
- ¼ teaspoon pepper
- 1 egg, slightly beaten
- ⅓ cup giblet or chicken broth (about)

Toss first 4 ingredients together. Sauté onion in butter about 2 minutes. Stir in seasonings. Add to crumb mixture. Add egg and just enough broth to moisten mixture so it holds together when pressed in hand. Shape in balls about 2 inches in diameter. Put on greased baking pan and bake in preheated moderate oven (375°F.) 15 minutes, or until crisp and browned. Top with half a piece of walnut, if desired. Recipe can be doubled. Makes 6 servings.

MUSHROOM-GIBLET STUFFING

- ½ pound mushrooms, sliced
- 1 medium onion, sliced
- ½ cup chopped parsley
- 1 teaspoon each dried marjoram and sage leaves and salt
- ½ teaspoon pepper
- ¼ cup butter or margarine
- Chopped cooked giblets and neck meat from roasting chicken
- 1 cup giblet broth
- 3 cups soft stale-bread crumbs

Sauté mushrooms, onion and parsley with seasonings in butter 5 minutes. Add remaining ingredients and mix well. Use as stuffing for chicken. Makes about 4 cups.

SOUTHERN SAUSAGE-PECAN STUFFING

- 1 pound hot pork-sausage meat
- ½ cup butter or margarine
- ¾ cup chopped onion
- ½ cup chopped celery
- 1 teaspoon poultry seasoning
- 3 cups crumbled Corn Bread
- 4 cups seasoned herb stuffing (7 ounce package)
- ¾ cup coarsely chopped pecans
- 2 eggs
- 2 cups chicken broth

Cook sausage, stirring, until lightly browned; drain. Melt butter, add onion and celery; sauté until tender. Stir in poultry seasoning. Combine crumbled Corn Bread, herb stuffing, pecans and onion mixture. Beat eggs and broth and pour over mixture, tossing gently (add more broth if necessary for desired moistness). Use as stuffing for poultry. Makes about 2½ quarts.

STURGEON

STURGEON—Various species of fish of the genus *Acipenser* are known as sturgeon. They are distributed throughout the coastal waters and rivers of the north temperate zone. Most species inhabit the sea for most of the year but ascend rivers to spawn; some are completely fresh-water fishes. One related genus, *Scaphirhynchus,* is recognized as a sturgeon; this is the shovelhead, or shovel-nosed, fresh-water sturgeon found in the Mississippi and other North American rivers.

Sturgeon have a projecting tapering snout, bony plates, and an asymmetrical tail fin. They range in size from the under three-foot-long snouted sterlet of the Volga River to the huge beluga of the Black and Caspian Seas where sturgeon is king among fish. This last fish is the largest of all fresh-water fish: it has been measured at twenty-six feet long, weighing 3,221 pounds. Although sturgeon was once plentiful on the West Coast, in the Great Lakes, and in some eastern rivers of the United States, it is now very scarce in American waters.

Fresh sturgeon steaks are a prized delicacy, and the flavor is so distinctive that they require little seasoning. Smoked sturgeon is a delicious but expensive treat. Even more of a delicacy is the roe of the sturgeon, called caviar, which is usually served chilled with lemon juice and toast or dark bread.

Another product of the sturgeon is isinglass, made from the swim bladder of the fish. It is used nowadays as a clarifying agent and in making jellies and glues.

Availability—Smoked sturgeon and caviar are available in specialty food stores. Fresh sturgeon is occasionally available in fish stores on both east and west coasts.

Storage
Fresh, refrigerator shelf: 1 to 2 days
Smoked, refrigerator shelf: 2 to 3 weeks
Caviar, well wrapped, at 26°F.: 3 to 4 months (Do not store caviar in freezer.)

Nutritive Food Values—High in protein
Raw, meat only, 4 ounces = 107 calories
Smoked sturgeon, 4 ounces = 170 calories
Caviar, granular, 1 ounce = 74 calories
Caviar, pressed, 1 ounce = 90 calories

SHERRY SMOKED STURGEON IN RAMEKINS

½ pound smoked sturgeon
¾ cup butter or margarine
¼ cup all-purpose flour
¼ teaspoon salt
½ teaspoon celery seed
⅛ teaspoon ground nutmeg
2 teaspoons minced parsley
2 cups half-and-half (half cream, half milk)
¼ cup sherry
2 hard-cooked eggs, chopped
½ cup coarse dry bread crumbs

Cut sturgeon into 1-inch cubes. Melt ½ cup butter and blend in flour, salt, celery seed, nutmeg, and parsley. Gradually add half-and-half, stirring constantly. Cook, stirring, until smooth and thickened. Add sherry, eggs, and sturgeon; remove from heat. Divide mixture into 6 individual ramekins. Sprinkle lightly with crumbs and dot with remaining ¼ cup butter. Bake in preheated hot oven (400°F.) for 5 minutes, or until browned. Makes 6 servings.

SUCCOTASH—A native American dish consisting of corn and beans, usually Limas, combined after cooking and served together.

The word comes from the language of the Narraganset Indians; *msakwatas* means "something broken into pieces." The dish is a truly indigenous one, discovered by the early settlers who learned it from the Indians.

Different versions of succotash have been developed over the years, some containing tomatoes and other vegetables besides the Lima beans and corn. In addition to the homemade variety, canned and frozen succotash are widely available.

SUCCOTASH

2 cups cooked Lima beans (fresh, frozen, or canned)
2 cups whole kernel corn (fresh, frozen, or canned)
2 tablespoons butter
1 teaspoon salt
½ teaspoon sugar
¼ teaspoon pepper
¼ cup water
½ cup heavy cream (optional)

Combine all ingredients except cream. Simmer, covered, over lowest possible heat for 5 minutes. Stir occasionally and check for moisture; if necessary, add a little more water. Add cream, if desired, and heat through. Makes 4 to 6 servings.

OVEN SUCCOTASH

Put 1 box each (10 ounces each) frozen Fordhook lima beans and cut corn in buttered 2-quart casserole. Add 3 tablespoons butter or margarine, ¼ cup water, ½ teaspoon salt and ⅛ teaspoon pepper. Cover and bake in preheated moderate oven (375°F.) 1¼ hours. Stir before serving. Makes 6 servings.

SUCKER—A name popularly applied to various types of fresh-water fish closely related to carp that are, with two Asiatic exceptions, native to North America. Suckers live and feed near the bottom of streams. Their flesh is lean and they are eaten where they are abundant. Generally speaking, they are the kind of fish caught by youngsters on fishing expeditions and brought home for their mothers to prepare.

Suckers can be cooked in any way fish is cooked. If broiled, they must be well spread with oil or butter to counteract their leanness. Poached, braised, or pan-fried, they profit from a sauce such as mayonnaise, tartar, hollandaise, etc.

Nutritive Food Value—Suckers are a good source of protein and low in calories.
4 ounces, raw = 127 calories

SUET—The hard fat around the kidneys and loins in beef, mutton, and other carcasses which yields tallow. In cookery, unless the word is otherwise qualified, the reference is always to beef suet which has a bland taste. It is widely used in British cooking as a shortening for pastry and for savory and sweet puddings, to which it gives a rich smooth quality. For this purpose it is shredded or diced. Suet can also be melted down, strained, and used like any other solid fat. Although it has a low smoking point, suet can be used for shallow frying.

Suet is sold in meat markets by the pound in large pieces, or it is sold by weight and sliced and ready to be used for barding meats. Large pieces of suet can be finely cubed or shredded with a sharp knife, or they can be ground through the coarse blade of a meat grinder.

Caloric Value
Suet (beef kidney fat), 1 ounce, raw = 242 calories

SUET PUDDING

- 1¼ cups sultana raisins
- 1¼ cups dry currants
- 1 cup seedless raisins
- 1 cup mixed chopped candied fruits
- ½ cup chopped blanched almonds
- 2 cups sifted all-purpose flour
- 1 nutmeg, grated
- ½ teaspoon each ground allspice and ginger
- 10 ounces suet, finely chopped
- 2¼ cups (1 pound) dark brown sugar
- 6 cups soft bread crumbs
- 6 eggs
- ½ cup each milk and brandy

Chop large raisins and mix with other fruits and nuts. Mix flour with spices, suet, sugar, and bread crumbs. Beat eggs with milk and brandy. Stir into dry ingredients. Beat in fruits and nuts. Spoon mixture into two 6-cup molds which have been greased. Cover the top of the mold with paper that has been greased or with greased aluminum foil. Set molds in a large kettle filled with boiling water that comes halfway up molds. Boil puddings for 7 to 8 hours, adding more boiling water to keep up the level of the liquid. Remove molds from the water. Remove paper and cover puddings with dry paper or foil. Store puddings until ready to use. Some puddings are kept for as long as a year, which improves their flavor. When ready to serve, boil pudding again for 2 to 3 hours. Stick a branch of holly with berries into the top of each pudding. Serve with brandy set aflame, rum butter, or cream. Makes 16 to 20 servings.

SUGAR—The sweet crystallized substance obtained from cane and certain beets is what people usually mean when they use the word "sugar". North Americans have for years been consuming this sugar, or sucrose, at an average rate of nearly 100 pounds a year. In addition, the average consumption of sugars derived from corn starch has reached a level of more than 30 pounds a year, up from an estimated 13 pounds in 1960. These corn sweeteners consist mostly of dextrose, maltose, and more complex sugars.

The word sugar (derived from the Sanskrit of ancient India through the Arabic word *sukkar*) actually applies to more than a hundred carbohydrate substances, among them the lactose in milk and the fructose and levulose in fruit and honey. These are simpler sugars than the sucrose refined from cane and sugar beets. Some are less sweet than sucrose. The body turns them all into glucose — the blood sugar essential to energy. Our livers store excess amounts, from whatever source, in the form of glycogen, available for conversion to glucose when needed, or converts them into fat, which often defies our most determined efforts to shed.

Too much sugar can be dangerous to diabetics, who have a genetic problem of metabolism, but it cannot produce diabetes in people without the genetic problem. High intake of sugar has also been associated with elevated blood levels of trygliceride, which may lead to heart disease. Sugar is a major culprit in the high incidence of dental caries. And since sugar supplies no nutrients, it has often come under attack as a source of "empty calories".

Animal studies on man-made substitutes for natural sweeteners such as sugar, maple syrup, and honey have raised questions about the safety of these substitutes, but there are hazards associated with the natural sweeteners themselves.

Many foods today contain unexpectedly large amounts of sugar. Crackers are often more than 10 percent sugar, most ice cream 21 percent, catsup nearly 30 percent, to give just a few examples. It is not easy to reduce sugar intake, but there are no significant health advantages in replacing refined sugar with brown sugar, "raw" sugar, or honey.

When Alexander the Great's admiral Nearchus made the first known reference to sugar in 325 B.C., he wrote of Indian reeds "that produce honey, although there are no bees." Sugar cane was introduced into the Middle East 25 years later, and the Egyptians became so famous for their white sugar that Kublai Khan called in Egyptian experts to improve Chinese sugar refining techniques in 1279. The Crusaders had brought home sugar from the Holy Land to give Europe its first taste of the new substitute for honey, but sugar remained far too costly for any but the very rich. Christopher Columbus, whose first wife's mother had owned a sugar plantation in Madeira, brought the cane to Santo Domingo on his second voyage in 1493, and sugar cultivated with slave labor in the West Indies and South America became more economical in the 17th and 18th centuries.

It was in the middle of the 18th century that a Prussian chemist, Andreas Sigismund Marggraf, discovered that beets and carrots contain small amounts of sugar. Selective breeding produced beet strains with increased sugar content, and sugar beets helped France survive the British blockade during the Napoleonic wars. But it was not until the late 19th century that improved technology began to make beet sugar competitive with cane sugar. The two are identical in every way, and beet sugar now accounts for more than 40 percent of the world's total sugar production.

SUGAR

TYPES OF SUGAR

Granulated sugar is the product for general use. The terms "granulated," "fine granulated," and "extra fine granulated" are used. They are all universally available in different size packages.

Superfine or **powdered** sugar is a very fine granulated sugar for use in cold drinks, for fruits and cereals, and for special cake baking. Use in recipes which need a quick-dissolving sugar; 1 cup superfine equals 1 cup granulated.

Confectioners' sugar is granulated sugar that is crushed very fine and mixed with cornstarch to prevent caking. X's may be used to indicate grade. There is only a slight difference between the 10X or ultrafine, and the 4X or very fine. Confectioners' sugar is used for frostings, confections, hard sauce, and dusting; 1¾ cups confectioners' sugar equals 1 cup granulated.

Brown sugar is also called soft sugar and consists of extremely fine crystals that are covered with a film or coating of molasses. This coating gives the sugar the characteristic color and taste which is of primary value. At one time, 15 grades of soft sugar were produced ranging in color from white to yellow to brown. Now, fewer grades are light brown and dark (old-fashioned) brown. Sometimes a medium brown is available. The new granulated form of brown sugar contains enough molasses to provide a flavor intensity between the two brown sugars; its use in baking requires adjustments in recipes, so follow the manufacturer's directions. It may be made from the syrup that remains after the sugar is extracted from sugar cane or sugar beet, or by adding refined syrups to white sugar crystals.

The light brown sugar is milder in flavor and is used in baking, icings, and candy. The dark brown sugar is used in cookies, cakes, gingerbread, mincemeat, plum pudding, and baked beans.

Brown sugar often hardens. To avoid this, keep sugar in airtight container in refrigerator. To restore hardened sugar, heat in oven at low temperature until it is soft enough to crumble. The sugar may be rolled and sifted or crumbled in an electric blender. Or a piece of apple, or fresh bread, or damp paper towel, may be placed on a piece of wax paper and put in the container of brown sugar for 2 days. Replace if necessary.

When measuring, pack brown sugar firmly into container; it should retain the shape of the container when it is removed.

Also available is *brownulated* sugar which pours freely. Use substitution table on the package when using brownulated sugar instead of regular brown sugar.

Maple sugar is made from the sap of the sugar maple, concentrated and crystallized into sugar. It is sold loose or pressed into cakes or decorative molds.

Rock candy is made by immersing a string in a supersaturated solution of sugar and water. The sugar solution is not stirred, allowing large sugar crystals to form on the string. Also sold crystallized on small sticks for drink swizzle sticks.

Colored sugars are available and are used for decoration.

Cinnamon sugar, a combination of granulated sugar and ground cinnamon, is also sold. It is used for flavoring toast, cookies, coffeecakes, etc.

Storage—Lasts indefinitely; store in an airtight container to prevent caking or lumping.

Nutritive Food Values—Sugar is almost 100 per cent carbohydrate and is the most efficient source of energy that can be used by the human body.
Brown, 1 cup (7.5 ounces) = 791 calories
Brown, 1 tablespoon (½ ounce) = 48 calories
White, granulated, 1 cup (6.9 ounces) = 751 calories
White, 1 tablespoon (.4 ounce) = 46 calories

NONNUTRITIVE SWEETENERS

Diabetics and others with compelling medical reasons to restrict their intake of sugar have used saccharin as a sugar substitute for more than a century. Saccharin is a coal tar derivative. Since all coal tar derivatives have been associated with cancer in test animals, there have always been some doubts as to the safety of saccharin.

In 1907, the chief chemist of the U.S. Department of Agriculture proposed a ban on the use of saccharin. Harvey Washington Wiley had obtained passage the year before of the first U.S. pure food law, but President Theodore Roosevelt took exception to Wiley's proposal. "Anybody who says saccharin is injurious is an idiot! Dr. Rixey gives it to me every day," President Roosevelt said angrily, and some critics noted that Wiley had ties to the sugar industry.

There is still no evidence that saccharin has ever been injurious to anyone. This is also true with regard to cyclamates, the nonnutritive sweeteners developed at the University of Illinois in the late 1930's. Cyclamates are 30 times as sweet as sugar and do not have the bitter aftertaste of saccharin, which is 300 times as sweet as sugar.

Until the early 1950's, few people other than diabetics used either of the nonnutritive sweeteners. Then came the first cyclamate-sweetened soft drinks, followed in the early 1960's by cyclamate-sweetened cola drinks marketed by the giants of the soft drink industry. Coincidentally, a Food Additives Amendment passed by Congress in 1958 contained a "cancer clause" inserted by Congressman James J. Delaney of Brooklyn, N.Y. The so-called "Delaney clause" stated that if *any* amount of any additive could be shown to produce cancer when ingested by humans or test animals, *no* amount of that additive could be used in foods for human consumption.

Test animals given enormous feedings of cyclamates did develop cancer in the late 1960's. Many countries, including Canada, continued to permit the sale of cyclamates to diabetics and others, but the U.S. Food and Drug Administration was obliged by the "Delaney clause" to ban any sale of cyclamates. Saccharin came under fire in the late 1970's when some Canadian tests indicated that massive feedings of saccharin produced cancer in test animals.

Heated controversy over the safety of existing and proposed nonnutritive sweeteners continues, often obscuring the fact that natural sweeteners, which are "nutritive" only in that they supply calories, pose as great a hazard for some people as do sugar substitutes.

SUMMER COOKBOOK

With a wink at the weather and neat sleight of hand the summertime cook can conjure up satisfying meals without wilting in the process. For almost any dish there are acceptable shortcuts, detracting not at all from its taste but cutting down considerably on the time and effort involved in its preparation. Here are suggestions for quick summer soups, meat and vegetable dishes, salads, sandwiches and desserts. Also sprinkled in are some do-ahead recipes that will be ready whenever you are good and ready for them.

APPETIZERS AND SOUPS

COLD TOMATO-CLAM SOUP

Mix 2 (10½ ounces) tomato soup, 1 bottle (8 ounces) clam juice and 2 soup-cans water. And lemon juice to taste and garnish with sliced lemon and chopped parsley. Makes 6 servings.

JELLIED CONSOMMÉ

Chill canned red consommé (madrilène). Served topped with lemon slices and capers.

ORANGE-TOMATO BISQUE

- 1 can (10¼ ounces) condensed bisque of tomato soup
- 1⅓ cups orange juice
- ½ cup water
- ⅛ teaspoon dried basil
- ½ cup heavy cream, whipped
- Salt

Put soup in saucepan and gradually stir in orange juice and water. Add basil and heat, stirring occasionally. Pour into 4 soup cups and top each with a spoonful of whipped cream. Sprinkle cream lightly with salt. Makes 4 servings.
NOTE: Soup can be served chilled, if preferred.

BLENDER VEGETABLE COCKTAIL

Combine in blender 1½ cups tomato juice, 1 stalk celery (cut up), 1 carrot (cut up), 1 teaspoon instant minced onion, 1 tablespoon lemon juice, ½ teaspoon Worcestershire and a dash of pepper. Whirl until blended. Chill and serve over ice cubes in glasses. Makes 2 cups, or four 4-ounce servings.

COLD SHRIMPS WITH SPICY SAUCE

- 3 tablespoons horseradish
- 1 cup catsup
- ¼ cup chili sauce
- 3 tablespoons lemon juice
- 2 dashes of hot pepper sauce
- 1½ pounds cleaned cooked shrimps

Mix all ingredients, except shrimps, and use as a dip or sauce for the shrimps. Makes 6 servings.

Sauce Rémoulade for Shrimp

Mix 1 cup mayonnaise, ¼ cup minced sour pickle, 1 tablespoon minced capers, 1½ teaspoons prepared brown mustard, ½ teaspoon each minced parsley, tarragon and chives. Makes 1⅓ cups.

MAIN DISHES

HAMBURGER AND GREEN-BEAN MEDLEY

- 2 onions, sliced
- 1 tablespoon butter
- ¾ pound ground beef
- ½ teaspoon seasoned salt
- ⅛ teaspoon pepper
- 1 can (10¼ ounces) condensed chicken-rice soup
- ¼ teaspoon ground ginger
- 1 tablespoon soy sauce
- 1 box (10 ounces) frozen French-style green beans
- 3 cups hot cooked rice
- Additional soy sauce

Brown onions in butter in heavy saucepan. Add meat and cook, crumbling with fork, until meat loses its red color. Add remaining ingredients, except last 2, cover and cook about 10 minutes, stirring occasionally. Serve on rice with additional soy sauce. Makes 4 servings.

FRUITED HAM SLICES

- 1 canned ham (3 to 4 pounds)
- 1 can (1 pound) fruit cocktail
- ⅓ cup honey
- 1 tablespoon lemon juice
- 1 tablespoon cornstarch
- 1 teaspoon curry powder
- ¼ teaspoon nutmeg
- 2 bananas, cut in 1-inch diagonal slices

Remove gelatin from ham and slice meat about ¼-inch thick. Put in baking pan, keeping slices together. Bake in preheated moderate oven (350°F.) 40 minutes, or until heated through. Drain fruit cocktail, reserving ⅔ cup syrup. In saucepan, mix syrup with next 5 ingredients and cook, stirring, until thickened. Add fruit cocktail and heat. Arrange ham on serving platter, surround with banana chunks and pour on hot sauce. Makes 8 to 10 servings.

SUMMER

HAMBURGER SUPREME

- 1 pound ground beef
- 1 medium onion, chopped
- ½ cup diced celery
- 1 can (10½ ounces) condensed tomato soup
- ½ cup water
- ½ teaspoon salt
- ¼ teaspoon pepper
- ½ teaspoon chili powder
- ½ cup halved small stuffed olives
- 1 can (2 ounces) mushroom bits and pieces or 1 cup fresh mushrooms, chopped

Cook beef in skillet, crumbling with fork, until meat loses its red color. Add onion and celery and cook a few minutes longer. Add soup, water and seasonings. Bring to boil and simmer, covered, 30 minutes. Add olives and undrained mushrooms and bring to boil. If too thin, thicken with a flour-water paste. Good on mashed potatoes, rice or macaroni. Makes 4 servings.

SKILLET "LASAGNA"

- 1 pound ground beef
- 2 tablespoons butter or margarine
- 1 envelope spaghetti-sauce mix
- 1 pound creamed cottage cheese
- 3 cups broad noodles, uncooked
- 2 teaspoons fresh basil leaves
- 1 tablespoon parsley flakes
- 1 teaspoon salt
- 1 can (1 pound) tomatoes
- 1 can (8 ounces) tomato sauce
- 1 cup water
- 8 ounces mozzarella cheese, sliced and cut in pieces

Cook meat in butter in 12-inch skillet until it loses its red color. Sprinkle with half the spaghetti-sauce mix, then spoon cottage cheese over meat. Top with noodles in a layer and sprinkle with remaining spaghetti-sauce mix, basil, parsley and salt. Pour tomatoes, tomato sauce and water over top, making sure all is moistened. Bring to boil, cover and simmer 35 minutes, or until noodles are tender. Sprinkle cheese over top and let stand about 5 minutes. Makes 6 servings.

GLAZED HAM STEAK

- 1 ready-to-eat ham slice (1½ pounds), cut about 1 inch thick
- 2 tablespoons orange marmalade
- 1 teaspoon dry mustard

Brown ham slice on both slides in heavy skillet. Mix remaining ingredients and spread half on each side of ham. Cook about 2 minutes. Makes 4 servings.

CORN CHIPS AND CHILI

- 2 cups corn chips, slightly crushed
- 1 small onion, chopped
- 1 can (15½ ounces) chili con carne, without beans
- 4 slices of processed American cheese

Put 1½ cups corn chips in skillet. Sprinkle with onion. Add chili and heat. Sprinkle with remaining corn chips and add cheese. Cover and heat until cheese is melted. Makes 4 servings.

BOLOGNA-VEGETABLE DINNER

- 4 raw large potatoes, peeled and cut in ½-inch slices
- 1 to 2 cups sliced carrots
- 1 small head cabbage, cut in quarters and sliced lengthwise in 1-inch strips
- 1 can (8 ounces) tomato sauce
- 2 teaspoons salt
- 2 teaspoons whole cuminseed
- ¼ teaspoon black pepper
- 1 cup water
- 1½ pounds bologna, cut in ½-inch slices
- Chopped parsley
- Prepared mustard

Layer potatoes in large heavy saucepan. Add next 7 ingredients. Bring to boil, reduce heat, cover and simmer 20 minutes. Put bologna on top of cabbage, cover and simmer 6 to 8 minutes. Sprinkle generously with parsley and serve with mustard. Makes 6 servings.

STREAMLINED PAELLA

- 1 frying chicken (3 pounds), cut up
- Salt
- Paprika
- 3 tablespoons vegetable oil
- ¼ cup chopped onion
- ¼ cup chopped green pepper
- 1 garlic clove, minced
- 1 can (10½ ounces) condensed tomato soup
- 2½ cups canned beef broth
- 1 tablespoon lemon juice
- ⅛ teaspoon saffron
- 1 cup raw rice
- 1 can (4½ ounces) large or jumbo shrimps, drained
- 1 can (5 ounces) lobster (optional)
- ½ cup cooked peas
- 1 or 2 canned pimientos, cut up

Sprinkle chicken lightly with salt and paprika. In large skillet or Dutch oven, brown chicken on both sides in oil. Push chicken to one side of skillet, add onion, green pepper and garlic; cook 2 to 3 minutes, stirring. Stir in next 4 ingredients. Bring to boil, cover and simmer 30 minutes. Stir in rice, cover and simmer 30 minutes, stirring gently occasionally to prevent rice from sticking. Add remaining ingredients; heat. Makes 4 to 6 servings.

Streamlined Paella and Savory Toasted Breadsticks

SUMMER

SEAFOOD FONDUE

- 1 large garlic clove, halved
- 1 can (10½ ounces) condensed onion soup
- ½ cup Chablis or other dry white wine
- ½ cup chopped canned tomatoes
- 1 small bay leaf
- ¼ teaspoon dried oregano
- Large pinch dried thyme
- 1⅓ cups water
- ¾ pound raw sea scallops
- ¾ pound raw shrimps, shelled and deveined
- Toasted Italian-bread slices
- Grated Parmesan cheese

Rub inside of saucepan or fondue pot with garlic. Add next 7 ingredients. Bring to boil. Cut seafood in bite-size pieces. Spear with fondue forks or long skewers and cook in the soup mixture. Serve remaining soup with bread and cheese. Makes 4 servings.

CREAMY COTTAGE CHEESE AND NOODLES

- 8 ounces medium noodles
- Salt
- 1 cup creamed cottage cheese
- ¼ cup dairy sour cream
- 2 green onions, finely sliced
- ½ cup chopped parsley
- Freshly ground pepper

Cook noodles in lightly salted boiling water until tender; drain. Return to saucepan and add remaining ingredients, except pepper. Stir to combine. Heat slowly, stirring gently. Season to taste with salt and pepper. Makes 6 servings.

TUNA NOODLES ROMANOFF

- 1 package (5¾ ounces) noodles Romanoff
- 1 teaspoon salt
- 2 tablespoons butter or margarine
- ½ cup milk
- 1 can (6½ or 7 ounces) tuna, flaked
- 1 tablespoon dried chives
- 2 pimientos, chopped
- Pepper to taste

Cook noodles with salt in boiling water 7 to 8 minutes. Drain and add remaining ingredients, including sauce mix from package. Mix lightly and heat gently. Makes 4 servings.

VEGETABLES

CORN IN TOMATO SAUCE

Cook 2 packages (10 ounces each) frozen cut corn with 1 can (8 ounces) tomato sauce until corn is tender. Season to taste with salt and pepper. Makes 4 to 6 servings.

GREEN BEANS WITH HERB BUTTER SAUCE

- 2 cans (1 pound each) French-style green beans
- 1 small onion, minced
- ¼ cup butter
- 2 tablespoons minced parsley
- ½ teaspoon dried thyme
- 3 tablespoons lemon juice
- Salt and pepper to taste
- ¼ teaspoon paprika

Heat beans, drain and put in serving dish. Sauté onion lightly in butter, add remaining ingredients and mix well. Heat gently and pour over beans. Makes 6 servings.

CARROTS WITH MINT GLAZE

- 2 bunches carrots, peeled
- Salt
- ¼ cup butter or margarine
- ¼ cup sugar
- 1 teaspoon vinegar
- 1 tablespoon chopped fresh mint leaves

Cut carrots in half crosswise. Cook, covered, in skillet in boiling water to barely cover 15 minutes, or until just tender. Drain and sprinkle with salt. Melt butter in skillet and stir in remaining ingredients. Add carrots and heat, turning frequently, until lightly glazed. Makes 4 servings.

TOMATO BROCCOLI

Cook 1 box (10 ounces) frozen chopped broccoli or spears as directed on the package, using 1 can (8 ounces) tomato-cheese sauce, tomato-mushroom sauce or meatless spaghetti sauce as the liquid. Makes 2 or 3 servings.

SUMMER

SALADS AND RELISHES

ALL-IN-ONE SALAD

- 2 cups diced cooked potatoes
- 3 hard-cooked eggs, diced
- 1 cup diced celery
- ½ cup diced salami
- ½ cup diced liverwurst
- ½ cup diced sharp Cheddar cheese
- 1 cup finely shredded cabbage
- 2 teaspoons instant minced onion or a few green onions, sliced
- ¼ cup olive oil
- Salt and pepper
- ½ cup mayonnaise
- Salad greens
- Chopped parsley

Combine first 7 ingredients. Add onion, oil, and salt and pepper to taste. Mix lightly but thoroughly. Toss lightly with mayonnaise. Arrange greens on platter. Top with salad and sprinkle with parsley. Makes 4 servings.

HAM-CHEESE-VEGETABLE SALAD

- ¼ pound sliced cooked ham
- ¼ pound Swiss cheese
- 4 stalks celery
- 2 tomatoes, peeled and cut in eighths
- French dressing
- Salad greens

Cut ham, cheese and celery in thin strips. Add tomatoes, and French dressing to moisten. Toss lightly and serve on greens. Makes 4 servings.

PICKLED GARDEN RELISH

- 1 small head cauliflower, broken in flowerets and sliced
- 2 medium carrots, cut in medium 2-inch strips
- 2 stalks celery, cut in 1-inch pieces
- 1 green pepper, cut in medium 2-inch strips
- 1 jar (4 ounces) pimiento, drained and cut in strips
- 1 jar (2 ounces) pimiento-stuffed olives, drained
- ¾ cup wine vinegar
- ½ cup salad oil
- 2 tablespoons sugar
- 1 teaspoon salt
- ½ teaspoon dried oregano
- ¼ teaspoon pepper
- ½ cup water

Combine all ingredients in large skillet. Bring to boil, stirring occasionally. Cover and simmer 5 to 7 minutes. Cool. Refrigerate, covered, about 24 hours before serving. Will keep, refrigerated, at least a week. Makes about 2 quarts.

SANDWICHES AND BREADS

HOT WESTERN SANDWICHES

- 8 frankfurter rolls
- Butter or margarine
- ⅓ cup each finely chopped green onion and green pepper
- ¾ cup minced ham
- 6 eggs, slightly beaten
- ¾ cup milk
- ½ teaspoon salt
- Freshly ground black pepper
- Grated Parmesan cheese

Open rolls, spread with butter and place, buttered side up, on baking sheet. In skillet, melt 1 tablespoon butter. Add green onion, pepper and ham and sauté, stirring, a few minutes. Transfer to mixing bowl. Cool slightly, then stir in eggs, milk and seasonings. In small buttered heated skillet, cook 8 individual omelets, using about ½ cup egg mixture for each. Cook only until still slightly creamy. Roll up and place one on bottom part of each roll. Sprinkle with cheese and, just before serving, toast under broiler 2 minutes. Close sandwiches and serve at once. Makes 8 servings.

QUICK SLOPPY JOES

- 1 pound ground beef
- ¼ cup chopped onion
- ⅛ teaspoon dried oregano
- 1 can (10¼ ounce) condensed minestrone soup
- ½ cup water
- ⅓ cup catsup
- 4 sandwich rolls, split and toasted

Brown beef and onion lightly. Add remaining ingredients, except rolls, and simmer about 5 minutes, stirring occasionally. Serve on rolls. Makes 4 servings.

SAN FRANCISCO SANDWICHES

Split sourdough (or hard) rolls and fill with thinly sliced salami and Monterey Jack cheese slices. Add thin rings of green pepper. (Use Cheddar if Monterey Jack is not available.)

TROPICAL SANDWICHES

- 1 cup creamed cottage cheese
- ¼ cup mayonnaise
- ⅓ cup drained crushed pineapple
- ⅓ cup chopped dates
- Sliced dark bread

Combine first 4 ingredients. Chill and serve between slices of bread. Makes enough filling for 4 to 6 sandwiches.

SUMMER

EGG-SALAD SANDWICHES

1 package (8 ounces) cream cheese, softened
¼ cup minced onion
¼ cup finely chopped green pepper
3 tablespoons chili sauce
⅔ cup chopped walnuts
5 hard-cooked eggs, finely chopped
½ teaspoon salt
Dash of pepper
12 slices bread
Butter or margarine, softened

Mix thoroughly all ingredients, except last 2. Spread 6 slices of bread with mixture. Spread remaining bread with butter and close sandwiches. Makes about 2½ cups filling, or enough for 6 sandwiches.

UPSIDE-DOWN APPLE ROLLS

⅓ cup butter or margarine
½ cup firmly packed light-brown sugar
1 cup finely chopped apple
½ cup seedless raisins
Ground nutmeg
4 or 5 sandwich rolls, split

Melt butter in 13 x 9 x 2-inch pan in preheated moderate oven (350°F.). Add next 3 ingredients and a sprinkling of nutmeg; mix in pan. Arrange roll halves on the mixture, cut sides down. Press down and bake about 10 minutes. Invert pan on platter or waxed paper and serve warm, fruit side up. Makes 8 to 10.

DEVILED-HAM PANCAKES WITH CHEESE SAUCE

3 eggs
1½ cups milk
1½ cups pancake mix
Butter or margarine
2 cans (4½ ounces each) deviled ham
1 cup (10½ ounces) condensed cheese soup, heated

Beat eggs, add milk and pancake mix and beat until smooth. Let stand ½ hour, then beat again. Melt 1 teaspoon butter in 7-inch skillet and pour in 2 tablespoons batter. Rotate pan so batter completely covers surface. Brown lightly on both sides. Spread with deviled ham, roll and put in warm serving dish. Repeat until all of batter is used, making about 18. Serve with cheese sauce. Makes 4 to 6 servings.

QUICK OLIVE-NUT BREAD

2¼ cups buttermilk biscuit mix
½ cup sugar
1 egg, slightly beaten
¾ cup milk
1 cup chopped walnuts or other nuts
1 cup chopped pimiento-stuffed olives

Put mix and sugar in bowl. Combine egg and milk and add to ingredients in bowl. Mix only enough to moisten dry ingredients. Fold in nuts and olives and put in greased 9 x 5 x 3-inch loaf pan. Bake in preheated moderate oven (350°F.) about 45 minutes. Turn out on rack, then turn right side up and cool thoroughly before cutting (use thin knife because loaf crumbles easily). Good with cream cheese.

PATIO CRACKLIN' BREAD

½ cup crushed cracklings (French fried pork rinds)
¾ cup crushed onion snacks
1¼ teaspoons lemon-pepper seasoning
2 cans (8 ounces each) refrigerated biscuits
⅓ cup butter or margarine, melted

In small plastic bag, crush separately with rolling pin enough cracklings and onion snacks to make desired amount. Put in bowl with seasoning and mix well. Butter a 9 x 5 x 3-inch loaf pan. Separate biscuits, dip in butter, then in crushed mixture on one side only. Alternating dipped and plain sides, set on edge in rows of 10 each in buttered pan (4 end biscuits can be dipped on both sides, if preferred; this makes a crunchier loaf). Sprinkle any remaining mixture over loaf and drizzle with any remaining butter. Bake in preheated moderate oven (375°F.) 20 minutes, or until a deep crusty brown. Invert on serving plate and serve hot.

Cheesed Onion Bread

Follow above recipe, substituting an equal amount of French-fried cheese snacks for the cracklings.

SAVORY TOASTED BREADSTICKS

Cut French bread in 4-inch lengths, then in quarters. Brush cut sides with melted butter or margarine. Put in shallow pan in one layer and sprinkle with any of the following: sesame seed, poppy seed, frozen chopped chives, grated Parmesan or Cheddar cheese sprinkled with caraway seed. Or put sprinkling ingredients on waxed paper and press cut sides of bread into ingredients. Bake in preheated hot oven (425°F.) 8 minutes, or until toasted. Serve hot.

DESSERTS

FROZEN RAINBOW DESSERT

1 dozen coconut macaroons
2 cups heavy cream
1 pint each lime, raspberry and lemon sherbets (or other available contrasting flavors and colors)

Toast macaroons in preheated slow oven (300°F.) 10 minutes. Cool, then crush into medium-fine crumbs. Whip cream just until thickened but not stiff. Fold in crumbs.

Line a 9 x 5 x 3-inch loaf pan with foil extending 2 inches above edge of pan. Spread about a third of mixture on bottom of pan. Using half of each, quickly spoon sherbets in layers on top. Cover with another third of cream mixture. Repeat layers (pan will be heaping full). Freeze overnight or until firm. About 15 minutes before serving, lift out of pan, remove foil and set right side up on serving dish. Let stand at room temperature about 10 minutes, then cut in slices. Makes 10 to 12 servings.

GLAZED FRUIT PIE

- 1 package (3¾ ounces) vanilla, banana, pineapple or coconut-cream instant pudding
- 2 cups milk
  Cointreau
- 1 baked 8 or 9-inch pastry shell
  Canned apricot halves and sliced peaches, well drained, or a combination of fruits such as sliced bananas, apricot halves, seedless grapes and blueberries
- 3 tablespoons apricot or peach jam

Prepare pudding with milk as directed on label, flavor with 2 teaspoons Cointreau and pour into shell; chill. Arrange fruit on top, then spread with jam mixed with 1 tablespoon Cointreau. Chill until ready to serve.
NOTE: If desired, substitute ice cream for the pudding; top with preferred fruit and glaze.

STOVE-TOP CHOCOLATE BREAD PUDDING

- 1 square (1 ounce) unsweetened chocolate
- 1½ cups milk
- 2 cups cubed bread, crusts trimmed
- 1 egg, beaten
- ¼ cup sugar
- ⅛ teaspoon salt
- 1 teaspoon vanilla extract
- 8 large marshmallows, quartered
  Cream

In top part of double boiler over boiling water, melt chocolate in milk. Add remaining ingredients, except last 2. Cook, stirring frequently, 5 minutes, or until thickened. Fold in marshmallows and serve warm with cream. Makes 4 servings.

SKILLET FRUIT BETTY

- 1½ cups soft stale-bread cubes
- 2 tablespoons butter or margarine
- ½ cup honey
- 2 cups berries or thinly sliced peeled peaches or apples
  Cream or milk

Brown bread cubes in butter in skillet. Add honey and fruit, cover and cook 8 minutes, or until fruit is tender. Serve hot or cool with cream. Makes 4 servings.

SUMMER

BUTTERSCOTCH PARFAIT

- ¼ cup cornstarch
- ¼ teaspoon salt
- 2 cups milk
- 2 eggs, slightly beaten
- 1 package (6 ounces) butterscotch morsels
- 3 tablespoons butter
- 2 teaspoons grated orange rind
- 1 teaspoon vanilla extract
  Whipped cream
  Toasted coconut or chopped almonds (optional)

Mix first 2 ingredients in saucepan. Stir in milk and cook, stirring, until smooth and thickened. Stir a little into eggs, then add to remaining hot mixture. Cook, stirring, 1 minute longer. Remove from heat and add remaining ingredients, except whipped cream and coconut. Stir until morsels are melted and blended. Spoon into parfait glasses, alternating with whipped cream, and chill. Top with toasted coconut or chopped almonds, if desired. Makes 6 servings.

GINGERY ORANGE DESSERT

- 1 package (3 ounces) orange-flavor gelatin
- 1 cup boiling water
- 1 pint orange sherbet
- ½ cup heavy cream
- 1 tablespoon sugar
- 2 tablespoons finely chopped crystallized ginger
- 1 can (11 ounces) mandarin oranges, drained and chilled
  Additional mandarin oranges and whipped cream (optional)

Dissolve gelatin in boiling water. Gradually add sherbet and stir until dissolved. Chill until partially set, then beat until frothy. Fold in cream whipped with sugar. Then fold in ginger and oranges. Pour into 1½-quart mold or individual molds and chill until firm. Unmold and decorate with additional mandarin oranges and whipped cream, if desired. Makes 5 or 6 servings.

FRESH-MINT SHERBET

- 2 cups sugar
- 2 cups water
- 1 cup chopped fresh mint leaves
  Juice of 2 lemons
- 1 cup orange juice
  Green food coloring

Bring sugar and water to boil and cool. Add mint leaves and lemon juice and let stand about 1 hour, crushing and mashing leaves to extract the flavor. Add orange juice and tint with food coloring. Pour into freezing tray and freeze until mushy. Stir well and freeze until just firm. Makes 4 servings.

SUNDAE

RASPBERRY-GLAZED PEACHES

Put partially thawed frozen raspberries in blender and blend until thick. Serve over chilled canned peach halves.

CHOCOLATE-PUDDING FUDGE

- 1 box (4 ounces) chocolate pudding-and-pie-filling mix
- ⅓ cup firmly packed light-brown sugar
- ⅓ cup milk
- 12 large marshmallows
- 1⅛ cups sifted confectioners' sugar
- 1 teaspoon vanilla extract
- Pecan or walnut halves (optional)

Put first 3 ingredients in saucepan, bring to boil and boil hard, stirring, 1 minute. Remove from heat, add marshmallows and beat with spoon until blended. (If necessary, return to heat a few seconds.) Stir in remaining ingredients, except nuts, and spread in buttered 9 x 5-inch loaf pan. If desired, press 10 to 12 nut halves at intervals in top. Cool and cut in squares. Makes about ¾ pound.

BEVERAGES

MINTED TEA LEMONADE

- 2 tablespoons mint jelly
- 1 quart hot tea
- 1 can (6 ounces) frozen lemonade, reconstituted

Dissolve jelly in the tea. Mix with lemonade and chill thoroughly before serving. Makes about 1¾ quarts as directed.

SPICED ICED TEA

- ½ cup sugar
- Grated rind and juice of 1 lemon
- Grated rind and juice of 1 orange
- 1 piece (1 inch) cinnamon stick
- ½ teaspoon whole cloves
- ½ cup water
- 4 cups hot double-strength tea
- Lemon slices (optional)

Put all ingredients, except last 2, in small saucepan, bring to boil and simmer, stirring occasionally, 5 minutes. Strain, add to tea and chill. When ready to serve, pour into ice-filled tall glasses. Serve with lemon, if desired. Makes about 1½ quarts.

FLAVORED MILK

Flavor 1 glass whole or skim milk with 1 teaspoon (or to taste) vanilla or other bottled extract, such as lemon, orange or almond.

DIETER'S ICE MILK SODA

Half-fill each glass with orange juice. Add ice milk and fill glass with cold low-calorie citrus-flavored carbonated beverage. Top with shredded orange rind.

ORANGE BLUSH

Combine in pitcher 1 can (6 ounces) partially thawed frozen orange-juice concentrate, 1½ cups cranberry-juice cocktail, ¼ cup sugar and 2 cups carbonated water. Serve over ice cubes. Makes 1 quart, or four 8-ounce servings.

BANANA-BERRY COOLER

Mix well 1 mashed ripe banana, 1 cup chilled cranberry-juice cocktail and the juice of ¼ lime. (Whirl in blender if available.) Pour into tall glass and top with a scoop of sherbet or ice milk.

SUNDAE—A dish consisting of ice cream topped with a sauce or sauces, with the optional addition of such garnishes as nuts, cherries, fruits, and whipped cream. There is no limit to the variations possible in sundaes.

SUNFISH—One of a large group of fresh-water fish which are closely related to the perches and include the bluegill, crappie, and calico bass, commonly called "sunnies." Their bright coloring and interesting shapes as well as their courage make them an excellent game fish for fishermen. They are not fished commercially.

Sunfish are generally panfried or broiled.

PANFRIED SUNFISH WITH DILL SAUCE

- 4 sunfish, cleaned
- Undiluted evaporated milk
- ¼ cup each all-purpose flour and cornmeal
- ½ teaspoon salt
- Dash of pepper
- Cooking oil
- Dill Sauce

Wipe fish with a damp cloth or paper towel. Dip into evaporated milk and roll in mixture of flour, cornmeal, and seasonings. Fry in small amount of hot oil for 3 to 5 minutes on each side, turning carefully with fork or flat turner. Add more oil as needed. Do not overcook. Serve with Dill Sauce. Makes 4 servings.

Dill Sauce

Melt 2 tablespoons butter or margarine and blend in 2 tablespoons all-purpose flour. Gradually add 1 cup milk and cook, stirring constantly, until thickened. Add 3 tablespoons minced fresh dill and season to taste.

SWEDISH COOKERY

by Nika Hazelton

Sweden is a prosperous country, and her standard of living is reflected in her food, which is by far the most varied of all Scandinavian food. The Swedes eat well. Although their food is bland, as is all Scandinavian food, it is not nearly as bland as that of other countries. The Swedes like flavorings; anchovies are much admired, dill is the national food plant, cardamom and spices are used in baking. The Swedes are also fond of sweetened foods. In all of Scandinavia sugar is used far more in nonsweet cooking than it is in America, but the Swedes use much more sugar than other Scandinavians.

The one thing the Swedes don't serve any more is the enormous smorgasbord that we Americans find in our Swedish restaurants and on such festive occasions as weddings, church suppers, or club socials. At a dinner party, the usual smorgasbord consists of four or five appetizers at the outside. There will be herring in some form or other, smoked salmon, a homemade liver pâté, and a cheese.

The Swedes eat a good many nourishing soups, including fruit soups, and much fish and seafood. The salmon is excellent, and so is the fresh-water fish such as pike. Lobsters are hightly thought of, and boiled crayfish, which look like miniature lobsters and are not shrimps, are the national passion. Their season is August to September, and they are the reason for most congenial parties, open-air ones preferably, held under a shiny moon, with much *akvavit,* beer, and all-round merriment.

Far more meat is eaten at everyday family meals in Sweden than in the other Scandinavian countries. Pork, lamb, and veal are boiled, pot-roasted, or minced in the ubiquitous meatballs. Oven roasts such as we and the English like, are not common, and beef is not as good as in the United States. The meats, of course, come with rich, delicious cream gravies. Chicken, as in all Scandinavia, is a party dish and a treat, although it is becoming less expensive. Goose, on the other hand, is a national bird, roasted with a stuffing of apples and prunes. Game and game birds, from the enormous Swedish forests, are common, and they are usually pot-roasted with bacon and cream.

The variety and excellence of baked foods is staggering. The American visitor in a Swedish home, especially in the country districts, finds it almost impossible to believe that Swedish women can bake so much, so well, and so often. Swedish home baking, to be consumed with coffee, is about the best in the world.

Sweden's present food habits are in an interesting state of transition between the old and the new. On one hand we have a national cuisine of traditional foods, to be eaten in a ritual manner especially on holidays. Among them are the sausages, the Shrove Tuesday buns, the Christmas lutfisk, to mention a few—all of them dishes which for the conservative Swedes have an almost mystical significance. On the other hand, these same Swedes—prosperous, traveled, and well versed in foreign affairs—are the producers and consumer of the most modern canned and frozen foods. They are also thoroughly sophisticated in their restaruant food, which is French influenced, as is the restaurant food in all of Scandinavia. In the clear air of the North, their cuisine seems infinitely richer than other European countries, with combinations of meats and vegetables, or fish and vegetables, and a predilection for cream sauces that are typically Swedish.

APPETIZERS

FÅGELBON
[Birds' Nests]

- 12 to 16 anchovy fillets, chopped
- 4 egg yolks
- 4 tablespoons minced onion
- 2 tablespoons capers
- 4 tablespoons minced parsley
- 4 tablespoons minced pickled beets

Make nests on a large platter or on 4 individual serving plates. Allowing one-fourth of the ingredients for each serving, arrange each ingredient in a circle. First, arrange anchovies, leaving space for an egg yolk in the center. Surround anchovies with a circle of onion. Then follow with circles of capers, parsley, and beets. Drop an egg yolk into center of each dish. If nests are on a large platter, the first person served mixes the ingredients together well. If on individual plates, each person mixes his own. Makes 4 servings.

GRAVAD LAX MED SENAPSSÅS
[Marinated Salmon with Mustard Sauce]

- 1 middle-cut piece of salmon (3 pounds)
- 6 tablespoons salt
- 3 tablespoons sugar
- 3 teaspoons coarsely crushed white peppercorns
- 1 large bunch of fresh dill
  Lemon wedges, freshly ground pepper, and dill for garnish
  Mustard Sauce

Cut fish along the back into 2 fillets. Carefully remove backbone. Wipe fillets with damp paper towel. Mix salt, sugar, and crushed pepper. Rub part of mixture into fish fillets. Put a thick layer of dill sprigs in the bottom of a dish about the size of salmon fillets. Put 1 fillet, skin side down, on dill layer. Sprinkle with salt mixture. Add more dill sprigs. Put remaining fish fillet, skin side up, on dill. Sprinkle with remaining seasonings and dill. Put a board or plate on top of fish and weight down. Refrigerate for 16 to 24 hours. Scrape fish and cut away from the skin into ⅛-inch slices or ½-inch slices if served as a main dish. Arrange on platter and garnish with lemon wedges,

SWEDISH COOKERY

pepper, and dill. Serve with the Mustard Sauce. If desired, serve salmon with tiny, piping hot dill potatoes, or with toast. Keeps for 2 weeks in refrigerator. Makes 8 to 10 servings.
NOTE: The skin is delicious cut into ½-inch-wide strips and panbroiled for 5 or 6 minutes, or until crisp and well browned.

Senapssås
[Mustard Sauce]

With wire whisk, blend 3 tablespoons prepared mustard, 3 tablespoons sugar, 1 tablespoon cider vinegar, 3 tablespoons salad oil, and ¼ teaspoon salt. Add freshly ground pepper to taste. Chill. Just before serving, add 3 tablespoons finely chopped fresh dill.

SMÅ KÖTTBULLAR
[Small Meatballs]

- 2 tablespoons fine dry bread crumbs
- ⅓ cup water
- ⅓ cup light cream
- ¾ pound ground lean beef
- ¼ pound ground veal
- 1 teaspoon salt
  Freshly ground pepper
- 1 teaspoon cornstarch
- 1 tablespoon grated onion
- ⅓ cup butter or margarine

Mix crumbs, water, and cream and let stand for 10 to 15 minutes. Add remaining ingredients except butter and mix well. Dip hands into cold water and shape meat into small balls about ¾ inch in diameter. Fry a few at a time in browned butter, shaking pan now and then to make balls round and browned on all sides and of desired doneness. Serve warm in a chafing dish, or cold for sandwiches. Makes about 5 dozen meatballs.

SILL OCH SKINKSALAD
[Herring and Ham Salad]

- 1 salt herring
- 1 cup each diced cooked potatoes, pickled beets, and diced apples
- 1 cup diced cooked ham (optional)
- ½ cup diced dill pickles
- ¼ cup minced onion
- ¼ cup liquid from pickled beets
- 2 tablespoons sugar
  Freshly ground pepper
- 2 hard-cooked eggs, chopped
  Parsley
- 1 cup dairy sour cream
  Hot toast

Clean herring and cut into boneless fillets. Cover generously with cold water and let stand for 10 to 12 hours. Drain and rinse; drain. With scissors, cut fish into ⅛-inch pieces. Combine fish, potatoes, beets, apples, ham (if used), pickles, and onion. Mix lightly but thoroughly. Mix liquid from beets with sugar and pepper. Gently stir into fish mixture. Pack into 1-quart mold rinsed with cold water; chill. Unmold and garnish with chopped egg and parsley. Serve with sour cream and toast. Salad may be arranged on lettuce, if desired. Makes 6 to 8 servings.

SOUPS

BRUNKÅLSSOPPA
[Brown Cabbage Soup]

- 1 large head cabbage, cored and shredded
- ¼ cup butter or margarine
- 3 tablespoons firmly packed brown sugar
- 4 cups beef bouillon or more, depending on consistency of soup desired
- 1 teaspoon salt
- ½ teaspoon pepper
- ¼ teaspoon ground allspice

In a deep kettle brown cabbage in hot butter on all sides. The color should be a light brown. Stir occasionally. Add sugar and cook, stirring constantly, until sugar is completely dissolved. Add bouillon, salt, pepper, and allspice. Simmer, covered, about 1 hour. Serve with dumplings. Makes 6 to 8 servings.

ÄRTER OCH FLÄSK
[Yellow Pea Soup]

- 1 pound dried yellow Swedish peas (see Note)
- 3 quarts water
- 1 pound fresh pork shoulder
- 1 smoked ham shank (about 2 pounds)
- 1 large onion
- 1 celery stalk
  Salt
- 3 whole cloves
  Prepared mustard
- ½ teaspoon ground ginger
- ½ teaspoon dried thyme

Wash peas and put in heavy kettle. Add water and let stand overnight. Do not discard water. Bring quickly to boil and boil vigorously about 10 minutes. Remove any scum or skins from top. Reduce heat and simmer for 2 hours. Add meats, whole onion, celery, 3 teaspoons salt, and cloves. Simmer for 1 hour longer, or until meat and peas are tender. Remove meat, cut into slices, and serve separately with prepared mustard. Season soup with ginger, thyme leaves, and more salt, if necessary. If too thick, add a little water. Makes about 2 quarts.
NOTE: Dried yellow Swedish peas are available in Scandinavian food stores. Dried yellow split peas can be substituted.

ÄPPELSOPPA
[Apple Soup]

- 6 juicy fairly tart apples
- 1½ cups dried apples, washed and soaked
- Water
- Thin peel of ¼ lemon
- 1 cinnamon stick
- ⅔ cup sugar
- 1½ to 2 tablespoons cornstarch or potato flour
- ¼ cup Madeira, white wine, or fresh lemon juice
- Whipped cream
- Rusks
- Garnish: mint sprig, cluster of ripe currants, or cherry

Wash apples, drain, core, and cube; combine with drained soaked dried apples in enamelware saucepan; add 7 cups water and bring to boil. Add lemon peel and cinnamon stick. Cook only until apples are tender; put through wire sieve. Reheat with sugar. When boiling, mix the cornstarch with ½ cup cold water and stir into boiling soup. Stir and boil for 3 minutes, or until clear. (With potato flour, boil about 10 minutes.) Add wine. Remove from heat. Chill thoroughly. Serve in iced bowls, with whipped cream and rusks. Garnish each serving as desired. Makes 6 or more servings.

FISH

STEKT SILL ELLER STRÖMMING
[Fried Herring or Smelt Fillets]

Excellent also when made with filleted mackerel

- 2 pounds herring or smelt fillets
- 1 teaspoon salt
- ¼ teaspoon white pepper
- ½ cup butter or margarine
- 1 cup chopped parsley or ½ cup chopped dill
- 2 eggs, beaten
- 2 cups fine dry bread crumbs

Wash fish fillets in ice water. Dry on absorbent paper. Sprinkle with salt and pepper. Blend ¼ cup butter with parsley. Spread on fish fillets and put together like a sandwich. Dip fish sandwiches into beaten eggs and roll in bread crumbs. Shake free of excessive crumbs. Chill for 15 to 30 minutes. (This is not strictly necessary, but fish fries more easily.) Melt remaining ¼ cup butter and fry fish sandwiches until golden on all sides. Serve with mashed potatoes and a salad. Makes 6 servings.

KOKT LUTFISK
[Boiled Lutfisk]

A must for a Swedish Christmas. Lutfisk is cod treated with lime, and in the old days this treatment took place at home.

- 3 pounds prepared lutfisk, cut into serving pieces
- Salt
- ½ cup boiling water (about)
- Pepper
- Dry mustard
- Ground allspice

Lutfisk is delicate to handle and it is best to place the pieces in a piece of cheesecloth, tying the ends.

Boil salt and water in large deep frying pan. Add lutfisk, either wrapped in a cheesecloth or in pieces, skin side down. Cover pan and bring to simmering, not boiling, point. Simmer for 10 to 15 minutes, or until fish flakes easily. Lift out fish carefully and drain well. Place on hot platter and remove skin and fins. Serve with pepper, a dash of dry mustard, and a dash of ground allspice; good with boiled potatoes and a cream sauce. These are the classic Swedish Christmas foods to go with lutfisk. Makes 6 servings.

FISKGRYTA
[Fish with Onions and Tomatoes]

- 2 medium onions, sliced
- 2 tablespoons butter or margarine
- 1½ pounds fillet of sole, cod, or flounder
- 1 tablespoon lemon juice
- 1 teaspoon salt
- 4 medium tomatoes, sliced ¼ inch thick
- Pepper
- ¼ cup white wine
- 3 tablespoons chopped parsley or dill

In a heavy saucepan, sauté onions in butter until soft and golden. Wipe fish with a damp cloth and cut into serving pieces. Sprinkle with lemon juice and salt. Arrange fish pieces on top of onions. Cover with tomato slices and sprinkle with pepper. Pour wine over top, cover, and simmer for 10 to 15 minutes. Add parsley. Good with riced potatoes. Makes 4 to 6 servings.

MEAT

BIFF À LA LINDSTRÖM
[Beef Lindström]

- 2 pounds ground steak
- 3 egg yolks
- ¾ cup mashed potatoes
- 2 teaspoons salt
- ½ teaspoon pepper
- ¼ cup heavy cream
- ¾ cup finely chopped cooked beets or pickled beets
- ⅓ cup finely chopped onion
- ⅓ cup chopped capers
- Butter

Blend together meat, egg yolks, mashed potatoes, and salt and pepper. Gradually beat in cream. Combine beets, onion, and capers, and blend into mixture. Shape into large flat patties and fry quickly in butter on both sides. Makes 6 to 8 servings.

NOTE: In Sweden, Beef Lindström is often served with a fried egg on top.

Kalvkotlett à la Oscar

KALVKOTLETT À LA OSCAR
[Veal Cutlet à la Oscar]

This combination of the tenderest veal, lobster, asparagus, and Béarnaise sauce is a specialty of first-class Scandinavian restaurants. The asparagus used in Sweden is snow white and very tender. This kind of asparagus can be bought here in specialty stores imported in glass jars.

- 2½ pounds boneless rump of veal, cut ¾ inch thick
- 1 teaspoon salt
- ¼ teaspoon white pepper
- ¼ cup butter or margarine
- 12 stalks of hot cooked asparagus, tender part only
- 1½ cups cut up cooked lobster meat
- 1½ cups Béarnaise Sauce
- Parsley sprigs

Cut meat into 6 round serving pieces and trim away all fat and gristle. Rub meat with salt and pepper. Melt butter in large skillet. Over medium heat cook meat until golden on both sides. Reduce heat and simmer, covered, for 10 to 15 minutes, or until meat is tender and cooked through. Arrange meat on hot serving platter. Place 2 asparagus spears on top of each round. Top with lobster. Cover with Béarnaise sauce and decorate with parsley sprigs. Serve with browned potatoes and a tossed green salad. Makes 6 servings.

PYTT I PANNA
[Swedish Hash]

- 6 tablespoons butter or margarine
- 3 medium onions, diced
- 3 cups diced peeled boiled potatoes
- 3 cups diced cooked meat
- Salt and pepper to taste
- 4 to 6 fried eggs
- Cucumber pickles, sliced

Heat 2 tablespoons butter and cook onions until soft and golden. Transfer to hot plate. Brown potatoes in 2 tablespoons butter and transfer to hot plate. Brown meat in remaining 2 tablespoons butter. Return onions and potatoes to skillet and mix thoroughly with meat. Season with salt and pepper and heat through. Arrange on hot platter and garnish with fried eggs (1 for each serving) and sliced cucumber pickles. Makes 4 to 6 servings.

VEGETABLES AND SALADS

KÅLSALLAD MED LINGON
[Cabbage Salad with Lingonberries]

- 2 cups finely shredded white cabbage
- ¾ cup lingonberries

Mix ingredients and toss lightly. Serve with any kind of meat. Especially good with broiled or fried liver, also with fried fish. Makes 4 servings.

SKÅNSK POTATIS
[Swedish Creamed Potatoes]

- 6 tablespoons butter or margarine
- 2 medium onions, sliced thin
- 6 cups diced peeled raw potatoes
- 1½ teaspoons salt
- ¼ teaspoon white pepper
- 1 cup light cream, or more (see Note)
- 3 tablespoons minced parsley or fresh dill

Heat 2 tablespoons butter in skillet and cook onions until soft and golden. Transfer onions to casserole. Heat remaining ¼ cup butter and sauté potatoes until golden-brown and half-cooked. Transfer potatoes to casserole. Season with salt and pepper and mix thoroughly with onions; add cream. Simmer, covered, over lowest possible heat about 15 minutes, or until potatoes are done. The cream should be absorbed and the potatoes creamy. Stir occasionally and check for dryness; if necessary add more cream, a little at a time. Before serving, sprinkle with parsley. Makes 6 servings.

NOTE: It is impossible to give accurate amounts for cream. Different kinds of potatoes will absorb different amounts of cream, and the absorption of cream depends also on the shape of the casserole. However, the dish is very easy to make; all it needs is a little attention.

POTATIS OCH SVAMP
[Potatoes and Mushrooms]

- 4 cups hot mashed potatoes
- 2 eggs, beaten
- 1 teaspoon salt
- ½ teaspoon pepper
- ⅛ teaspoon ground cardamom
- 1 pound mushrooms, sliced
- 6 tablespoons butter or margarine
- ⅓ cup chopped chives or parsley

Combine potatoes, eggs, salt, pepper, and cardamom and mix thoroughly. Sauté mushrooms in ¼ cup hot butter until just limp. They must be still firm. Place mushrooms into the bottoms of 4 individual well-buttered baking dishes 4½ x 6 inches. Top with a border of mashed potatoes piped through a tube in decorative swirls. Or else, use a fork and score the border with the fork to make a pattern. Paint potatoes with remaining 2 tablespoons butter, melted, and sprinkle with chives. Bake in preheated hot oven (425°F.) about 15 minutes, or until potatoes are slightly browned. Or broil under medium broiler for about 5 minutes. Makes 4 servings.

SWEDISH COOKERY

RÖDBETSSALLAD MED ÄPPLEN
[Beet Salad with Apples]

- 1 jar (1 pound) pickled sliced beets
- 2 medium tart apples
- 2 tablespoons mayonnaise
- 1 tablespoon sugar
- ⅛ teaspoon salt
- Freshly ground pepper
- 2 tablespoons chopped parsley

Drain beets and cut into strips ¼ inch thick. Peel apples and dice finely. Mix beets, apples, mayonnaise, sugar, salt, and pepper to taste. Toss ingredients lightly together. Garnish with chopped parsley. Serve with meat or fish. Makes 4 to 6 servings.

SAUCES

SAUCES FOR FISH AND MEATS

Swedish cooks are famous for their sharp dill-flavored sauces and those in which mustard and wine combine for pungent good flavor. Many Scandinavian sauces are well known to American cooks, such as currant-jelly sauces for game, caper sauces for boiled fish, wine sauces for ham and game. But their piquant sauces created for shellfish and smoked salmon are among the great sauces of the world's cuisine. Here is the famous *Skarpsås* which is served with any cold fish or shellfish, and as dressing for meat and fish salads.

KAPRISSÅS
[Caper Sauce]

For pork chops and for fried fish and meats

- 1 small onion, chopped
- 1 tablespoon butter
- 3 anchovy fillets, minced, or 2 tablespoons anchovy paste
- 3 tablespoons capers
- 3 tablespoons chopped parsley
- 1½ teaspoons all-purpose flour
- ½ cup chicken bouillon
- ½ cup mild vinegar

Brown onion in butter. Add anchovies, capers, and parsley; stir in flour. Add bouillon and vinegar and simmer, covered, for 10 minutes, stirring frequently. (For a thinner sauce, add a little more bouillon.) If made for pork chops, pour sauce over chops before serving. If for fried fish or meats, serve separately. Makes about 1½ cups.

SKARPSÅS
[Sharp Dill Sauce]

- 1 cup wine vinegar
- 1 tablespoon lemon juice
- ¼ cup sugar
- Dash of hot pepper sauce
- 1 tablespoon onion juice
- 1 tablespoon dry mustard
- ⅛ teaspoon cayenne
- 2 tablespoons chopped fresh dill

Combine all ingredients in wide-mouthed bottle or glass jar and shake it well. Chill. Shake sauce again before using. Makes about 1½ cups.

BREADS AND DUMPLINGS

RÅGBRÖD
[Rye Bread]

A very good, easy bread

- 1 cup milk
- 1 package active dry yeast or 1 cake compressed yeast
- 2 tablespoons sugar
- Water*
- 4½ cups all-purpose flour
- ¾ cup dark corn syrup
- 1 teaspoon fennel seeds
- 1 teaspoon aniseed
- ⅓ cup butter or margarine
- Grated rind of 1 orange
- 1½ teaspoons salt
- 3 cups rye flour

Scald milk and cool to lukewarm. Sprinkle or crumble yeast and sugar into 1 cup water. *Use very warm water (105°F. to 115°F.) for dry yeast; use lukewarm (80°F. to 90°F.) for compressed. Let stand for a few minutes, then stir until dissolved. Stir in milk. Beat in 3 cups all-purpose flour. Cover and let rise until doubled in bulk, 1 to 1½ hours. Combine syrup, fennel, and aniseed in saucepan and bring to boiling point. Cool to lukewarm. Beat syrup, butter, orange rind, and salt into risen batter. Stir in rye flour and 1 cup all-purpose flour. Use remaining ½ cup flour for kneading; sprinkle some on bread board and turn dough onto it. Knead with floured hands until smooth and elastic. Place in greased bowl, turn to grease on all sides, and let rise until doubled in bulk, 30 minutes to 2 hours. Shape dough into 2 loaves. Grease 2 bread pans 9 x 5 x 3 inches and place loaves in pans. Cover and let rise until doubled in bulk, about 50 minutes. Bake in preheated moderate oven (375°F.) for 35 minutes. Brush with lukewarm water and bake for 5 minutes longer. Makes 2 loaves.

SEMLOR
[Shrove Tuesday Buns]

Traditionally served on Shrove Tuesday and throughout Lent, and often accompanied by hot milk with cinnamon

- 1 package active dry yeast or 1 cake compressed yeast
- ¼ cup water*
- 1 egg, slightly beaten
- ⅔ cup lukewarm light cream
- ¼ cup sugar
- 1 teaspoon salt
- ½ teaspoon ground cinnamon
- ½ cup butter or margarine, at room temperature
- 3 to 3¼ cups sifted all-purpose flour
- Almond paste
- Whipped cream
- Confectioners' sugar

Sprinkle or crumble yeast into water. *Use very warm water (105°F. to 115°F.) for dry yeast; use lukewarm (80°F. to 90°F.) for compressed. Let stand for a few minutes, then stir until dissolved. Stir in half of beaten egg (reserve other half), cream, sugar, salt, cinnamon, and butter. Mix thoroughly. Add flour, a little at a time, and beat to make a soft dough. Turn out dough on floured surface and knead about 10 minutes, or until dough is smooth and elastic. Place dough in greased bowl and turn to grease on all sides. Cover and let rise until doubled in bulk, 1 to 1½ hours. Punch down risen dough and knead on floured board until smooth. Shape dough into 10 or 12 round buns. Place buns on greased cookie sheet. Cover and let rise until almost doubled in size. Brush with reserved egg. Bake in preheated hot oven (400°F.) for 10 to 12 minutes, or until golden brown. Cool on racks. Cut off tops of buns with a sharp knife. Insert a wafer-thin piece of almond paste into each bun. Top with whipped cream. Replace top of bun and sprinkle with confectioners' sugar. Makes 10 to 12.

POTATISBULLAR
[Swedish Potato Dumplings]

For soup or as a main course, served with butter or a sauce

- ¼ cup butter or margarine
- 2 egg yolks
- ½ cup fine dry bread crumbs
- ½ cup firmly packed mashed potatoes
- ¼ teaspoon salt
- 1 cup ½-inch cubes ham or luncheon meat

Cream butter and beat in egg yolks. Stir in bread crumbs, potatoes, and salt. Mix thoroughly. Knead and shape into a long roll. Cut off pieces about the size of a walnut. Flatten each piece in the hand and place a cube of ham in middle. Shape into a round dumpling enclosing ham completely. Cook uncovered in simmering soup or simmering water for 10 minutes. Cover and cook for 5 minutes longer. Makes 6 servings.

SWEDISH COOKERY

CAKE, PASTRY AND COOKIES

MAZARINTÅRTA
[Mazarin Torte]

One of the most famous of Swedish cakes

- 1⅓ cups sifted all-purpose flour
- 1 teaspoon baking powder
- ⅓ cup sugar
- ½ cup butter
- 1 egg
- ⅔ cup raspberry jam
- Filling
- Lemon Icing

Into deep bowl sift together flour, baking powder, and sugar. Cut in butter and add egg. Mix together and knead with hands or spoon into a smooth dough. Chill while preparing Filling. Roll out chilled dough between 2 sheets of wax paper to fit bottom of 9-inch springform pan. Cut remaining dough into a strip and line sides of pan with it. Bring the dough at the bottom of the pan and the dough on the sides together so that they are tightly joined. This is done to prevent filling from oozing out during baking. Spread ⅓ cup raspberry jam over dough at bottom of the pan. Top with Filling. Bake in preheated moderate over (350°F.) about 50 minutes, or until torte tests done. Cool torte for 10 minutes. Remove sides of spring form pan and let torte cool entirely. When cold, spread with remaining ⅓ cup jam. Dribble Lemon Icing over top of jam. Makes 10 servings.

Filling

- ½ cup butter
- ⅔ cup sugar
- 1 cup ground blanched almonds
- ½ teaspoon vanilla extract
- 2 eggs

Cream butter; add sugar gradually and beat until fluffy. Add almonds and vanilla. Add eggs, one at a time, beating well after each addition.

Lemon Icing

Stir lemon juice gradually into 1 cup sifted confectioners' sugar, beating constantly until a good spreading consistency is reached.

SWEDISH COOKERY

PUNSCHKAKOR
[Punch Rings]

- ½ cup butter or margarine
- 1¼ cups sifted all-purpose flour
- 2 tablespoons Swedish punch or rum
- 1 egg, beaten
- ½ cup finely chopped almonds
- 2 tablespoons sugar

Cream butter until fluffy. Add flour and Swedish punch. Mix thoroughly with spoon or with hands. Roll out on wax paper to strips ½ x 4 inches. Shape strips into rings. Brush with egg. Combine almonds and sugar and sprinkle on top of cookies. Bake on buttered and floured cookie sheets in preheated moderate oven (350°F.) for 8 to 10 minutes, or until golden. Makes about 9 dozen.

KANELKAKOR
[Swedish Cinnamon Cookies]

These cookies are not the usual Central European cinnamon stars which are made with white of egg. They are very tender and flavorful cookies.

- ⅔ cup butter
- Sugar
- 1 egg
- 1 teaspoon vanilla extract
- 1⅓ cups sifted all-purpose flour
- 1 teaspoon baking powder
- Ground cinnamon
- ½ cup walnuts, finely chopped
- 2 tablespoons each ground cinnamon and sugar, mixed

Cream butter and gradually add 1 cup sugar. Beat in egg and vanilla. Sift flour with baking powder and 1 teaspoon cinnamon. Add to egg mixture and blend thoroughly. Chill for 30 minutes. Combine walnuts, and 2 tablespoons each cinnamon and sugar. Roll chilled dough into balls the size of walnuts. Roll each ball in walnut-cinnamon sugar. Place cookies on greased and floured cookie sheets about 3 inches apart. Bake about 12 minutes in preheated moderate oven (350°F.). Makes about 3 dozen cookies.

GOD JUL!

Christmas in Sweden is the most joyous and most important holiday of the entire year. It's a festival of lights when the nights are long and the days are dark and a season of feasting when the earth is bare and frozen—a celebration of faith and expectancy. Beginning with the first Sunday in Advent, when the first candle is lighted on the small Advent tree or wreath and a lighted star is hung in the window; continuing through Lucia Day, December 13, when the eldest daughter in the family, wearing a crown of seven candles, serves coffee, saffron buns and gingersnaps to her parents; and ending on January 13, Saint Canute's Day, when the children "rob" the Christmas tree, Swedish families follow their traditional Jul customs. High point of the holiday season is Christmas Eve, when the most elaborate meal of the year is served. Christmas Day is reserved for the family, and dinner is an intimate, rather simple, yet still special affair. The day after Christmas, also a holiday in Sweden, friends again come to call, and many of the Christmas Eve dishes are repeated. In fact, the same traditional dishes are served all during the holiday season.

PICKLED CUCUMBERS

- ½ cup white vinegar
- ¼ cup sugar
- ½ teaspoon salt
- ⅛ teaspoon white pepper
- 2 tablespoons water
- 2 medium cucumbers
- 2 tablespoons chopped parsley or dill

In small saucepan, mix first 5 ingredients; bring to boil. Cool. Partially peel cucumbers and slice thin. Put in serving dish and add vinegar mixture. Sprinkle with parsley. Refrigerate 2 to 3 hours before serving. Serve with Liver Pâté or other meats. Makes 4 servings.

Christmas Eve Menu: Christmas Ham; Spiced Prunes, Matjes Herring, Swedish Style, and Cumin Rye Rings

SWEDISH COOKERY

MATJESSILL, SVENSK STIL
[Matjes Herring, Swedish Style]

Herring, a great favorite of the Swedes, is usually accompanied by ice-cold aquavit and a beer chaser. These herring fillets, marinated in water, sugar, vinegar, salt and spices, have a mild salty flavor and are served as an hors d'oeuvre.

- 1 can (5 to 6 ounces) matjes herring, chilled
- 2 hard-cooked eggs, chopped
- Minced green onions, chives or red onions, or a mixture of all
- Dairy sour cream
- Dill sprigs (optional)
- Boiled potatoes
- Swedish crisp bread or Cumin Rye Rings

Drain herring well and cut in ½-inch slices. Arrange on platter and garnish with eggs, onions, sour cream and dill. Serve with additional sour cream, hot potatoes and crisp bread. Makes 4 servings.

NOTE: Herring and crisp bread are available in supermarkets or Scandinavian delicatessens.

LEVERPASTE
[Liver Pâté]

This can be made ahead and frozen. Serve as an hors d'oeuvre.

- 1 pound pork liver
- Milk
- 2 eggs
- ½ cup all-purpose flour
- 1 cup light cream
- 2 teaspoons salt
- 1½ teaspoons sugar
- ½ teaspoon white pepper
- ¼ teaspoon ground ginger
- ¼ teaspoon ground allspice
- ¼ pound fresh-pork fat
- 1 small onion
- Parsley
- Pickled Cucumbers

Cover liver with milk and let stand while preparing other ingredients. Combine ½ cup milk with next 8 ingredients and beat until smooth. Drain liver and pat dry with paper towels. Cut liver, fat and onion in small cubes. Put half the amount at a time in electric blender and whirl until smooth. Put in mixing bowl and add spice mixture a little at a time, beating well after each addition until smooth and well blended. Pour into buttered 9 x 5 x 3-inch loaf pan, cover with foil and bake in a water bath in preheated slow oven (325°F.) 1 hour. Remove foil and bake 30 minutes longer. Cool, then run a small spatula around edges to loosen; turn out on platter. Garnish with parsley and serve with cucumbers. Makes 20 servings.

JULSKINKA
[Christmas Ham]

The pride of the Swedish Christmas table is the ham. Many housewives still cure their own and bake or boil it for hours. Glazes and icings take on an astonishing variety. "Come taste my ham" is a typical invitation.

Traditionally, a carving or roasting fork decorated with paper frills is inserted into the ham for serving. To **make the frills,** cut two 20 x 5-inch strips of glazed colored gift wrap, colored tissue paper or colored foil. Fold each strip in half lengthwise with wrong side of paper facing out. Fold in half a second time (fold line will be 1¼ inches down); unfold second fold. Use second fold line as guide for depth of slits. Cut slits about ⅛ inch wide along folded side of strip. Unfold, turn so that right side is facing out and refold; fluff frills. Secure edges with plastic tape so strip will not unfold. Place one strip on top of other. Secure one end of strips with plastic tape to top of fork handle (handle should be about 5 inches long) and carefully twist both strips at once around handle. At base of handle, secure end strips with plastic tape.

NOTE: A skewer can be decorated in same manner. Frills can be a combination of colors or all one color.

The ham in recipe below can be baked and glazed a day or so ahead and iced just before serving.

- 1 ready-to-eat ham (10 to 12 pounds)
- 1 egg yolk
- 1½ teaspoons sugar
- 1 tablespoon prepared mustard
- 2 tablespoons fine dry bread crumbs
- Confectioners' Sugar Icing
- Spiced Prunes
- 1 polished red apple
- Homemade Mustard

Place ham in baking pan and bake in preheated slow oven (325°F.) 10 minutes per pound. Remove skin. Mix egg yolk, sugar and mustard until smooth, spread on ham and sprinkle with bread crumbs. Bake in preheated hot oven (400°F.) 15 to 20 minutes, or until golden brown; cool. Using heavy white paper, make a cone with a fine opening, fill with icing and decorate ham as desired. Garnish platter with prunes and apple. Serve ham cold in thin slices with Homemade Mustard. Makes 15 to 20 servings.

NOTE: Ham can also be baked, glazed and served warm with red cabbage. Store leftover ham, well wrapped in foil, in refrigerator.

HEMLAGAD SENAP
[Homemade Mustard]

An absolute must for Swedes; many housewives make their own.

- 1 tablespoon dry mustard
- 1 tablespoon sugar
- 1½ teaspoons all-purpose flour
- 1 tablespoon vegetable oil
- 1 teaspoon red-wine vinegar
- 2 tablespoons heavy cream

SWEDISH COOKERY

Combine dry ingredients. Add remaining ingredients and beat until smooth. Store, covered, in refrigerator. If mustard gets too thick, add more cream. Makes ¼ cup.

KALVSYLTA
[Jellied Veal]

Serve as an hors d'oeuvre or luncheon dish.

- 3½ to 4 pounds veal shanks, neck or breast
- 1 pound pork shank
- Water
- Salt
- 5 whole white peppercorns
- 5 whole allspice
- 2 bay leaves
- 1 medium onion, quartered
- Ground white pepper
- Pickled beets

Put meats in heavy kettle. Add water to cover and 1½ tablespoons salt. Bring to rapid boil and skim well. Add remaining ingredients, except last 2, and simmer slowly, covered, 1½ hours, or until meat is very tender. Take meat from broth and remove bones and gristle. Put bones back in broth and reduce broth while chopping meat very fine. Strain broth, return to kettle (you should have about equal parts broth and chopped meat) and add meat. Bring to boil and season with salt and white pepper to taste. Pour into mold rinsed in cold water and refrigerate overnight. Run small spatula around edge, dip mold in warm water and shake out on platter. Serve in slices with pickled beets. Makes 12 servings.

KUMMIN RÅG RINGAR
[Cumin Rye Rings]

Serve with herring.

- 3 envelopes active dry yeast
- 1½ cups whole rye flour
- 1½ cups all-purpose flour
- 2 teaspoons cumin seed
- 1½ teaspoons aniseed
- ½ teaspoon salt
- 3 tablespoons butter or margarine
- 1 cup milk
- 2 tablespoons dark corn syrup
- 2 tablespoons hot water

Combine first 6 ingredients in mixing bowl. Melt 2 tablespoons butter in small saucepan over low heat; add milk and syrup and heat until lukewarm. Pour over dry ingredients. With wooden spoon, beat until dough is smooth and leaves sides of bowl. Turn out on floured board and knead until smooth and elastic. Put in greased bowl, turning to grease top. Cover with plastic wrap or put bowl into large plastic bag. Let rise in warm place free from drafts 20 minutes, or until doubled in bulk. Punch down, turn out on lightly floured board and knead until smooth. Roll or pat dough ½ inch thick and prick with fork. Cut out 2½-inch rounds and, with thimble, cut ¾-inch hole just off center. Reroll scraps and cut. Put on greased baking sheet and let rise 10 minutes. Bake in preheated hot oven (425°F.) 10 minutes, or until well browned and light. Move to cake rack and brush with a mixture of hot water and remaining 1 tablespoon butter. Cover with towel. When cool, split rings with fork and serve with butter. Makes about 1 dozen.

NOTE: The large amount of yeast causes dough to rise quickly. Don't let it over-rise especially during second rising, or dough will fall flat. Rye flour can be obtained in healthfood or other specialty stores.

SPICED PRUNES

- 1 pound prunes with pits
- ½ cup sugar
- 1 to 2 teaspoons whole cloves
- 2 small strips lemon peel
- 1½ cups water

Put ingredients in saucepan. Slowly bring to boil, cover and simmer, stirring gently to cover prunes with syrup, about 20 minutes. Cool; chill. Makes 4 to 6 servings.

SAFFRANSBRÖD
[Saffron Bread]

Some kind of saffron bread is always served on Lucia Day, December 13. Saffron and raisins go together.

- 5 to 5½ cups all-purpose flour
- 2 envelopes active dry yeast
- ½ cup granulated sugar
- ½ teaspoon salt
- ½ teaspoon powdered saffron
- ½ cup margarine
- 1½ cups milk
- 2 eggs
- ½ cup seedless raisins
- Pearl sugar (see Note)
- Chopped almonds or other nuts

Measure flour onto waxed paper. Combine 3 cups flour and next 4 ingredients in large mixing bowl. Melt margarine over low heat and add milk (mixture should be lukewarm). Pour over dry ingredients, add 1 egg, beaten, and raisins. Beat with wooden spoon until smooth. Gradually add 2 cups flour or more if necessary to stiffen dough, beating until dough leaves sides of bowl. Turn out on floured board and knead until smooth and elastic. Put in greased bowl, turning to grease top. Cover and let rise in warm place free from drafts 30 minutes, or until doubled in bulk. Punch down, turn out on lightly floured board and knead until smooth. Divide dough in 2 equal parts. Pat or roll one part to 10-inch round and put on greased baking sheet. Divide remaining dough in 3 parts. Shape each part to ¾ inch thick rope. Braid and shape in wreath. Put wreath on top of circle and let rise in warm place about 20 minutes. Brush with remaining egg, beaten, and sprinkle with mixture of pearl sugar and nuts. Bake in preheated moderate oven (350°F.) 20 minutes, or until golden brown and done. Remove to cake rack, cover with towel and cool. Serve in wedges.

NOTE: Pearl sugar is available in Scandinavian delicatessens, or substitute granulated sugar.

SWEDISH COOKERY

MANDELMUSSLOR
[Almond Shells]

Serve plain, bottom up, or, as a dessert, filled with whipped cream and preserves.

- ½ cup blanched almonds, minced in blender or very finely chopped
- ½ cup sugar
- 2 cups all-purpose flour
- ¾ cup butter
- 1 egg, slightly beaten
- ¼ teaspoon almond extract

Combine first 3 ingredients in mixing bowl. Cut in butter until particles are very fine; add egg and almond extract. Gather mixture into ball, wrap in waxed paper and chill 1 hour. Working with one fourth of dough at a time, pinch off pieces size of walnut. Dip thumb in flour and press dough evenly into tiny fluted molds. Put molds on baking sheet and bake in preheated slow oven (325°F.) 12 minutes, or until golden. Let stand 2 minutes, then turn molds upside down on baking sheet and tap gently on bottoms to loosen. Cool and store airtight in cool place. Makes about 42.

PEPPARKAKOR
[Gingersnaps]

Small undecorated gingersnaps in any desired shape — hearts, trees, stars, etc. — are baked to be served with coffee on the first Sunday in Advent after the family returns from church and on Lucia Day. Every household has its own special recipe, and the cookies actually seem to improve with age. The heart, of course, is the Swedes' favorite shape for Christmas.

- 10 cups all-purpose flour
- 1 pound butter or margarine, softened
- 3 cups sugar
- 1½ cups water
- 2 tablespoons each ground cloves, ginger and cinnamon
- 1 tablespoon ground cardamom (optional)
- 1 tablespoon baking soda
- 2 tablespoons dark corn syrup
- Icing

Put flour in mixing bowl. Combine butter and sugar in large mixing bowl. In small saucepan, mix water and remaining ingredients, except Icing; bring to boil and pour over butter and sugar. Stir until sugar is dissolved. Add flour about 1 cup at a time, blending well after each addition. Store, well covered, overnight in refrigerator. (Dough will be quite soft but will stiffen overnight.) Roll a small amount at a time on lightly floured surface ⅛ inch thick. (Pastry cloth and stockinet rolling-pin cover rubbed with flour, and excess shaken off, are a great help.) Cut in any desired shapes or in 3½-inch heart shape for tree ornaments. Bake on ungreased cookie sheets in preheated moderate oven (375°F.) 6 minutes, or until well browned. Cool on sheets. Using a small pastry tube with fine point for writing, decorate cookies with Icing. Let stand until firm. Put in tins and store airtight in cool dry place. Makes about 25 dozen small cookies or 11 dozen large hearts.

NOTE: Dough can be kept, covered, in refrigerator up to 2 weeks. To hang cookies on Christmas tree, cut small hole in center of each before baking.

Icing

Blend 2 cups sifted confectioners' sugar, 1 egg white and 1 teaspoon lemon juice.

JULSTJÄRNOR
[Christmas Stars]

Serve as dessert with coffee.

- 1 recipe Puff Paste
- 1 cup chopped cooked pitted prunes, sweetened to taste

Divide puff paste in 2 parts. Roll out each part to form a rectangle 12 x 9 inches and cut in 3-inch squares. Slit each corner 1½ inches from tip to center. Place a rounded teaspoonful of filling in center and fold every other tip to center, like a pinwheel. Press firmly in center and put on ungreased cookie sheets. Bake in preheated hot oven (425°F.) 10 minutes, or until golden brown. Remove to rack. Serve slightly warm. Makes 24.

SVENSK SMÖRDEG
[Puff Paste, Swedish Style]

- 2 cups all-purpose flour
- 1 cup margarine
- 5 tablespoons ice water
- ½ teaspoon white vinegar

Measure flour into mixing bowl. Cut in margarine until mixture is very fine. Mix ice water with vinegar and add to flour mixture. Quickly gather in a ball and roll out on lightly floured board to 14 x 10-inch rectangle. Fold in 3 layers. Make a quarter turn; repeat rolling, folding and turning 3 times. Chill, well wrapped in foil or plastic, 1 hour or overnight.

NOTE: Stockinet rolling-pin cover and pastry cloth are helpful in rolling puff paste.

SWEDISH COOKERY

PLÄTTAR MED LINGONGRÄDDE
[Pancakes With Lingonberry Cream]

A Swedish pancake pan is cast iron with seven 1/4-inch-deep depressions 3 inches in diameter. Batter is runny and must be held in molds. If you don't have a Swedish pan, make Thin Pancakes which have no leavening and are flat and tender.

- 1 cup all-purpose flour
- 2 tablespoons sugar
- ¼ teaspoon salt
- 3 eggs, beaten
- 3 cups milk
- ¼ cup butter or margarine, melted
- ½ cup heavy cream, whipped
- ½ cup lingonberry preserves

Mix flour, sugar and salt. Mix eggs and milk and add to dry ingredients. Heat Swedish pancake pan slowly. Brush individual sections of hot pan with melted butter. Stir batter before putting about 1 measuring-tablespoonful into each section. Brown on both sides. Pile pancakes on top of each other and transfer to hot serving platter. Keep platter warm over pan of boiling water. Mix whipped cream and preserves and serve with pancakes. Makes 8 servings.

NOTE: Pancakes can be served with sugar and other preserves instead of whipped cream and lingonberries.

TUNNA PANNKAKOR
[Thin Pancakes]

Prepare Pancakes, increasing flour to 1½ cups. For each pancake, put ¼ cup batter into 8-inch skillet. Turn with narrow spatula. Fold pancakes in quarters. Makes 16.

KNÄCK
[Toffee]

Children help make the Christmas candies and wrap them in fancy paper. On January 13, Saint Canute's Day, they rob the Christmas tree of all its candies and gingersnap hearts.

- 1 cup sugar
- 1 cup dark corn syrup
- 1 cup heavy cream
- ½ cup chopped blanched almonds
- ¼ teaspoon baking powder

Combine first 3 ingredients in heavy 2-quart saucepan. Cook over low heat, stirring occasionally, 50 minutes, or until mixture forms a firm ball when small amount is dropped into ice water (or 246°F. on candy thermometer). Add almonds and baking powder and mix well. Spoon into small fluted paper or foil cups. (Or pour mixture into measuring cup with spout and pour into fluted cups.) Let stand at room temperature until firm. Store in single layers between waxed paper in tightly covered box in cool place. Makes about 5 dozen.

JULGLÖGG
[Spiced Wine]

The good-cheer drink when friends drop in, especially on Lucia Day, December 13.

- ½ cup sugar
- ½ cup seedless raisins
- ¼ teaspoon cardamom seed
- 5 whole cloves
- 1 piece (2 inches) cinnamon stick
- 1 small piece whole ginger
- 1 cup Swedish aquavit, gin or vodka
- 1 bottle Burgundy
- ¼ cup Madeira or port wine
- ½ cup blanched whole almonds

Combine first 7 ingredients in heavy saucepan. Heat slowly until hot (do not boil). Add wine and continue to heat (do not boil) about 30 minutes. Add almonds. Serve hot in small china cups or punch cups with teaspoons for eating raisins and almonds. Makes about 10 servings.

JULMUMMA
[Christmas Beverage]

A hearty mealtime beverage

- ¼ teaspoon cardamom seed
- ½ cup sugar
- ½ cup Madeira or port wine
- 2 bottles (about 12 ounces each) stout or porter, chilled
- 2 bottles (12 ounces each) beer, chilled

Crush cardamom seed and mix with sugar and wine. Shortly before serving, add stout and beer. Makes about 8 servings.

SWEETBREAD

SWEETBREAD—The thymus glands of lamb, veal, or young beef (under 1 year; the thymus disappears in mature beef). Sweetbreads consist of two parts: the heart sweetbread and the throat sweetbread. Lamb and veal sweetbreads are white and tender; beef sweetbreads are redder in color and a little less tender.

Availability and Purchasing Guide—Widely available year round fresh and frozen.

Fresh sweetbreads should be absolutely fresh when purchased; this means firm and clear in appearance.

Storage—Sweetbreads are very perishable and should be used at once. They may be precooked and kept covered in the refrigerator but even so they should be used quickly. If frozen, keep frozen until ready to use.
Fresh, refrigerator shelf, raw or cooked: 1 day
Frozen, refrigerator frozen-food compartment: 2 to 3 weeks
Frozen, freezer: 3 to 4 months

Nutritive Food Values—A good source of protein.
Young beef, 4 ounces, raw = 235 calories
Young beef, 4 ounces, cooked = 363 calories
Veal, 4 ounces, raw = 107 calories
Veal, 4 ounces, cooked = 191 calories
Lamb, 4 ounces, raw = 107 calories
Lamb, 4 ounces, cooked = 178 calories

Basic Preparation—Sweetbreads should be precooked before using them in recipes. Put in a saucepan with water to cover. Add 1 teaspoon salt and 1 tablespoon vinegar or fresh lemon juice for each 4 cups of water used. (The acid helps to keep the sweetbreads white and firm.) Simmer for 20 minutes. Then, hold sweetbreads under cold running water and slip off membrane with fingers. Cut out dark veins and thick connective tissue. Cut very thick sweetbreads into halves lengthwise. Use at once or refrigerate.

To Broil—Precook sweetbreads as directed above. Split them and brush with melted butter or cooking oil. Sprinkle with salt and pepper. Then broil about 3 inches from broiler unit until golden brown, 4 to 6 minutes on each side. Spread with soft butter or margarine.

To Sauté—Precook sweetbreads as directed above; then split. Dip into fine dry bread crumbs or cracker crumbs, then into beaten egg, then again into crumbs. Sauté in hot butter or margarine in skillet until delicately browned on both sides. Serve with lemon quarters.

CREAMED SWEETBREADS

- 1 pair large sweetbreads
- 1 large onion, minced
- 12 medium mushrooms, sliced
- 6 tablespoons butter or margarine
- ¼ cup all-purpose flour
- 1 teaspoon salt
- ½ teaspoon curry powder
- 2½ cups light cream
- 1 tablespoon brandy
- ¼ cup sherry

Prepare sweetbreads as in Basic Preparation. Break into pieces. Cook onion and mushrooms in butter for 5 minutes. Blend in flour and seasonings. Gradually add cream and cook, stirring constantly, until thickened. Add sweetbreads, brandy, and sherry; heat. Makes 4 servings.

SWEETBREADS, NORMANDY STYLE

- 3 pairs sweetbreads
- ½ pound mushroom caps
- 6 tablespoons butter
  Salt and pepper to taste
- 3 ounces Calvados or applejack
- 1 cup light cream
- 2 egg yolks
  Sautéed Apples

Prepare sweetbreads as in Basic Preparation. Cut into ¼-inch slices. Slice mushroom caps. Melt butter in a large skillet. Add sweetbreads and sauté for 10 minutes. Add mushrooms, and continue cooking until mushrooms are tender. Season with salt and pepper. Remove to a hot platter. Add Calvados to pan, then cream mixed with egg yolks. Stir until thickened, being careful mixture does not boil. Pour over the sweetbreads, and serve with Sautéed Apples. Makes 6 servings.

Sautéed Apples

Peel 5 cooking apples; slice thinly. Sauté in butter until soft but not mushy.

SWEETBREAD AND CUCUMBER SALAD

- 1 pair sweetbreads
  Salted water
- 1 onion, sliced
- 2 whole cloves
- ⅓ bay leaf
- 1 parsley sprig
- 1 lemon slice
- 2 cucumbers
- 3 celery stalks, chopped very fine
  Mustard-flavored mayonnaise
  Green pepper and pimiento, chopped (optional)

Poach sweetbreads in salted water, together with onion, cloves, bay leaf, parsley, and lemon, for 20 minutes. Remove sweetbreads. Hold under cold running water and slip off membrane with fingers. Cut out dark veins and thick connective tissue. Cut sweetbreads into bite-size pieces and chill. Peel and seed 1 cucumber and cut into small dice. Add celery and sweetbreads and toss with mayonnaise flavored lightly with mustard. Arrange on greens and garnish with the second cucumber, peeled, seeded, and chopped. Chopped green pepper and pimiento can be added if desired. Makes 4 servings.

SWEET CICELY [*Myrrhis odorata*]

—A perennial plant with aromatic leaves which are excellent, finely chopped, in salads and stews. The leaves have a mild aniselike flavor. The seeds can be eaten fresh. This herb is said to improve the flavor of all other herbs with which it is combined. The seeds are especially good in beverages and cordials, fruit salads, and fruit cups.

SWEET POTATO COOKBOOK

SWEET POTATO—The enlarged or swollen roots of a perennial vine of the morning-glory family. There are hundreds of varieties with skins of many colors although yellow tones predominate. They can be slender or globular, forked or beet-shape. The flesh is usually yellow-red, but some sweet potatoes are white. The majority are sweet, but there are also sweet potatoes which are no sweeter than a white potato. Some sweet potatoes have a jellylike consistency, while others are so dry that they have to be moistened with butter or a lubricant in order to be swallowed.

The sweet potato, *Ipomoea batatas,* is often confused with the yam which it resembles. Yams, however, belong to the completely different botanical genus *Dioscorea.* For the cook, sweet potatoes and yams are interchangeable in recipes.

The sweet potato is a truly native American vegetable, from the tropical parts of the continent. The Indians cultivated them long before the coming of the white man. Sweet potatoes grew in colonial gardens in the South. From the Americas they traveled to such countries as the South Seas, China, Japan, and Indonesia, where they have become an indispensable and basic food. Sweet potatoes have given the name "potato" to the white variety, but in tropical America *Batatas* invariably means the sweet potato. The same is true for our southern states, where sweet potatoes are an important staple food. There, a "potato" is a sweet potato and a white potato is an "Irish potato."

Availability and Purchasing Guide—All year round fresh, canned, dehydrated, and also frozen. There are two main types of sweet potatoes, the dry meaty type and the moist-flesh type. Varieties of the dry meaty type are: Little Stem Jersey, Big Stem Jersey, Yellow Jersey, Gold Jersey. Varieties of the moist-flesh type are: Nancy Hall, Puerto Rica. The dry meaty type is of a very light yellow or orange flesh. The moist-flesh type ranges from light yellow to orange-reddish tint and is much sweeter.

Select smooth plump potatoes that are clean, dry, and uniform in shape and color.

Storage—Refrigerate; or store at room temperature if a cool dry place is available.
Refrigerator shelf, raw: 1 month
Refrigerator shelf, cooked and covered: 4 to 5 days
Refrigerator frozen-food compartment, prepared for freezing: 2 to 3 months
Freezer, prepared for freezing: 1 year
Canned, kitchen shelf: 1 year
Canned, refrigerator shelf, opened but covered: 4 to 5 days
Dried, kitchen shelf: 6 to 8 months

Nutritive Food Values—Excellent source of ascorbic acid and vitamin A.
4 ounces, baked in skin = 155 calories
5 ounces, boiled in skin = 168 calories
Canned, 4 ounces, syrup pack = 129 calories
Canned, 4 ounces, dietary pack = 52 calories
Dehydrated, reconstituted with water, ½ cup (4.4 ounces) = 120 calories

Basic Preparation—Scrub and trim off woody or bruised portions. Sweet potatoes are usually cooked before peeling.
To Boil—Cook in boiling salted water to cover. Cover and boil until tender, 20 to 30 minutes. Drain; remove skins. Cooked potatoes are then mashed, candied, glazed, etc.
To French-Fry—Boil for 10 minutes only; drain, peel, and cut into strips. Fry in deep hot fat (375°F. on a frying thermometer) until browned and tender.
To Bake—Grease the skins of clean potatoes and bake in preheated hot oven (400°F.) for 30 to 40 minutes. Potatoes that are greased before baking peel easily.
To Charcoal-Broil—Grease sweet-potato skins. Wrap double foil loosely around potatoes. Cook in coals about 45 minutes. Keep warm on edge of grill.
To Panroast—Peel sweet potatoes and cover with boiling salted water. Cook for 10 minutes. Drain and put in pan with meat for 1 hour before meat is done. Baste 4 or 5 times with pan drippings.
To Freeze—Wash potatoes and cook by any method until just tender. Dip cooled slices or whole sweet potatoes into a solution of ½ teaspoon ascorbic acid and 5 cups cold water. Add 2 tablespoons fresh orange or lemon juice to each 4 cups mashed sweet potatoes. For candied sweet potatoes, after dipping pieces or whole potatoes, roll them in brown or granulated sugar.

Pack into freezer containers, leaving ½-inch headspace.

SOUPS

CHICKEN AND SWEET-POTATO SOUP

1½ quarts chicken bouillon
1 cup diced cooked chicken
2 carrots, diced
¾ cup diced celery
1 onion, thinly sliced
4 raw medium sweet potatoes, peeled and diced
⅛ teaspoon each dried thyme and poultry seasoning
Seasoned salt and pepper to taste

In kettle mix all ingredients except salt and pepper. Bring to boil. Simmer, covered, for about 25 minutes. Season with salt and pepper. Makes about 2 quarts.

SWEET POTATO

CREAM-OF-SWEET-POTATO SOUP

- 3 raw sweet potatoes
- 2 cups chicken bouillon
- 1 teaspoon sugar
- ⅛ teaspoon each ground nutmeg and cloves
- 1½ cups milk
- Salt to taste

Peel and slice potatoes. Add to bouillon and bring to a boil. Simmer, covered, about 20 minutes, or until tender. Force through food mill or purée in blender. Reheat with remaining ingredients. Serve hot, or chilled with a dollop of sour cream. Makes 1 quart.

MAIN DISHES

TURKEY AND SWEET-POTATO CASSEROLE

- 3 tablespoons butter or margarine
- 3 tablespoons all-purpose flour
- 1½ teaspoons salt
- ¼ teaspoon pepper
- ⅛ teaspoon poultry seasoning
- 2 cups milk
- 1 cup grated Cheddar cheese
- 2 cups diced cooked turkey
- 12 small white onions, cooked
- 6 sweet potatoes, cooked, peeled, and halved

Melt butter and blend in flour and seasonings. Gradually add milk and cook, stirring constantly, until thickened. Add cheese. Stir until melted. Fold in remaining ingredients and put in greased 2-quart casserole. Bake in preheated moderate oven (350°F.) for 30 minutes. Makes 6 servings.

BAKED CHICKEN AND SWEET POTATOES

- 1 frying chicken (about 3 pounds), cut up
- Salt and pepper to taste
- Fine dry bread crumbs
- 1 egg
- 3 tablespoons water
- 4 sweet potatoes, cooked and peeled
- ½ cup butter, melted

Sprinkle chicken with salt and pepper. Roll in crumbs. Beat egg and water together. Dip chicken into egg mixture and roll again in crumbs. Put in greased shallow baking dish or pan without piling up pieces. Put sweets around chicken. Baste with ¼ cup butter. Bake in preheated hot oven (400°F.) for about 1 hour, basting several times with remaining ¼ cup butter. Makes 4 servings.

PORK-CHOP AND SWEET-POTATO SKILLET

- 4 pork chops
- 1 tablespoon shortening
- Salt and pepper to taste
- ¼ teaspoon each dried thyme and marjoram
- 1 onion, sliced
- 4 raw sweet potatoes, peeled, and sliced
- 1 green pepper, cut into rings
- 1 can (1 pound 3 ounces) tomatoes

Brown chops on both sides in shortening in skillet. Season with salt, pepper, and herbs. Top with onion, potatoes, and green pepper; add tomatoes. Cover; cook slowly for 45 minutes. Makes 4 servings.

CANDIED SWEET POTATOES AND HAM BALLS

- 1 egg
- ½ cup water
- ⅓ cup instant powdered cream
- 1½ cups soft stale-bread crumbs
- 1 teaspoon dry mustard
- 2 cups ground cooked ham
- 4 sweet potatoes, cooked, peeled, and halved
- ¾ cup firmly packed brown sugar
- ¼ cup cider vinegar

Beat egg lightly; add ⅓ cup water, cream, crumbs, ½ teaspoon mustard, and ham. Mix well and shape into 12 balls. Put in greased large shallow baking dish, making 1 layer only. Arrange potatoes around edge. Mix sugar, remaining ½ teaspoon mustard and water, and vinegar. Pour over ham balls and potatoes. Bake in preheated moderate oven (375°F.) about 45 minutes, basting several times with the syrup in bottom of dish. Makes 4 servings.

SIDE DISHES

BROWN-SUGAR CANDIED SWEET POTATOES

- 4 raw medium sweet potatoes
- Salt
- ¾ cup firmly packed brown sugar
- ⅓ cup water
- 2 tablespoons butter or margarine

Cook sweet potatoes until tender. Peel, halve, and sprinkle with salt. In skillet mix sugar, water, and butter. Bring to boil. Put potatoes in syrup and cook over low heat, turning occasionally, until potatoes are candied, about 15 minutes. Makes 4 servings.

SWEET POTATO

SWEETS À LA RECTOR

- 8 medium sweet potatoes, cooked
- ½ cup firmly packed brown sugar
- 2 tablespoons butter or margarine
- ½ teaspoon salt
- ¼ teaspoon paprika
- ½ cup sherry

Peel and slice potatoes. Arrange in greased shallow baking dish. Sprinkle with sugar and dot with butter. Add seasonings and sherry. Bake in preheated moderate oven (350°F.) about 30 minutes. Makes 6 servings.

SWEET POTATOES WITH MINCEMEAT

Bake 6 raw medium sweet potatoes as directed for Baked Sweet Potatoes. Remove pulp from shells and mash with 1 tablespoon butter and 1 teaspoon salt. Add 1 cup prepared mincemeat. Fill custard cups with mixture and bake in preheated slow oven (325°F.) for 30 minutes, or until lightly browned. Makes 4 to 6 servings.

PEANUT SWEET POTATOES

- 4 medium sweet potatoes
- ⅔ cup milk
- ¼ cup peanut butter
- ½ teaspoon salt
- ½ cup chopped salted peanuts

Wash sweet potatoes, and bake in preheated moderate oven (350°F.) for 45 minutes, or until done. Cut potatoes into halves and remove potato from shells. Reserve shells and mash potato. Beat in milk, peanut butter, and salt. Refill shells with the mixture and sprinkle with chopped peanuts. Put on baking sheet and brown lightly in oven. Makes 4 servings.

DOUGHNUTS, PANCAKES, AND STUFFING

LOUISIANA PANCAKES

- 1½ cups sifted all-purpose flour
- 3½ teaspoons baking powder
- 1 teaspoon salt
- ½ teaspoon ground nutmeg
- 1¼ cups mashed cooked sweet potatoes
- 2 eggs, beaten
- 1½ cups milk
- ¼ cup butter, melted

Sift dry ingredients into bowl. Combine remaining ingredients and add to flour. Mix only until blended. Drop by tablespoonfuls onto hot greased griddle and fry until browned. Makes 24 pancakes.

SWEET-POTATO DOUGHNUTS

- 2 eggs, beaten
- ¾ cup sugar
- 3 tablespoons shortening
- ¾ cup mashed sweet potatoes
- ¼ cup milk
- 3½ cups sifted all-purpose flour
- 4 teaspoons baking powder
- ½ teaspoon salt
- ¼ teaspoon each ground nutmeg and cinnamon
- Fat for deep frying

Combine first 4 ingredients and beat until well blended. Add milk and sifted dry ingredients; mix well. Chill for 1 hour, or until firm enough to roll. Roll on lightly floured board ½ inch thick and cut with floured 3-inch cutter. Fry in deep hot fat (375°F. on a frying thermometer) until golden brown and done. Drain. Makes 30.

SWEET-POTATO SAVORY STUFFING

- ½ pound sausage
- 1 onion, minced
- ½ cup diced celery
- ¼ teaspoon poultry seasoning
- ½ teaspoon salt
- Dash of pepper
- 1½ cups soft stale-bread cubes
- 2 cups mashed sweet potatoes

Cook sausage until half done, breaking up meat with fork. Add onion, celery, poultry seasoning, salt, and pepper. Cook, stirring constantly, until sausage is cooked. Add bread cubes and potatoes. Mix well. Use as stuffing for poultry or pork. Makes 4 cups.

DESSERTS

SWEET POTATO-PECAN PIE

- ¼ cup soft butter
- ¼ cup firmly packed brown sugar
- ⅛ teaspoon salt
- 3 eggs
- ¾ cup dark corn syrup
- 1¼ cups mashed sweet potatoes
- 1 teaspoon vanilla extract
- 1½ cups pecans
- Pastry for 1-crust 9-inch pie

Cream butter and sugar. Beat in salt, eggs, corn syrup, sweet potatoes, and vanilla. Add 1 cup nuts and pour into pastry-lined pie pan. Sprinkle remaining ½ cup nuts over top. Bake in preheated moderate oven (375°F.) for 50 to 55 minutes. Cool. Makes 6 to 8 servings.

SWEETSOP

SWEET-POTATO APPLE CRISP

- 1 can (1 pound 4 ounces) apple slices
- Water
- 2 cups very thin slices peeled raw sweet potatoes
- 1 teaspoon ground cinnamon
- ½ teaspoon salt
- 2 tablespoons lemon juice
- ½ cup all-purpose flour
- ½ cup firmly packed brown sugar
- ⅓ cup butter or margarine

Drain apples; add enough water to juice to make 6 tablespoons liquid. Alternate layers of apples and potatoes in greased shallow 1½-quart baking dish. Sprinkle with mixed cinnamon and salt. Mix apple liquid and lemon juice; pour over apples and potatoes. Combine flour and sugar; cut in butter. Sprinkle over top. Cover and bake in preheated moderate oven (350°F.) for 30 minutes. Uncover and bake for 15 minutes longer. Makes 6 servings.

SPICY SWEET-POTATO PUDDING

- 6 raw sweet potatoes
- ¾ cup cane or corn syrup
- 1 egg
- 3 tablespoons butter or margarine, melted
- 1 cup milk
- ½ cup all-purpose flour
- ½ teaspoon ground nutmeg
- 1 teaspoon ground cinnamon
- ¾ teaspoon salt

Peel and grate potatoes, 1 cup at a time. Add syrup to prevent darkening. There should be 4 cups in all. Add egg, butter, and milk. Sift in dry ingredients and mix well. Pour into greased 1½-quart casserole. Bake, uncovered, in preheated slow oven (300°F.) about 2½ hours, stirring every 30 minutes for first 2 hours. Makes 4 to 6 servings.

GOLDEN CHEESECAKE

- 1⅔ cups fine graham-cracker crumbs
- ⅓ cup butter or margarine, melted
- 2 envelopes unflavored gelatin
- ½ cup water
- ¾ cup sugar
- ½ teaspoon salt
- ⅓ cup milk
- 3 eggs, separated
- 2 packages (8 ounces each) cream cheese, softened
- 1¼ cups puréed cooked sweet potatoes
- 1 cup heavy cream
- 2 teaspoons vanilla extract
- 1 teaspoon grated orange rind

Mix crumbs and butter; reserve ¼ cup and press remainder onto bottom of 9-inch springform pan. Chill. Soften gelatin in cold water in top part of a small double boiler. Add ½ cup sugar, salt, milk, and slightly beaten egg yolks. Cook, stirring constantly, over boiling water until slightly thickened. Pour over cheese and potatoes; beat until smooth and blended. Cool. Beat egg whites until foamy; add remaining ¼ cup sugar and beat until stiff. Whip cream and fold into potato mixture with egg whites. Add flavorings. Pour into prepared pan. Sprinkle with reserved crumbs. Chill until firm.

MOLASSES DROP COOKIES

- ½ cup butter or margarine
- ¼ cup sugar
- 1 egg
- ½ cup light molasses
- 1 cup grated raw sweet potatoes
- 1 teaspoon grated orange rind
- 2 cups sifted all-purpose flour
- ½ teaspoon each salt and baking soda
- 1 teaspoon baking powder
- ½ teaspoon ground ginger
- ⅓ cup buttermilk
- 1 cup sliced pitted dates
- ½ cup chopped nuts

Cream butter and sugar. Beat in egg, molasses, sweet potatoes, and orange rind. Sift together flour, salt, baking soda, baking powder, and ginger. Add to egg mixture alternately with buttermilk. Mix well. Add dates and nuts. Drop by teaspoonfuls onto greased cookie sheets. Bake in preheated moderate oven (375°F.) for 12 to 15 minutes. Makes 48 cookies.

SWEETSOP
—A small tropical American tree and its sweet pulpy fruit. Also called the sugar apple, the skin of the heart-shape fruit is yellow-green, thick and rough. It is custardlike and very sweet, similar to the cherimoya but not so piquant in flavor. Numerous dark-brown or black seeds are embedded in the pulp. The sweetsop is eaten raw, and used for desserts and ices.

Grown in southern Florida and California, the fruit is in season from mid-summer to about December and is available in limited supplies in local food stores in the area where it is grown.

SWISS CHARD
—Another name for chard, a type of beet which does not develop the fleshy roots of ordinary beets. It is grown for its large leaves which have thickened midribs and are used as are other green vegetables.

SWISS COOKERY

by James A. Beard

Eating the Swiss way is an interesting and varied experience, for the cuisine of Switzerland is most cosmopolitan. Although the Swiss have for centuries been a firmly independent people, peacefully cultivating their mountain-rimmed valleys and minding their own business, they are a people banded together from three distinct national cultures. There are German Swiss, French Swiss, and Italian Swiss. There is also a fourth Switzerland, Romanic or Romansh Switzerland, to use the local dialect. It is part of the Grisons, in the eastern part of the country, centered in the region that contains the famous resort of St. Moritz. The people of these valleys speak a distinctive language derived from Latin, and they have many original recipes.

In spite of the many generations of being united, the country is still trilingual and Swiss cooking is trilingual, too. Around Lausanne and Geneva the cusine is similar to French. Around Bern and Zurich it has overtones of German and Austrian cooking. In the Savoy region, bordering on the lakes, it takes on a distinct Italian flavor. In addition, Switzerland has developed some special and unique favorites of her own. Being a lush dairy country, Swiss cuisine includes many dishes lavish with cheese, cream, and butter. Veal and young beef liver are exceptionally good and used in interesting ways. And the Swiss make tasty unusual dishes with fine beef.

OPEN SANDWICHES

SWISS OPEN-FACE SANDWICHES

Among the most attractive foods found in all sections of Switzerland are the open sandwiches. They are served in Zurich, in Bern, in Lausanne, in practically every town. They are made with squares or rounds of rye bread, firm white bread, pumpernickel, almost any good bread you choose. The pieces of bread are topped with a great variety of meats, fish, cheese, and garnishes and then each one is delicately coated with a gelatin aspic to keep it firm and fresh. An array of these sandwiches is a most appetizing and colorful mosaic.

To make, spread the bread with a seasoned butter, add toppings of your choice, and an appropriate garnish. (See suggestions below.) Chill the sandwiches well, and then brush each lightly with meat-flavored aspic made with canned beef broth or jellied consommé with a little more unflavored gelatin added to make it firm. (Soak gelatin in a little cold water, then melt over hot water.) Do not cake the sandwich heavily with aspic; give it just a gentle coating so that it will have a sparkling finish. A wide pastry brush or paint brush does a good job.

Seasoned Butters

Cream butter before spreading on bread; to ½ cup soft butter, add one of the following.

2 teaspoons dry mustard and 1 teaspoon prepared mustard

1 teaspoon finely chopped sweet or sour pickle

2 teaspoons anchovy paste or finely chopped anchovy

2 teaspoons chopped onion and 2 teaspoons finely chopped green pepper

2 teaspoons finely chopped peeled seeded tomato and ½ teaspoon fresh or crumbled dried basil

1 finely chopped garlic clove and 2 teaspoons minced parsley

½ teaspoon fresh or dried rosemary and 2 teaspoons minced onion

2 tablespoons finely chopped cooked shrimps and 1 tablespoon finely chopped parsley with 1 teaspoon fresh lemon juice

Toppings

Paper-thin slices of prosciutto with a green-olive garnish

Thin slices of baked ham with a garnish of 2 tiny asparagus tips

Slices of thinly cut salami arranged in a pattern and garnished with a tiny gherkin or pickled onion

Slices of white meat of chicken, garnished with a tiny wedge of tomato or a green-pepper ring centered with a slice of stuffed olive

Small shrimps nicely arranged on a thin spread of mayonnaise and topped with a tiny rosette of mayonnaise and a tiny sprig of parsley

Thin slice of rare roast beef with a small bowknot of pimiento and a slice of gherkin

Anchovy fillets with a slice of hard-cooked egg and a caper

Thin slices of smoked salmon with an onion ring and capers

Rolls of thinly sliced bologna with black and green olives speared on a toothpick

Thin slices of chicken-liver pâté topped with a small pickle

Whole boneless skinless sardines with a slice of lemon and a slice of hard-cooked egg

Thin slices of smoked sturgeon with a dash of red caviar and a cucumber slice

Thin fillets of herring with a thin slice of dill pickle

Alternating slices of tongue and Swiss cheese with prepared mustard and a thin slice of tomato

Fillets of smoked eel with a bit of chopped onion, parsley, and capers

Thin rounds of lobster with a green-pepper ring and a slice of hard-cooked egg

Rare roast beef on a spread of mustard butter and topped with a rosette of mustard butter

SWISS COOKERY

Garnishes

- Stuffed egg
- Crisp fried onion rings
- Switzerland Emmentaler or Gruyère cut into fine julienne strips
- Roquefort-cheese-flavored mayonnaise
- Tiny pickled capers
- Slices of raw mushroom

FISH AND MEAT

BASLER LACHS
[Sautéed Salmon]

- 2 medium onions, thinly sliced
- 6 tablespoons butter
- All-purpose flour
- 4 salmon steaks
- Salt and pepper to taste
- Juice of ½ lemon
- Sherry
- Lemon slices

Sauté onions in ¼ cup butter until evenly browned. Remove onions and keep warm. Add remaining 2 tablespoons butter. Lightly flour salmon steaks, season, and brown evenly on both sides in hot butter. Cook until fish flakes easily when tested with a toothpick or fork. Add lemon juice and transfer fish to hot platter. Rinse out pan with a little sherry. Spoon onion on salmon steaks and pour sauce over all. Garnish with lemon slices. Makes 4 servings.

POISSON EN PAPILLOTE
[Fish Baked in Foil]

In Switzerland the fish might be perch or trout or other lake or stream fish. Choose any local fresh fish that is available.

- Cooking oil
- 6 to 8 small whole fish, cleaned
- 3 tablespoons chopped parsley
- ¼ cup chopped mushrooms
- Salt and pepper to taste
- 2 tomatoes, peeled and sliced
- 6 to 8 lemon slices

Cut 6 to 8 heart-shape pieces of foil large enough to hold the fish with some room left for expansion. Place a well-oiled fish to one side of each piece of paper. Sprinkle with parsley, mushrooms, and salt and pepper. Top with a slice of tomato and a slice of lemon. Fold over the other half of the foil or parchment to envelop the fish, and crimp the edges together to make the package airtight. Arrange the *papillotes* in a baking pan and bake in preheated hot oven (400°F.) for 20 to 25 minutes. Place the fish in their envelopes on plates and serve. Makes 6 to 8 servings.

FILET DE BOEUF À LA SUISSE
[Roast Beef]

- 1 filet of beef (3 to 4 pounds)
- Cooking oil
- 1 cup dry red wine (about)
- Salt and pepper

Heat oven to very hot (475°F.). Rub filet well with oil and arrange on a rack in a roasting pan. Roast for 15 minutes and then baste with wine. Season to taste. Roast for another 15 minutes. Baste with pan juices and additional red wine. Roast for 10 minutes more. Baste again and let stand for 10 minutes. Makes 8 to 12 servings.

BIFTECKS TARTARE
[Tartar Sandwiches]

- 1 pound filet of beef without fat
- Thin slices of pumpernickel
- Mustard butter
- Onion rings
- 1 hard-cooked egg

Accompaniments:
- Minced onion
- Capers
- Mustard
- Chopped parsley
- Worcestershire
- Salt and pepper

Chop the beef fairly fine. Spread the bread slices, toasted or not as you choose, with mustard butter and then spread on very smoothly the chopped raw beef. Garnish each with an onion ring and a slice of egg and serve with the accompaniments. Makes 4 servings.

Variation—You can combine the beef with the seasonings and blend in 1 raw egg. Mix well and spread on bread or toast. Garnish with onion ring, sliced egg, capers, and chopped parsley.

ROGNONS BOLO
[Flambéed Kidneys]

- 3 tablespoons butter
- 2 tablespoons cooking oil
- 4 veal kidney (most of the fat removed), cut into ½-inch slices
- All-purpose flour
- Salt and pepper to taste
- ⅓ cup brandy
- 1 teaspoon Dijon mustard
- Juice of ½ lemon
- Hot cooked rice

Heat butter and oil in a chafing dish or skillet until very hot. Dust kidneys lightly with flour and brown quickly on each side. Season with salt and pepper and flame with heated brandy. Remove to a hot serving dish and add mustard and lemon juice to pan. Blend and spoon over the kidneys. Serve with rice. Makes 4 to 6 servings.

SWISS COOKERY

BERNER LEBERLI
[Sautéed Liver Bernese]

- 8 thin slices young beef liver (1½ pounds)
- 2 cups milk
- All-purpose flour
- 8 slices of bacon
- ¼ cup butter
- Salt and pepper
- Juice of ½ lemon
- 8 leaves fresh sage
- 8 lemon slices

Soak liver in milk for 30 minutes. Remove, wipe dry, and roll in flour. Sauté bacon and keep warm. Pour off fat. Melt butter in same skillet and heat until bubbly. Sauté liver gently, turning once to brown on both sides. Season to taste. Remove to a hot platter. Add lemon juice to pan. Pour over liver. Garnish with bacon, sage, and lemon slices; serve with *Rösti*. Makes 4 servings.

GESCHNETZELTES
[Minced Veal]

- ⅓ cup butter
- 3 tablespoons minced onion
- 1½ pounds veal cutlet, cut ½ inch thick and into 1-inch strips
- All-purpose flour
- Salt and pepper to taste
- 1 teaspoon chopped fresh or ¼ teaspoon dried tarragon
- ½ cup dry white wine
- 1 tablespoon lemon juice
- ½ cup dairy sour cream

Heat butter in a heavy skillet. Sauté onion until just wilted. Dredge veal strips lightly with flour and add to pan. Brown evenly. Season with salt and pepper and add tarragon and wine. Cover and cook gently for 4 minutes. Add lemon juice. Toss veal in the seasonings and sauce and test for tenderness. When done, slowly stir in sour cream. Heat through, but do not boil. Makes 6 servings.
NOTE: This dish should be served with noodles, dressed with butter and chopped parsley.

BRATWURST
[Cooked Sausage]

This sausage appears on almost every Swiss menu. It is of very fine texture, delicately flavored, and varies in size from 4 to 7 inches. It may be broiled until crisply browned or sliced and sautéed in butter. It is sometimes sold in the streets of Zurich with big hard rolls to accompany it and good mustard, a delicious snack on a brisk day.

I find bratwurst available in many areas of this country. Try it the Swiss way, sautéed, served with onions sautéed in butter until brown and tender, mashed potatoes, and sometimes sauerkraut. Or try it as a tasty addition to your outdoor grill menus. Grill it over charcoal and serve with mustard, fresh corn on-the-cob, and hot French bread.

CÔTELETTES DE PORC AU FROMAGE
[Pork Chops with Cheese]

Allow 2 pork chops per person and sauté them until nicely browned on both sides and done through. Grill the same number of thick slices of tomato and top with thin slices of Swiss or Gruyère cheese to melt at the last minute. Serve each chop with a tomato on top and a little cream sauce if you like.

BERNERPLATTE
[The Dish from Bern]

This is the Swiss version of the French choucroute garnie. *In short, it is sauerkraut surrounded with a variety of smoked meats and sausage.*

For 6 persons, drain and rinse 3 pounds fresh sauerkraut. Place in a large pot lined with strips of salt pork or bacon, add 5 or 6 juniper berries, some pepper, 1 cup beer or white wine, and 1 cup broth or water. Bring to a boil, cover, reduce heat, and simmer for 2 to 3 hours. Heap sauerkraut on a large platter; surround it with any or all of the following meats, and serve with boiled potatoes and a variety of mustards.

1. Smoked loin of pork, sliced. This can be purchased in most areas across the country. Roast in preheated slow oven (325°F.) about 15 minutes per pound.
2. Slices of boiled or baked ham.
3. Half-inch slices of cooked salt pork or pickled pork. For the last 1½ hours of cooking add to the sauerkraut a 2-pound piece of the pork with even streaks of fat and lean.
4. A selection of sausages. In Switzerland, the selection would probably include bratwurst, simple coarse pork sausages, and perhaps *saucisson de Frankfort,* which to us is frankfurter. The sausages can be braised or added to the sauerkraut. Cooking time varies from 30 minutes for large sausages to about 10 minutes for the frankfurter.

MIXED GRILL

This is one of the most popular of all Swiss entrées and is found in all sections of the country. Its combinations may vary but it always has a selection of 4 or 5 broiled meats usually with a broiled mushroom cap and a broiled tomato for garnish.

1. A small half slice of beef filet grilled rare; a slice of veal cutlet grilled to well done; Brockwurst or other sausage, grilled; a kidney (lamb or veal), grilled; a strip of bacon.
2. A cut of calf's liver, grilled; a small pork chop, well done; 2 or 3 mushroom caps; a small lamb chop.
3. Veal sweetbreads; a cut of filet of beef; chicken livers; a pork sausage; 1 or 2 slices of bacon.

NOTE: These are usually served with watercress and *Rösti*. The mixed grill may also be prepared on an outdoor grill.

Ramequins au Fromage

Croquettes au Fromage

Bernerplatte

SWISS COOKERY

GEFÜLLTES BROT
[Stuffed Bread]

- 2 cups ground cold meat (rare beef, ham, pork, veal, or a combination; or a combination of ground chicken, gizzards, and livers)
- 2 pickles, finely chopped
- 3 tablespoons minced onion
- 3 tablespoons minced parsley
- Dash of hot pepper sauce
- 2 hard-cooked eggs, chopped
- 1 tablespoon Worcestershire
- Mayonnaise
- 1 large loaf well-crusted French or Vienna bread
- Butter, softened

Mix ground meat with next 6 ingredients. Bind well with mayonnaise to make a stiff paste. Cut both ends from loaf of bread; with fork, remove crumbs, leaving a shell about ½ inch thick. Brush the interior well with soft butter and then force the meat mixture into the bread firmly so that it has no air holes in it. Wrap in foil and keep in refrigerator for several hours before slicing. Makes 6 servings.

FONDUE BOURGUIGNONNE

Tiny cubes of beef sautéed in peanut oil, then dipped into sauce

- 1 cup butter and 1 cup peanut oil, or 2 cups oil
- 2½ pounds fillet of beef, well trimmed and cut into ½-inch cubes

Melt butter in a fondue pan over an alcohol burner or in an electric skillet. Add oil and heat thoroughly. Give each guest 2 long-handled, two-pronged fondue forks (one for cooking and one for eating). Warn them not to eat with the fork they use in cooking or they may burn themselves severely. Each guest spears a piece of meat and cooks it to suit his taste; rare, medium, or well done. He then dips the meat into any of several sauces and eats. Sauces may include Béarnaise or Bordelaise barbecue sauce, or any favorites that you choose. With this meat dish go potatoes and a good salad. Allow a generous ¼ pound of beef per person. This recipe serves 6 to 8. Prepare at least 1 cup of each kind of sauce.

FONDUES

FONDUE
[Melted Cheese Dish]

- 1 garlic clove
- 2 cups dry white wine
- 1 pound Swiss cheese, finely cut
- 1 teaspoon cornstarch
- 3 tablespoons kirsch, brandy, applejack, or vodka
- Dash of ground nutmeg
- Dash of hot pepper sauce
- 2 loaves Italian or French bread with hard crust, cut into bite-size pieces, each with at least one side of crust

Rub an enameled metal casserole with garlic. Pour in wine and set over low heat. Heat until air bubbles rise to the surface. Add cheese by handfuls, stirring constantly with a wooden spoon or fork. Keep stirring until the cheese is melted. Dissolve cornstarch in kirsch and add to cheese mixture. Stir again for 2 or 3 minutes and season with nutmeg and hot pepper sauce. Place casserole on the table on a hot plate, over an alcohol burner, or on a hot tray to keep it faintly bubbling. Guests spear pieces of bread on fondue forks and dip them into the cheese. Tradition says that if a lady drops bread into the fondue the men at the table may kiss her; if a man drops bread into the cheese, he may kiss any girl he chooses. Makes 6 servings.

CHEESE, EGGS, AND POTATOES

STEAK DE FROMAGE
[Batter-Fried Cheese]

- 1 pound Swiss or Gruyère cheese
- Beer Batter
- Butter
- 8 eggs
- 2 teaspoons water
- Dash of hot pepper sauce
- Salt and pepper to taste

Cut slices of cheese 3 x 5 inches and ½ inch thick. Dip into Beer Batter and sauté in butter to brown on both sides. Arrange in a baking pan 15 x 10 inches. Beat eggs well; add remaining ingredients. Pour over cheese and bake in preheated moderate oven (375°F.) about 12 minutes. Makes 6 servings.

Beer Batter

Combine 2 slightly beaten eggs, ⅔ cup beer, and ¼ teaspoon hot pepper sauce. Slowly beat in 1 cup all-purpose flour, ½ teaspoon salt, and 2 tablespoons cooking oil.

SWISS COOKERY

CROQUETTES AU FROMAGE
[Cheese Croquettes with Green Noodles]

- ½ pound green noodles
- ⅓ cup butter
- ½ pound Gruyère, cut into strips 2 inches by 1 inch
- 1 egg, beaten
- Fine dry bread crumbs
- Olive or peanut oil
- ½ cup grated Romano cheese
- 2 tablespoons chopped parsley
- Pine nuts
- Paprika

Cook noodles in boiling salted water until just tender. Drain and combine with butter. Dip strips of cheese into egg and roll in crumbs. Brown in hot oil. Sprinkle Romano cheese and parsley on noodles in a serving dish. Arrange cheese croquettes on the noodles and sprinkle with pine nuts and paprika. Makes 4 to 6 servings.

KÄSESALAT
[Cheese Salad]

- ½ pound Swiss cheese (Emmentaler)
- 6 hard-cooked eggs
- ¾ cup dairy sour cream
- 1½ teaspoons Dijon mustard
- ½ teaspoon dry mustard
- 1 teaspoon prepared horseradish
- Salt and pepper to taste
- 1 teaspoon grated lemon rind
- 1 teaspoon caraway seeds
- Greens

Cut cheese into ½-inch cubes; chop eggs coarsely. Combine and toss with sour cream and seasonings. Arrange on a bed of greens. Makes 4 servings.

GNOCCHI
[Dumplings]

- 1 recipe Pâte à Choux
- 2 cups rich cream sauce
- ¼ pound (1 cup) Swiss or Gruyère cheese, grated

Drop teaspoonfuls of *Pâte à Choux* (or force it through a pastry bag with a plain tube, cutting off 1-inch pieces) into boiling salted water. Poach about 5 minutes, or until puffy and cooked. Drain well. Put in greased baking dish. Pour over cream sauce and sprinkle with grated cheese. Bake in preheated moderate oven (375°F.) for 15 to 20 minutes, or until cheese is melted and lightly browned. Makes 4 servings.

Pâte à Choux

Place ¼ cup butter and ½ cup hot water in a heavy saucepan over medium heat; when butter melts and water boils, add ½ cup all-purpose flour and ¼ teaspoon each salt and sugar. Stir vigorously until the mixture leaves the sides of the pan. Beat in 2 eggs, one at a time, until the mixture is waxy and shiny.

RÖSTI
[Home-Fried Potatoes]

New, very waxy potatoes should be boiled in their jackets or baked, although the former is desirable as baked ones will require much more butter. Cool cooked potatoes, peel, and grate them coarsely. A rounded-edge 8-inch skillet or sauté pan is the preferred one. The small black iron pans are excellent. Melt a little lard or shortening in pan. Add 1½ to 2 cups grated potatoes and cook over brisk heat, shaking the pan from time to time. Add bits of butter, in all about 1 tablespoon, to the potatoes and push the potatoes over the butter with a spatula, lifting the edge of the potatoes to see if they are becoming too brown on the bottom. Continue shaking the pan. When they are nicely browned on the bottom, turn the potatoes with a heavy spatula and continue in the same manner on the other side. You may have to add additional butter. Press the potatoes more firmly so that you have a beautifully browned cake which will slide out of the pan easily. Each cake will serve 2 or 3.

NOTE: Sometimes a little grated onion is added to the *Rösti;* at other times, grated Gruyère or sapsago cheese.

PASTRIES

KUCHENTEIF
[Tart Pastry]

Use for tart shells or open fruit pies

- 2 cups all-purpose flour
- 3 tablespoons sugar
- ¾ cup butter or margarine at room temperature
- 1¼ teaspoons grated lemon rind
- 3 hard-cooked egg yolks, mashed
- 2 raw egg yolks
- ½ teaspoon salt

Make a well in center of flour in a bowl. Put all remaining ingredients in well. Butter should not be ice cold, nor so soft it is oily. Using fingertips, make a paste of center ingredients, gradually incorporating flour to make a firm smooth ball of paste. Work as quickly as possible so butter won't become greasy. When bowl has been left clean, chill dough until firm enough to roll between sheets of wax paper.

NOTE: To use this pastry for quickies, hors-d'oeuvre, etc., omit sugar and lemon rind.

RAMEQUINS AU FROMAGE
[Cheese Tartlets]

    Pastry (2-cups flour recipe)
- 2 cups grated Swiss cheese
- 1 cup milk
- 2 eggs
- ¼ teaspoon salt
- ¼ teaspoon dry mustard
-     Dash of hot pepper sauce

Line 16 well-greased 3-inch tartlet pans, 1 inch deep, with pastry. Beat together cheese, milk, eggs, salt, mustard, and hot pepper sauce. Half fill tartlet shells with mixture. Bake in preheated hot oven (425°F.) for 15 minutes. Makes 16.

BEIGNETS SOUFFLÉS
[Fritters]

Prepare 1 recipe of Pâte à Choux. Heat cooking oil in a deep fryer to 370°F. on a frying thermometer. Drop in the dough by spoonfuls, or make small balls with lightly floured hands. Fry in hot oil until brown and puffy. They may be kept warm in a medium oven until ready to serve, but are best served freshly made. Roll in granulated sugar and serve quite hot, or serve with a raspberry syrup, or flambé with heated brandy and additional sugar. Makes 16.

REHRUECKEN
[Chocolate Almond Torte]

This torte is sometimes called a "larded saddle of venison" because it is baked in a loaf pan with a rounded bottom, and when inverted its shape and brown color resemble a saddle of meat.

- ⅓ cup butter (about)
-     Fine dry bread crumbs
- 5 eggs, separated
- 2 whole eggs
- ½ cup granulated sugar
- ½ teaspoon ground cinnamon
- 2½ tablespoons finely chopped citron
- ¼ pound blanched almonds, grated (¾ cup)
- ⅓ cup grated unsweetened chocolate
- 4 squares (4 ounces) unsweetened chocolate
- ¼ cup boiling water
- 2 cups sifted confectioners' sugar
- ⅛ teaspoon salt
- ½ teaspoon vanilla extract
-     Slivered blanched almonds

You need two 10½-inch *rehruecken* pans or one large one; or you can use two 9-inch loose-bottomed layer-cake pans. Butter pans well and dust with bread crumbs. Shake out excess crumbs. Combine egg yolks, whole eggs, and granulated sugar; beat until light and lemon-colored. Add cinnamon, citron, grated almonds, and grated chocolate. Mix well. Beat egg whites until stiff but not dry. Fold into chocolate mixture until whites are no longer visible. Pour into pans and bake in preheated moderate oven (350°F.) about 30 minutes for small pans, or 45 minutes for large. Remove from pans and cool on a rack. To make glaze, melt together ¼ cup butter and 4 ounces chocolate. Beat in boiling water and next 3 ingredients. Spread smoothly over cakes, let harden slightly, and stud with slivered almonds. Makes 12 to 16 servings.

APFELTORTE
[Apple Tart]

-     Kuchenteig or pastry (2-cups flour recipe)
- ⅓ cup butter
- 8 large cooking apples, peeled and cut into eighths
- ½ cup sugar (about)
- 1 teaspoon vanilla extract
- 2 apples, peeled and sliced thin
- 1 cup water
-     Juice of 1 lemon
- 1 egg
- 3 to 4 tablespoons heavy cream
-     Apricot preserves, melted (optional)

Line a 10-inch flan ring or pie pan with pastry, and chill. Melt butter in skillet and add 8 apples. Cover and cook, stirring occasionally, until apples are just soft. Add ⅓ cup sugar and vanilla; break the apples into small pieces. Cool slightly and spoon into pastry-lined pan. Cook thinly sliced apples in water with lemon juice about 5 minutes. Drain apples and dry. Arrange slices in a pattern on top of pie. Sprinkle with sugar. Bake in preheated hot oven (425°F.) for 10 minutes. Reduce heat to moderate (350°F.) and bake for 20 minutes longer. Beat egg and cream and pour over tart. Bake about 10 minutes longer. Serve warm. If desired, glaze top with preserves melted over hot water. Makes 8 to 10 servings.

SWORDFISH—An oceanic food and sport fish of heroic proportions; swordfish may weigh between 200 and 600 pounds. Strong muscles, a powerful forked tail, a saillike dorsal fin and other strong fins, as well as the characteristic flattened "sword," which is a prolongation of the forepart of the skull, make the swordfish a very fast swimmer as well as a powerful predator on lesser fish.

The swordfish is found throughout the world in tropical and temperate seas. It is numerous in both the eastern and western Atlantic, with a considerable fishery in the Mediterranean.

Swordfish are among the world's best game fish; they are also fished commercially. Their flesh is red, meaty, and rich.

SYLLABUB

Availability—Scientists have found traces of mercury above the level of safe human consumption in swordfish. For health reasons when this is discovered swordfish is removed from sale in many markets. The season for fresh **swordfish** is from June to October. Frozen swordfish steaks are available year round. Some swordfish is sold canned.

Storage
Fresh, refrigerator shelf, raw: 1 to 2 days
Fresh, refrigerator shelf, cooked: 3 to 4 days
Fresh, prepared for freezing; and frozen, refrigerator frozen-food compartment: 2 months
Fresh, prepared for freezing; and frozen, freezer: 1 year
Canned, kitchen shelf: 1 year

Nutritive Food Values—Good source of protein and vitamin A.
Fresh, broiled with butter (4.4 ounces) = 218 calories
Canned, 4 ounces, solids and liquid = 116 calories

Basic Preparation
To Sauté—Cut swordfish steaks into serving pieces and sauté in hot butter or margarine until well browned on both sides and fish flakes easily with a fork. Remove to a hot platter and season with salt and pepper. Add a little more butter to the pan, and a little wine, if desired. Heat and pour over fish. Serve with lemon wedges.
To Broil—Put slices of swordfish in shallow pan. Brush with melted butter or margarine. Broil under medium heat for 5 to 7 minutes on each side, basting with drippings in pan; be careful not to let fish become dry. Spread lightly with mayonnaise. Season with salt and pepper and sprinkle top with fine dry bread crumbs; baste again with drippings. Broil for a few minutes longer, or until crumbs are crisp and brown.
To Bake—Cut swordfish steaks into serving pieces and season with salt and pepper. Dip into a mixture of ¼ cup melted butter or margarine and 2 tablespoons fresh lemon juice. Put in greased shallow baking dish and pour any remaining butter mixture over top. Bake in preheated moderate oven (350°F.) for 25 to 30 minutes, or until fish flakes easily with a fork. Sprinkle with paprika, if desired.
To Freeze—Clean fish and eviscerate. Cut fish into steaks. Dip pieces of fish into a solution of 4 cups water and 1 tablespoon ascorbic acid for 20 seconds. Wrap pieces of fish in moisture-**vaporproof wrapping**, excluding as much air as possible. Seal.

SWORDFISH AMANDINE

½ cup chopped almonds
½ cup butter
Parsley
1 lemon
4 swordfish steaks
Sherry
Pepper
2 green onions, chopped
8 slices of crisp bacon, crumbled
Paprika

Brown almonds lightly in 2 tablespoons of the butter. Melt remaining butter; add few parsley sprigs, chopped, and grated rind and juice of ½ lemon. Put fish on foil-covered broiler pan. Put 1 tablespoon sherry on each steak, and sprinkle with pepper. Spoon under medium heat for 10 minutes, basting with sherry-butter mixture. Turn fish; baste. Broil for 10 minutes longer. Sprinkle with almonds, green onions, and bacon. Garnish with lemon slices and paprika. Makes 4 servings.

DEEP-FRIED SWORDFISH

1½ pounds swordfish steaks
2 eggs
3 tablespoons water
Fine dry bread crumbs
Cooking oil or shortening for deep frying
Salt

Cut steaks into bite-size chunks. Dip into eggs and water beaten together, then into crumbs. Fry until golden brown in deep hot oil (375°F. on a frying thermometer). Drain on absorbent paper; sprinkle with salt. Serve very hot with tartar sauce. Makes 4 servings.

SWORDFISH WITH TOMATO SAUCE

1½ pounds swordfish, 1½ inches thick
7 tablespoons olive oil
1 cup finely chopped parsley
2 garlic cloves, minced
Juice of 1 lemon
1 can (8 ounces) tomato sauce
Salt and pepper to taste

Cut fish into serving pieces; put in baking dish. Simmer next 3 ingredients for 10 minutes. Add lemon juice and sauce; heat. Season and pour over fish. Bake in preheated hot oven (425°F.) for 25 minutes. Makes 3 or 4 servings.

MAYONNAISE SWORDFISH

Season 2 pounds swordfish with salt and pepper. Spread generously with mayonnaise and sprinkle lightly with instant minced onion, then with packaged cornflake crumbs, fine dry bread crumbs, or cracker crumbs. Bake in preheated hot oven (400°F.) about 30 minutes. Makes 4 servings.

SYLLABUB
—A drink or dessert made with milk or cream and a wine or liquor. It is of two kinds: curdled and fresh. In the curdled kind, which an 18th-century Williamsburg writer described as "everlasting," the milk or cream is curdled with wine or other acid. The best-known type of syllabub, however, is the frothy kind, made by beating the milk or cream to a foam (sometimes made with egg white, although this is not the classic method) and flavoring it with wine of some sort. This type should be served immediately.

The origin of the word is unknown, but it is thought that it may have come from a kind of wine of the Champagne district, Sill or Sille, and the Elizabethan slang word "bub," which meant a bubbling drink. Syllabub is thought to have been made with Sille and frothing cream, hence, to make a Sille Bub. Whatever the correct origin is, the spelling of the word is anything but consistent. It may be spelled sillabub, sillebub, sulebubbles, or even silly-bubbles. The drink is probably of English origin, and has been popular since pre-Elizabethan times. The early colonists of this country brought with them their love of the foaming drink or dessert, and it was popular through the 19th century. There are as many recipes for syllabub as there are spellings of the word, but they fall into the two main categories mentioned above.

OLD ENGLISH SYLLABUB

2 cup heavy cream*
1 cup sugar
½ cup sherry
Grated rind and juice of 1 lemon

Combine ingredients in deep bowl. Beat with rotary beater or whisk in the same direction for 30 minutes. Or use an electric beater at medium to high speed for about 6 minutes, or until stiff but not curdled. The mixture should be very stiff. Set a large, very fine sieve over another bowl. Pour mixture onto sieve. Refrigerate about 1 hour. Spoon the froth that remains on the sieve into sherbet glasses. Serve with thin crisp cookies. Makes about 6 servings.

*The cream should be very thick; use heavy cream that has been refrigerated for 3 to 4 days.

SYRUP or SIRUP

—A sweet, thick, sticky liquid made from a concentrated solution of sugar and water, with or without the addition of a flavoring agent such as chocolate; or from a concentrated solution of sugar and the juice of a plant, for example, corn syrup; or from the concentrated juice of such plants, as sugar cane, etc., which results in cane syrup and molasses, the sugar maple from which maple syrup is made, and the sugar sorghum from which sorghum syrup is made.

The word comes from the Arabic *sharab,* "drink."

Many commercial syrups are widely available in food stores: maple syrup and blends of maple and cane syrup, cane syrup, sorghum cane syrup, corn syrup (both light and dark), and molasses (both light and dark). These syrups are used for pancakes, waffles, etc. Other syrups for use in making beverages are chocolate syrup, and fruit syrups such as lemon, lime, orange, pineapple, and raspberry.

SUGAR SYRUPS FOR STEWED FRUITS

These syrups can be used to great advantage when stewing fruit, since fruit stewed in a hot syrup will preserve its shape and not become mushy. Make the syrup appropriate for the fruit to be stewed. Drop a few pieces of fruit into the hot syrup; they should not crowd each other. Simmer gently until fruit is just tender. Remove with slotted spoon and put in serving dish. Repeat until fruit is used. Pour remaining syrup over fruit.

	Sugar Cups	Water Cups	Yield in Cups
Thin—for apples, grapes, rhubarb	2	4	5
Medium—for apricots, berries, cherries, figs, grapefruit, grapes, peaches, pears, plums, prunes	3	4	5½
Heavy—for berries, figs, peaches, plums	4¾	4	6½

To make syrup: Add sugar to water, cover, and bring to a boil. Remove cover, lower heat, and simmer for 3 minutes.

CHOCOLATE SYRUP

3 squares (3 ounces) unsweetened chocolate
⅔ cup water
½ cup sugar
Dash of salt
½ cup corn syrup
½ teaspoon vanilla extract

Put chocolate and water in saucepan. Bring to boil and simmer until thick and well blended, stirring constantly. Add sugar and salt; bring to a boil and boil gently for 2 minutes, stirring. (For a thicker syrup, boil for 4 minutes.) Add corn syrup and bring again to a boil. Remove from heat, cool slightly, and add vanilla. Pour into a jar and cover tightly. Keep in refrigerator. Serve hot or cold as sauce or for use in chocolate drinks. Makes about 1½ cups syrup.

NOTE: For chocolate drinks, use 2 tablespoons syrup to 1 cup milk.

ORANGE SYRUP

Grated rind of 1 orange
½ cup orange juice
1 cup sugar
Dash of salt
Sections from 1 orange

Mix grated rind, orange juice, sugar, and salt and boil until the consistency of maple syrup, 4 or 5 minutes. Add orange sections free of seeds and membrane. Serve hot or cold on pancakes or waffles. Makes 1 cup.

HOT SPICED SYRUP

2 cups maple or maple-blended syrup
1 cup butter or margarine
1 teaspoon ground cinnamon
¼ teaspoon each ground allspice and mace

Combine all ingredients in saucepan. Boil for 2 or 3 minutes over medium heat. Beat with rotary beater until blended. Serve hot on pancakes or waffles. Makes about 3 cups.

Menus

50 Menus to help you plan more varied meals

BREAKFASTS AND BRUNCHES

Fruit Salad
Walnut Waffles
Hot Spiced Syrup
Coffee

Strawberries
Honey and
Sour-Cream Dressing
Minute Steaks
Scones   Butter
Tea or Coffee

Cold Plum Soup
Berner Leberli
(Sautéed Liver Bernese)
Sweet-Potato Biscuits
Café au Lait

Sautéed Pear Wedges
Poached Salmon Steaks
Spinach Frittata
Coffee

Spiced Apple Juice
Stekt Sill eller Strömming
(Fried Herring or Smelt Fillets)
Rye Rolls   Butter
Coffee

Sliced Fresh Pineapple
Shirred Eggs with Cream
Soy-Wheat Muffins
Hot Chocolate

Tangerines
Zucchini Frittata
Arizona's Biscuits
Butter   Mesquite Honey
Coffee

Mixed Fruit
Louisiana Pancakes
Pineapple Syrup
Country Bacon
Coffee with Chicory

LUNCHES AND SUPPERS

Oyster Stew
Corn Muffins
Whipped Butter
Apricot Jam
Sliced Oranges

Peanut-Butter and Red-Onion
Sandwiches with Alfalfa
Sprouts on Cracked-Wheat Bread
Rugola and Plum-Tomato Salad
Italian Dressing
Raspberry-Leaf Tea

Spaghettini with
Crab-Meat Sauce
Green- and Red-Pepper Salad
Italian Dressing
Ginger Cookies

Baked Whole Cauliflower Stuffed
with Veal and Bread Crumbs
Mushroom Sauce
Fried Tomatoes, Country Style
Green and Red Grapes
Coffee

Biff à la Lindström
(Beef Lindström)
Rye Toast
Tangerines and Apple Salad
Iced Coffee

Egg and Tomato Scramble
Semlor (Shrove Tuesday Buns)
Huckleberries and Cream
Tea

Cream-of-Sweet Potato Soup
Sliced Cold Roast Veal
Cranberry Mold
Watercress
Apple and Almond Tarts

Greek Spinach Pie
Tomato and Black-Olive Salad
Feta Cheese Dressing
Lemon-Lime Ice
Tea

Rice Pilaf with
Diced Sweetbreads
Cucumber Relish
Grapes and Peaches
Kanelkakor
(Swedish Cinnamon Cookies)

Dried Beef in Sour-Cream Sauce
Popovers
Wilted Raw Spinach
Sweet-Potato Apple Crisp

Whole Artichokes
Hollandaise Sauce
Sweetbread and Cucumber Salad
Toasted Sesame Rolls
Carob Mousse

Panned Sunfish with Dill Sauce
Rösti
(Home-Fried Potatoes)
Apfeltorte
(Apple Tart)
Coffee

Turkey and Sweet Potato
Casserole
Chinese Cabbage and Radish Slaw
Sponge Cake
Blackberry Sauce

Tomato-and-Herb Soup
on the Rocks
Candied Sweet Potatoes
and Ham Balls
Cheese Toast
Chocolate-Covered Raisins

Corn-Frankfurter Soup
Croquettes au Fromage
(Cheese Croquettes with
Green Noodles)
Poached Pears and
Mandarin Oranges
Beverage

Cream of Zucchini Soup
Biftecks Tartare
(Tartare Sandwiches)
Sliced Bananas and Pineapple

DINNERS

Braised Sweetbreads
with Foie Gras
Madeira Sauce
Herbed Wild Rice
Snow Peas with Julienne
Celery Knob
Apple Strudel

Rolled Fish Fillets with
Shrimp Sauce
Riced Potatoes
Zucchini with Tomatoes
Cherry Strudel

Spinach-Stuffed Fish Fillets
Stewed Green Tomatoes
and Peppers
Creamed Sweet Potatoes
Lemon-Cheese Cake

Purée of Asparagus
Breast of Veal with Sausage
Stuffing
Ratatouille
Strawberry Cake Roll

Pork Chops Baked in
Orange Juice
Mustard Greens with
Irish Potatoes
Marinated Tomatoes
Strawberry Mousse

Ärter och Fläsk
(Yellow Pea Soup)
Mustard Greens and Bibb
Lettuce Salad
Lemon and Olive Dressing
Tiny Pancakes
Lingonberry Preserves

Geschnetzeltes (Minced Veal)
Parsleyed Noodles
White Asparagus
Drawn Butter Sauce
Plum and Hazelnut Tarts

Poisson en Papillote
(Fish Baked in Foil)
Sautéed Mushrooms
Boiled Potatoes
Fennel and Red-Apple Salad
Frozen Vanilla Custard
Pecan and Cointreau Sauce

Brunkålssoppa
(Brown Cabbage Soup)
Fiskgryta (Fish with Onions
and Tomatoes)
Riced Potatoes
Rye Rolls
Raspberry Compote

Mixed Grill
Baked Duchess Potato Loaves
Watercress Salad
Beignets Soufflés
(Fritters)

Basler Lachs
(Sautéed Salmon)
Gnocchi (Dumplings)
Mixed Green Salad
Rehruecken
(Chocolate Almond Torte)

Two-Cheese Fusilli
Mixed Salad Greens
French Dressing
Hot Buttered Italian Bread
Strawberry-Almond Roll

Braised Lamb Shoulder
Dill Sauce
Pan-Roasted Potatoes
Green Peas
Äppelsoppa (Apple Soup)
with Rusks

Basque Barbecue
Roasted Onions
Stuffed Tomatoes, Las Vegas
Biscuits
Apple-Raisin-Nut Tarts

Avocado Soup
Gallina Rellena (Stuffed Turkey,
Southwestern Style)
Grapefruit and Melon Salad
Sopaipillas
Southwestern Mocha

Spicy Barbecued Spareribs
Squash Fritters
Cucumbers
Onion Toast
Italian Strawberry Ice

Trucha Frita
(Southwestern Fried Trout)
Sweet Potatoes, New Indian
Style
Baked Zucchini
Iced Pineapple

Steak Fry
Frijolitos (Mashed Beans)
Spicy Tomato Relish
Chuck Wagon Pecan Bread
"Piebox" Special Vinegar Pie

Merluza Asado al Horno
(Baked Fish)
Judias Verdes a la Vasca
(Basque Green Beans)
Squash with Mexican-Corn
Stuffing
Rosquillas (Fried Cakes)
Black Coffee with Anisette

Cocido (Spanish Boiled Beef)
Verduras (Vegetable Side Dish
for Cocido)
Tortillas
Whole Oranges Stuffed with
Orange and Lime Ice

Spaghetti with Meatballs
Tossed Salad
Herbed French Dressing
Deviled Toast
Spumoni
Espresso Coffee

Chili con Carne Verde
Fruit Salad
(Casaba and Grapefruit)
Burritos from Taos
Caramela
Aniseed Cookies

Fågelbon (Birds' Nests)
Gravad Lax med Senapssås
(Marinated Salmon with
Mustard Sauce)
Små Köttbullar (Small Meatballs)
Silloch Skinksallad
(Herring and Ham Salad)
Rågbröd (Rye Bread)
Butter
Fruit and Cheese

Kalvkotlett à la Oscar
(Veal Cutlet à la Oscar)
Oven-Browned Potatoes
Tossed Green Salad
Mazarintårta
(Mazarin Torte)
Demitasse

Steak with Onions
Quelites (Lamb's-Quarters)
Tomato and Green-Olive Salad
White-Wine Dressing
Melon Cup

Zarzuela de Mariscos
(Musical Comedy of Shellfish)
Ensalada a la Andaluza
(Andalusian Vinaigrette Salad)
Seeded Bread
Baked Pear Soufflé with
Pear Brandy

Table of Equivalents

few grains = less than 1/8 teaspoon (tsp.)

3 tsp. = 1 Tablespoon (Tb.)

4 Tb. = ¼ cup

8 Tb. = ½ cup

5 Tb. plus 1 tsp. = ⅓ cup

16 Tb. = 1 cup

1 cup = ½ pint (pt.)

2 cups = 1 pt.

4 cups = 1 quart (qt.)

4 qts. = 1 gallon

16 ounces (oz.) = 1 pound (dry weight)

16 oz. = 1 pt. (liquid measure)